AMONG THE BRAVES

HOPE, STRUGGLE, AND EXILE IN
THE BATTLE FOR HONG KONG AND
THE FUTURE OF GLOBAL DEMOCRACY

AMONG THE BRAVES

SHIBANI MAHTANI AND TIMOTHY McLAUGHLIN

hachette
BOOKS

New York

Hachette Books
Hachette Book Group
1290 Avenue of the Americas
New York, NY 10104
HachetteBooks.com
Twitter.com/HachetteBooks
Instagram.com/HachetteBooks

First Edition: November 2023

Published by Hachette Books, a subsidiary of Hachette Book Group, Inc. The Hachette Books name and logo is a trademark of the Hachette Book Group.

The Hachette Speakers Bureau provides a wide range of authors for speaking events. To find out more, go to hachettespeakersbureau.com or email HachetteSpeakers@hbgusa.com.

Books by Hachette Books may be purchased in bulk for business, educational, or promotional use. For information, please contact your local bookseller or Hachette Book Group Special Markets Department at: special.markets@hbgusa.com.

The publisher is not responsible for websites (or their content) that are not owned by the publisher.

Print book interior design by Amy Quinn

Library of Congress Control Number: 2023943890

ISBNs: 978-0-306-83036-5 (hardcover), 978-0-306-83038-9 (ebook)

Printed in the United States of America

LSC-C

Printing 1, 2023

To our mothers.

CONTENTS

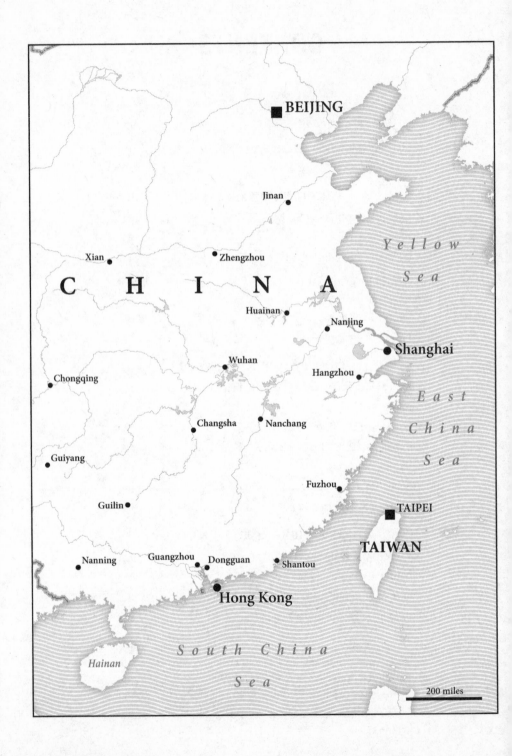

BEIJING

Jinan

Xian • • Zhengzhou

C H I N A

Huainan
Nanjing
Shanghai

Wuhan
Hangzhou

Chongqing

East

China

Changsha Nanchang

Sea

Guiyang

Fuzhou

Guilin •
TAIPEI

Nanning
Guangzhou Dongguan
Shantou
TAIWAN

Hong Kong

South China

Hainan

Sea

Yellow

Sea

200 miles

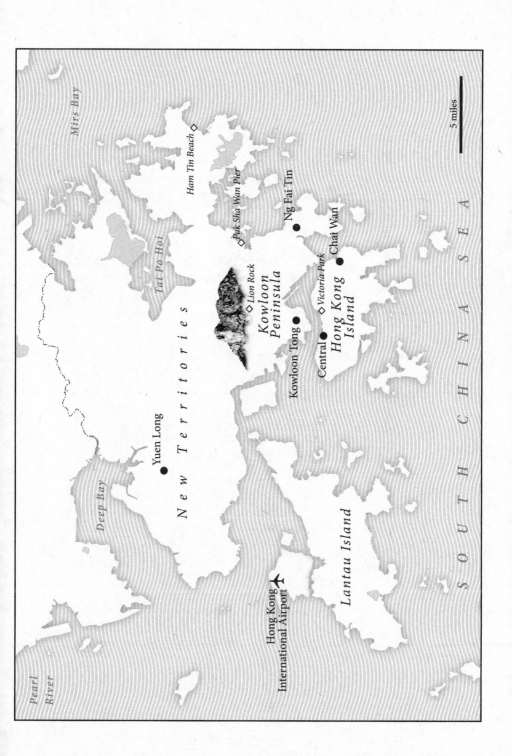

Mirs Bay

Ham Tin Beach ◇

Pak Sha Wan Pier ◇

Ng Fai Tin ●

Chai Wan ●

◇ Victoria Park

Hong Kong Island

Central ●

Kowloon Tong ●

◇ Lion Rock

Kowloon Peninsula

Tai Po Hoi

New Territories

Yuen Long ●

Deep Bay

Pearl River

Hong Kong ✈ International Airport

Lantau Island

SOUTH CHINA SEA

5 miles

"In an age when it is so common for progressive, cosmopolitan intellectuals to insist on the near-pathological character of nationalism . . . it is useful to remind ourselves that nations inspire love, and often profoundly self-sacrificing love."

—Benedict Anderson, *Imagined Communities:*
Reflections on the Origin and Spread of Nationalism

"Your Honour, the people of Hong Kong who took part needed no person or organization to incite them. If there was a provocateur, it is the regime that fired at its own people."

—Lee Cheuk-yan, former chairman of the Hong Kong Alliance
in Support of Patriotic Democratic Movements of China

BOUNDLESS OCEANS, VAST SKIES

TOMMY CLUMSILY SHUFFLED OUT OF HIS SLEEPING BAG, REACHING OVER to rouse the friend dozing beside him before unzipping the small door of their tent and stepping outside. The soft sand of Ham Tin beach, still cold in the predawn darkness, shifted under his weight. The breeze carried his wavy, shoulder-length hair up in wisps, brushing a face framed by circular, thick-rimmed glasses—a defining accessory that he had worn since his teens. In front of him, the waters of Tai Long Wan on the east coast of Hong Kong stretched out under the sky as it shifted from deep indigo to violet.

In English, Tai Long Wan translates to "Big Wave Bay," and it often lives up to the name, producing swells that attract the city's contingent of surfers on holidays and weekends. But at that early hour, the strip of sand was quiet, dotted with colorful tents like Tommy's, and the water was relatively calm and empty. Tommy watched as a few sets of knee-high waves rolled in. Around him, other campers began to stir, the swish of nylon tents and hiss of propane stoves boiling water for instant coffee and noodles just audible. The campers chatted in hushed voices and stifled laughter, trying not to disturb those still sleeping off New Year's Eve overindulgences from the night before.

For some years, Tommy and his friends had shared this tradition: camping out on one of Hong Kong's easternmost points, where they would be among the first to watch the new year's sun rise. Here, surrounded by lush rolling hills, they found respite from their cramped apartments in towering public-housing complexes and their overbearing parents. The night before, his friends had gathered a pile of brush and fallen tree branches and built a roaring bonfire. They clinked the green bottles of soju they'd bought at a convenience store before their hike. Their conversation—irreverent and meandering—lasted long into the night, the towering fire reduced to a pile of ash, embers flickering in the sand.

What Tommy couldn't tell his friends was that this would be his final New Year's Day sunrise on Ham Tin. It would, in fact, be his last new year in Hong Kong. In a few weeks he wouldn't be staring out at the sea. He would be racing across it in a desperate dash for freedom in Taiwan.

He tried not to dwell as the sky pinked and he ambled back toward his tent to join his drowsy friends. Tommy took a mug full of warm water. He liked to refer to himself as a barista and believed he was above the instant coffee that his friends prepared, although his training as a coffee connoisseur was in a humble McCafé in a suburban shopping mall. It wasn't quite pour-over or cold brew, but he did learn how to create latte art, making swirls and illustrations in the foam on customers' orders. (Sometimes, he'd practice making phallic doodles in the steamed milk.)

Warm drinks in hand, the early risers stood as the sun began edging over the horizon, just a sliver visible at first and then filling the sky in its entirety. Sunrises and the new year symbolized a hopeful new start, but Tommy tried not to think of the one awaiting him. It made him queasy.

Since middle school, Tommy had found peace in Hong Kong's vast country parks, the hills and beaches seemingly incongruous with the skyscrapers that most people associated with the global financial center. He had spent much of his free time exploring an extensive network of hiking trails that traversed the territory. Some snaked through the hills high above packed neighborhoods, and Tommy would peer down at the blocks of towers and ribbons of roads, wondering what they might look like in a decade or so. Others ran along the border with the Chinese mainland, where the modern high-rises of Shenzhen competed for stature with the peaks that Tommy climbed. Once a backwater, the city was now a physical manifestation of China's dizzying rise, symbolizing for many Chinese the kind of promise that Hong Kong once held.

As the mid-morning sun rose higher, Tommy and two friends folded up their tents, strapped on their backpacks, and hiked to retrieve the car they'd left parked at the trailhead the night before. They chucked their gear in the trunk and made the hour-long drive south to Victoria Park, a forty-seven-acre expanse of green space and sports facilities nestled in the popular Causeway Bay shopping district on Hong Kong Island. No excuse, not even their slight hangovers, could keep them away.

Hong Kong at the start of 2020 was in its seventh month of a sustained, city-wide revolt against the Chinese Communist Party and its rule over the city. Tommy was a foot soldier in this movement, living a double life as both the carefree class clown and the black-clad protester, unidentifiable in the mass of fighters. By then, some 6,000 people had been arrested, including Tommy—twice. Police had fired more than 16,000 tear-gas rounds, 10,000 rubber bullets, 1,850 sponge grenades, 2,000 bean-bag rounds, and a handful of live bullets.[1] But the movement persisted. On that New Year's Day, the veteran protest organizers who stunned the world with their million-strong marches had called for people to turn up again in the afternoon at Victoria Park. The Civil Human Rights Front was an organization now synonymous with Hong Kong's larger civil society, and it wanted to set the tone for the year. The organizers did everything by the book—applying for a police letter of "no objection" to hold their demonstration—consistent with laws in Hong Kong meant to preserve free speech, the freedom of assembly, and the right to peaceful opposition. These were the fundamentals that, more than the Shenzhen border, set the boisterous city apart from the mainland.

Tommy sat in the backseat. The car was not his; he couldn't afford one as a second-year visual arts student. His parents, a cook at a local restaurant and a part-time car-wash attendant, didn't own one either. His friend sped across the hinterlands known as the New Territories— named for when the British took even more land from China in 1898— onto the highways of Kowloon and under Victoria Harbor. The wild country parks gave way to village homes and low-rise buildings; then towering apartments and skyscrapers formed angular blocks under the blue sky. For most of Tommy's life, these landmarks had seemed largely meaningless, but now some were imbued with memories of tear-gas shrouded battles between his compatriots and the Hong Kong police. There was Polytechnic University, besieged by the police several months earlier. The police headquarters in Wan Chai, which he had pelted with eggs before he knew how to mix a Molotov cocktail. As the car sailed down Harcourt Road, Tommy remembered the asphalt stained with blood and littered with broken gas masks, the remnants of a violent mass arrest that had ensnared him.

The group cursed as they crawled through the streets around Victoria Park, struggling to find a parking spot. Clusters of people, almost all dressed in black, were filling the sidewalks, some spilling into the streets, weaving between traffic. Tommy checked his phone obsessively, scrolling through a stream of messages and toggling between groups on the encrypted messaging app Telegram. Thousands were posting updates in different channels: locations of police vans and riot officers, subway delays, and possible emergency exit routes from the park.

They finally spotted a parking garage and guided the car into a space. The group jumped out.

Tommy looped a black surgical mask around his ears and slipped into a small opening in the thronging crowd. The surgical mask was part of the uniform of protesters, keen to stay anonymous even before a mysterious new virus from Wuhan would prompt wearing them for an entirely different reason.

This was a seasoned movement by January 1, 2020, and everyone had their role. There were the "braves" like Tommy, front liners who strategically vandalized businesses owned by Beijing's supporters, snuffed out tear-gas canisters and threw them back at police, and took on officers, beating them with rods and sticks at the risk of certain jail if arrested. Behind them were the 和理非 or "wo, lei, fei," Cantonese for the "peaceful, rational, and nonviolent" crowd: those who held banners and shouted slogans. They often had their kids in tow and avoided conflict. There were those operating behind the scenes, organizing gear, supplying snacks and bottles of water, and providing transport at the end of marches. Together, they had spent the past months united, presenting the Chinese Communist Party with the greatest challenge to its rule on Chinese soil since the Tiananmen Square protests of 1989—in a city that was meant to be placated and subdued by wealth, too seduced by the trappings of modernity and glitz to ever rock the boat.

The discontent started in the spring of 2019 with a proposed bill that would allow fugitives to be transferred to countries and territories with which Hong Kong had no formal extradition agreements, most notably mainland China. It triggered anxieties about Beijing's control over Hong Kong that went back decades. The movement that followed was the last stand of an in-between place: not China but not independent, fiercely proud of its democratic culture but without the luxury of democratic governance, designed as a cushion between two systems that were no longer velveting their hostility toward each other.

Tommy would have normally packed a standard "braves" kit with a half-face mask fitted with lurid magenta 3M filters, the most widely available respirators used to protect from the stinging tear gas. A helmet was mandatory too, and sometimes he brought a hammer to smash glass doors and deface subway stations. But if he was being honest with himself, he was not quite as brave anymore. After his second arrest, Tommy's singular goal was to avoid becoming a victim of the penal system. Still, he showed up to the march that day. The Civil Human Rights Front was made up of veteran rally organizers and was widely respected. The march was authorized. In theory, no one would get arrested for being there.

Tommy saw families that looked just like his, ambling out of the park and down the narrow streets of Causeway Bay. He briefly thought about his mother at home. It still hurt that she never quite understood his motivations, not even after she attended her first protest—which was also her last. Even without her, it seemed like most of the city was present, a swell of undeterred grandparents, couples, and toddlers. Every now and then their jumble of voices would turn into one, crying— "Liberate Hong Kong, Revolution of Our Times!" "Five Demands, Not One Less!"—until the leader of the chant grew tired, their voices cracking and fading back against the incoherent chatter. Organizers eventually tallied more than a million people at the height of the demonstration, almost one-seventh of the city's population.

The demonstration abruptly halted three hours after it started. Several men in nearly identical dark windbreakers and balaclavas were arrested, allegedly for vandalizing an HSBC bank branch along the path of the march in Wan Chai. Protest marches often ran the familiar route from Victoria Park through the neighborhoods just west, and then down to the government headquarters, Admiralty, ending in the central business district.

Some ten plainclothes officers stood on the sidewalk, screaming and swinging metal batons at marchers who stopped to watch and film the arrests of the supposed vandals. Demonstrators were angry about HSBC freezing crowd-sourced funds meant to help detained protesters. But amid the bedlam, it was difficult to tell the officers and the arrestees apart, an approach the police adopted to sow distrust and paranoia among protesters. By disguising themselves, police forced demonstrators to think twice about sharing too much information or welcoming new, unvetted members to their small crews.

Two officers near the door of the bank branch reached into athletic bags they were carrying and pulled out sawed-off shotguns that they pointed toward the crowd. As people cursed at the police, one officer rushed forward, kicking a man on the street. Another officer shook a can of pepper spray menacingly toward the hecklers before opening fire. Soon, the percussions of the exploding tear-gas grenades echoed down the streets, followed by plumes of the choking gas.

It was a descent to chaos that had become familiar to the people of Hong Kong. The image of the police had degenerated into that of a band of thugs, neither respected nor particularly feared even after months of heavy-handed methods. Although they proclaimed themselves "Asia's Finest" and had been lionized in popular crime films, the city's law enforcement now more closely resembled a paramilitary outfit occupying by force. Kitted out in tactical gear, their faces shielded by masks and dark sunglasses, police smashed protesters' faces into the concrete and waved batons at reporters to keep them away from documenting their brutality. Officers deployed large cans of pepper spray, unleashing torrents of thick stinging foam indiscriminately on protesters and the public, regardless of age. They used high-powered flashlights to blot out cameras and derided demonstrators as "cockroaches." In a notorious incident, one hurled a trash can off an elevated walkway down on marchers, and others regularly tossed tear-gas grenades directly into crowds, sometimes from the open door of a speeding van.

January 1, 2020, was the last police-sanctioned pro-democracy protest in Hong Kong. Officers went on to corral and arrest more than four hundred demonstrators near a department store in Causeway Bay later that evening. Among them were three observers from Civil Rights Observer, a local police watchdog group. They wore oversized white vests with the group's logo and the word "OBSERVER" in English and Chinese characters stamped on them. There were so many held in the police station overnight that they had to sleep on chairs, sitting upright. By then, Tommy had already left. His lawyer had advised that a third arrest at a protest would be the final strike against him, sending him straight into detention before trial, without the option of bail.

From the air-conditioned comfort of his favorite noodle shop, TamJai SamGor, sipping spicy soup and chewing strips of pork belly, he watched a live stream on his phone of what was unfolding, too numb to be surprised. As darkness fell, Telegram alerts flooded his iPhone, piling up one after another with angry emojis. Officers were herding hundreds behind their cordon line, their hands behind their backs in milky-white zip ties, piling them onto buses and carting them to police stations. Tommy had flashbacks of his own forty-eight-hour detention. Following news of these latest arrests, his main emotion was relief, peppered with unmistakable anger. He felt guilty for dipping out early, for not pushing on to Causeway Bay late into the night. But he thought back to the groups of supporters he saw at Victoria Park that afternoon when it was still calm, writing colorful New Year's cards to protesters in jail. He did not want to be one of the recipients.

Back at his family's apartment later that night, Tommy exchanged a nod and a few platitudes with his mother before he went into his room and shut the door. Lying on his bed, he again opened up Telegram. There he was "justfkingdoit," one of the several usernames he cycled through to hide his identity (another was "justfkingnotdoit"). He entered a groupchat filled with people known to him simply as "parents." He didn't know who they were or what they did, just that they were volunteers who were older, well-resourced, and sympathetic to young protesters like him on the front lines of the movement.

They made small talk about the protest and the arrests that ensued, but Tommy had other things on his mind. In recent days the volunteer parents had reached out with some news: they had found him a way out. It was an insane plan, one that involved trusting his life to anonymous people with ever-changing Telegram usernames who would sail him across the Taiwan Strait, one of the most militarized waters in the world, and on to a new life on the self-governing island. The risks included death. But he—like his city—had reached a point of desperation. When Hong Kong's government first proposed the extradition bill, blurring the lines between the British-modeled legal system and one that disappeared subjects before Potemkin trials, resistance took all forms. Cleavages that had previously defined Hong Kong's modern democracy movement all but disappeared in those months, giving way to a united front of opposition lawmakers, diplomats, tycoons, lawyers, and even some politicians aligned with the mainland. The goal was singular: to stop the bill.

The mass protests did stop work on the legislation, and within months it was officially withdrawn—dead. By then, it was too late. The movement mushroomed, anger within young people like Tommy swelling into something they could not control or even fully understand. It was directed at the police, at the broken promises of Hong Kong, at their government for its arrogance, and at China for trying to erode an identity they had only just discovered for themselves in the streets, standing beside like-minded others. It was directed at the lives they were told to achieve—a family, a house—but that were out of reach for their generation. They fought not because they knew it could work but because the cost of not doing anything was simply too much to bear.

They did so knowing that their time would soon come to an end. The stakes were getting higher. They had stamina, creativity, and their ideals, but the Chinese Communist Party and its enforcers in Hong Kong held the power. When the protesters took to the streets, they knew every fight could be their last. By January 1, 2020, top officials in Beijing were moving ahead on a solution, holding it close to their chests, working in secret in a secure hotel room. Just weeks before Tommy eventually made his move to Taiwan, Beijing would play that trump card: a new law tailored specifically for the kind of dissent and resistance of 2019 and 2020, from vandalizing subway stations to lobbying foreign countries for support. China would pass that law on its own, subverting Hong Kong's legislature in a brazen move reflecting the belligerence of this new global power. International criticism was brushed aside, dismissed as meddling in "internal affairs." Hong Kongers' victory in defeating the extradition bill was for naught. In the end the legal system was subverted anyway, killing the movement not by military force but by the prospect of life in prison or years-long detention without bail ahead of predetermined trials, much like on the mainland. It was Beijing's final answer to the question of how the territory could be neutralized, one that had its roots in colonial history and would have far-reaching global consequences.

Tommy's binary—jail or flight—would become the defining question for all the guardians of Hong Kong's civil society and democratic ideals. Tommy was just a few steps ahead and, in retrospect, incredibly lucky.

INTRODUCTION

W<small>E WERE SEATED IN A "YELLOW" CAFÉ ON JULY 2, 2020, THE DAY</small> after China's new national security law went into effect in Hong Kong. It was one of the hundreds of establishments—bubble-tea shops, traditional diners known as cha chaan teng, Japanese-style coffee cafés, bakeries peddling soft, sweet breads—that for the last year had proudly displayed their support for the pro-democracy protests. But over the past forty-eight hours, the posters, slogans, and banners had started to come down. Employees were packing away hundreds of neon Post-It notes into flimsy plastic bags, scrubbing bits of glue that remained after peeling off stickers featuring a smiling cartoon pig, the mascot of the local online forum LIHKG that had become an enduring symbol of the protests. People were afraid.

The frosted-glass door to the café was completely opaque. We had buzzed in and looked up at the CCTV. Our faces were covered with surgical masks, this being the height of the COVID-19 pandemic, but they'd know who we were. They were expecting us. The security was warranted. A raid on this café would have revealed folder after folder, each containing details of successful rescues, of people who were now living free, away from the grasp of the Chinese Communist Party.

Tommy, although we didn't know him yet, wasn't the only one looking for a way out. The national security law carried jail terms up to life, but that wasn't even the scariest part: its ambiguity was. No one knew how to define the vague crimes held within, such as "subversion" against the state. We had not yet seen how the British-modeled legal system, once Hong Kong's pride, would integrate the Chinese law and be corrupted by it. Looking to China's past, everyone feared the worst.

So dozens and dozens of young men and women across Hong Kong were calling up interlocutors like the two sitting before us, hoping for a solution.

Between puffs of their cigarettes, the two started explaining the process. If you had your passport, it was pretty simple. All you had to do was get on a plane. Canada, the UK, Australia—all were coming up with special immigration pathways for Hong Kongers in response to the new law. Get there, and they'd help with the rest, including sponsors or temporary housing. The pandemic offered some inconveniences—quarantine, COVID-19 tests, lockdowns—but that was nothing compared to the risk of staying put.

The more complicated cases involved those without passports and facing charges such as rioting, arson, or assaulting a police officer. Given that the city's only land border was with China, there was only one way out: over water. They told us that a small fishing boat would bring a group of escapees out to sea to a larger trawler more fit for the voyage, then on to Taiwan, where they'd slip away and disappear in the last part of "greater China" that still had democratic freedoms.

Frankly, this second part sounded like fiction.

We'd met in Myanmar in 2014, where we also started dating. There, we reported extensively on the Rohingya refugee crisis, following the rake-thin, stateless migrants as they set off from squalid camps on the far edge of the impoverished country to places like Malaysia and Indonesia. We'd heard of this process—first a small fishing boat, then on to a bigger boat, then out into the open sea. But it was in the context of people who had little to lose, gambling with death in the hope of a marginally better life. We'd never had that conversation sitting in Causeway Bay, where malls displayed the latest Cartier collection and elevators led up to trendy *izakayas*, hot-pot restaurants serving *wagyu* beef, and bars that stocked more than three hundred varieties of whiskey.

After Myanmar, and a stint in Chicago, we moved to Hong Kong in 2018. The city's media landscape was by far the most vibrant in Asia. Journalism jobs were plentiful. The *New York Times*, the *Wall Street Journal*, and financial newswires had for decades positioned their Asian headquarters in the city, aided by a seamless visa process. Hong Kong had a gregarious community of reporters, nothing like its closest rival, Singapore, which spent much of the 1990s and early 2000s suing foreign publications for supposedly defaming the government. Journalists even had a place to call their own: the Foreign Correspondents' Club Hong Kong, housed in a colonial-era brick and stucco building in central Hong Kong. It was a natural choice for the *Washington Post* to base regional correspondents there, and easy enough for both of us to get working visas. The bonus, *Post* editors said, was that Hong Kong was "quiet," a place where major news barely happened. That stability would be helpful when returning home from chaotic trips covering earthquakes in Indonesia and pseudo-elections in Cambodia.

That narrative was proven wrong within the first months of our arrival. Then it fell apart entirely in June 2019. The pro-democracy movement began to consume our lives, defining our everyday for eight months until the pandemic hit. We adjusted each other's gas masks to ensure there were no leaks. We reminded each other to eat, to drink water, to pack raincoats when it was about to pour, and an extra pair of socks. We became part of a community of journalists—of Hong Kongers—so much bigger than ourselves. And as Hong Kong moved from one trauma to the next, from the uprising to the pandemic to the crushing national security law, we moved with it, our emotions inseparable from the unraveling happening around us.

After we heard about them, the boats became somewhat of a fixation, something that seemed entirely possible yet equally outlandish. We set out to prove it was true—until we didn't have to. Just over a month after that meeting at the "yellow" café, a boat carrying twelve Hong Kongers arrested for allegedly violating the national security law was intercepted by the Chinese Coast Guard. They were trying to flee to Taiwan. As news trickled out about what had happened, there were rumors that another boat, carrying just five, had made it to the self-governing island. But no one had heard from them since.

When we managed to piece it together, we knew we had to tell that story, not just for the dramatics of the escape. It was testament to the fragility of institutions we know and trust, proof that even a place where Gucci and Louis Vuitton stores line the streets could become a dystopian nightmare that people would risk their lives to flee. Hong Kong was never a democracy. It is not even a country. But it stood as in-between, a space where completely oppositional ways of looking at the world coexisted. It had its own identity, a thriving protest culture, a free media, an independent judiciary. And then it was gone, with willing collaborators eager to brutally enforce the demands of authoritarians. The speed with which this happened holds urgent lessons. The world is standing at a precipice as an alliance of strongmen—Xi Jinping and Vladimir Putin—try to remake the world in their image. Hong Kong, Ukraine: they won't be the last targets.

We found parallels with Tommy's journey across the Taiwan Strait in his own family history. His grandmother escaped China during the Cultural Revolution, paddling across the Sham Chun River to British-run Hong Kong using a makeshift float. Then, after Chinese soldiers opened fire on students at Tiananmen Square in June 1989, a covert operation in Hong Kong came together to extract these dissidents from China. Except they were all fleeing *to* Hong Kong—not from it. They looked to the territory as a place to build their lives and families away from the Chinese Communist Party, only to witness the party create a new generation of political exiles.

Tommy and hundreds of others hoped to settle in Taiwan when Beijing crushed their city's freedoms. Yet the highest levels of Washington's foreign-policy and defense establishment predict that it is only a matter of years before Taiwan meets the same fate, just as Tibet and Xinjiang preceded Hong Kong's undoing.[1] With the focus now on Taiwan, Washington has largely abandoned Hong Kong after rushing to champion its cause when the media spotlight was on the city—a pattern in American foreign policy. The whole gamut of Hong Kong's pro-democracy movement, from the nativists supporting US president Donald J. Trump to the liberals who backed Black Lives Matter, believed that the US, the world's most powerful democracy, could help to save them. It did not.

We chose to tell the story of Hong Kong through Tommy and three others who encapsulate the spirit of its pro-democracy movement. We are not Hong Kong natives and will never be; our story is largely irrelevant in this narrative. In the few instances we believed that our presence or observations were helpful, we have used the collective "we" to avoid other awkward permutations. We also chose to use the term "Hong Kongers" to describe the people of the territory only when writing about 2014 onward, reflecting when it was added into the *Oxford English Dictionary* in a nod to strengthened local identity. Some names, specifically those of our main characters' family and friends, have been changed for their protection.

Our access to this story is a privilege, as are our foreign passports. It is worth noting that every single person with ties to Hong Kong who helped in the production of this book—from researchers to our fact-checker—did so on the condition of anonymity. We have never taken for granted our responsibility in telling this story from our positions of relative safety, recording facts when they are being actively and systematically erased.

There are so many more "braves" who are not mentioned in these pages, but we chose to focus largely on people currently in exile, considering the risk for those still in the city, and on those who want their voices preserved even if that means trading their freedom. We are deeply grateful for their trust.

PART ONE

TWO SYSTEMS

CHAPTER 1

PROMISED LAND

CHU YIU-MING WAS BORN IN JANUARY 1944 IN HONG KONG. A FEW months later, his parents tried to sell him.

Hong Kong was then under Japanese rule, an attempt by the imperial power to control the Pacific region. The invasion of Hong Kong, which started just hours after the attack on Pearl Harbor, left the city in near ruin. After three years of occupation, there were few ways to make money in Hong Kong. Rations of rice, flour, and oil were too scarce to feed another mouth. As a boy, Chu would have been highly regarded by Chinese couples who wanted a child but for whatever reason were unable to conceive. His grandmother, "Ah Ma," objected, and she decided to raise him as her own.

Chu's family had their roots, as many in Hong Kong do, in mainland China. The mainland and Hong Kong had been separated since 1841 by the opium war that would forever be remembered as a stain on Chinese history, its first great humiliation at the hands of a Western power. In the early nineteenth century, China was in a trade imbalance with Britain, exporting silk, porcelain, and tea but restricting imports from the West. British merchants responded by smuggling opium into the country, weakening a significant part of the Chinese population and profiting handsomely in silver.[1] The Chinese tried to get them to stop, but the opium merchants kept coming. In 1839 the Chinese confiscated all the opium stock from the merchants and destroyed it. Britain invaded that September, winning quickly in a war fought ostensibly for the principles of free trade and to put Britain's relations with China on "proper footing."[2] The Qing Dynasty was forced to sign the Treaty of Nanking, ceding the island of Hong Kong over to the British as a colony "in perpetuity." After a second opium war in 1860, the colony was extended to include the Kowloon peninsula. In 1898 the British added the New Territories to British Hong Kong, this time under different terms: a ninety-nine-year lease.

The treaties did little to change the reality of a porous border, or family ties that spanned both sides of Shenzhen Bay. Ah Ma asked another one of her sons to travel from Zhuwu village, a rural settlement in Guangdong Province in southern China where everyone shared their surname, and bring the toddler Chu to her. Together, they eked out a quiet life. They did almost everything together, sleeping in the same bed in a small brick house. The elderly woman made enough money to buy food for them both by repairing torn fishing nets. Though just a child, Chu quickly went to work as well. He kept an eye on small herds of cattle and helped guide them into the mountains to graze. Chu's parents cut ties with him as if they'd never had the boy. He soon couldn't remember anything about them: not their names, the contours of their faces, or if they ever held him.

Japan was losing the war by the time Chu was born, and surrendered in 1945 after the US dropped two atomic bombs on the cities of Hiroshima and Nagasaki. Hong Kong stabilized under the British, who sailed back to reclaim their colony that August. China fell deeper into civil war between Chiang Kai-shek's nationalist forces and Mao Zedong's People's Liberation Army. On October 1, 1949, the "liberation" came: Mao and the Chinese Communist Party founded the People's Republic of China. Chiang's nationalist government fled from the mainland to the island of Taiwan, establishing Taipei as the provisional capital of the Republic of China. Chu heard the "March of the Volunteers." "Arise, ye who refuse to be slaves!" the soaring anthem proclaimed. Village officials screened a film adaptation of *The White-Haired Girl*, an opera about a woman enslaved by a landlord and then saved by Communist soldiers. Chu was amazed; he had no idea that images could move.

When Chu was in fifth grade, a teacher in his village recruited him to the Chinese Communist Party's Young Pioneers. Chu was the perfect candidate. He and his grandmother had no land to build on, no rice fields to cultivate, and no money to spend. Chu joined the ideological struggle against the rich and bourgeois. He took the Young Pioneers pledge, promising to "follow the guidance of the Chinese Communist Party, to study hard, work hard, and be ready to devote all my strength to the Communist cause." Chu marched along with the other patriotic youths, a fake gun cradled in his arms. During mock battles he tossed dummy grenades at imaginary enemies. As they trained, the students with red scarves tied loosely around their necks worked themselves into a pro-Communist fervor. "Fight US imperialism! Fight US imperialism!" they shouted in unison, condemning the rising capitalist superpower that refused to recognize Mao's China and instead backed the Republic of China in Taiwan as the sole legitimate government of the country.

Sometimes, the enemies were real, flesh and blood. It was the time of land reform, where plots were taken from the rich and redistributed to poor residents like Chu and his grandmother. Landlords, the Communist Party told the villagers, were the root of evil. They were drivers of great inequality, the reason some were able to feast on rice and meat while others had only scraps for dinner. With this type of messaging fueling his strength, Chu meted out beatings. He lifted his rattan pole and swung it downward, landing heavy blows on accused landlords until they confessed to their crimes. He gathered with his young comrades to watch public trials where party officials violently interrogated landowners on how many acres they owned and what they charged for rent. The new state's red flag, emblazoned with five yellow stars, flapped above them. Sometimes the people found guilty were dragged not far from the stage and shot dead in full view. A few who were unwilling to be subjected to this humiliation took their own lives, jumping into the nearby river or hanging themselves.

One morning in his last year of elementary school, a neighbor anxiously sought out Chu, urging the boy to return home to check on his grandmother. Through the brick wall, neighbors could hear everything from Chu's home; the poor construction made keeping tabs inevitable. They had heard no sound all morning from the woman, who had recently fallen ill. Alarmed, Chu ran inside and over to the bed. He prodded his grandmother. "Ah Ma, Ah Ma!" he wailed, over and over. She didn't move.

There was no doctor in the village, so the neighbors pronounced her dead. Chu stayed with her for three days, per the custom of the countryside, watching over her body. When she was finally buried, his tears had run dry. He continued living in her small house, alone.

His loss compounded the difficulties of everyday life. The reforms promised equality, but Chu still went to bed hungry at night. Communist officials overestimated the amount of grain and harvest villagers could produce, and requisitioned so much food that they were left with little for themselves. Villagers began foraging, chopping leaves off banana trees and boiling them. Chu stole to survive. He and his friends used chicken cages to trap carp from ponds and rushed them back home, their slippery, scaled bodies writhing under the boys' shirts. Chu made sure that all the doors and windows were closed before frying the fish, worried that his neighbors would report him—as they were encouraged to do—if they caught a whiff of the aroma. He caught frogs, more difficult in the winter. Sometimes when he reached into a hole to find one, he accidentally pulled out a snake. Chu planted vegetables on a small plot of unused land. Officials discovered the illegal leafy greens, uprooted them, and threw them away.

His grandmother had been sick for some time before her death and, unbeknownst to Chu, started making plans for when she was gone. She had summoned another villager and asked him to gather the paperwork needed for Chu to return to Hong Kong when she died. She thought his fortunes would be better in the city than the countryside, and perhaps he would find someone to look after him. Within two years of her death, Communist officials signed off on his permit allowing him to leave China for Hong Kong.

Accompanied by a neighbor, Chu walked for a day from his village to a bus stop almost seventy miles away.[3] An immigration officer scolded him when he applied for his identification card. He was prepared with a birthday—had randomly picked January 21—but had no idea what his parents were called. "How," the officer asked in disbelief, "could you not know your parents' names?" Chu used his imagination.

His father, he decided, would be called Chu Kong-sing and his mother called Li Mui. For simplicity's sake, he told anyone who asked that they were both dead. The bus took him from Taicheng up to Guangzhou, where he stared out the window at the art deco Oi Kwan Hotel, which seemed impossibly tall. The bus continued down to Shenzhen and over the border. As Chu crossed from the Kowloon peninsula to Hong Kong Island, the arches and cupola of the four-story Queen's Building, one of the most prestigious office buildings in the city, with diplomatic tenants, became clearer.[4] Rickshaws and black cars jostled for space on the streets. The short boat ride across the harbor felt like crossing a vast ocean.

———

CHU WAS AMONG THE MILLIONS WHO ARRIVED IN HONG KONG FROM THE 1950s to the 1980s, fleeing the harsh reality the Chinese Communist Party had created.[5] He was among the lucky few with legitimate papers. About two million came to the city undocumented. Others died along the journey or were caught and repatriated. They believed that the risk was worth taking. The relatively porous border meant the difference between British rule and Chinese rule, poverty and opportunity, famine and sufficiency, and, most fundamentally, persecution and freedom.

Collectivization in rural China was escalating in the late 1950s, and the kind of changes Chu and his grandmother saw drove millions like them into extreme poverty. It would be the greatest famine in human history, with some thirty million deaths from starvation.[6] Just over the border from Hong Kong, in Bao'an County—or what we now call Shenzhen—local officials similarly forced families to grow crops according to state directives, pushing collectivization over private trade. Adhering to the rules meant going hungry; ignoring them meant being forcibly sent to a labor camp.[7]

Hong Kong, separated by just a narrow bay, was another world. The average income of a farmer in Bao'an County was about seventy cents per day; in Hong Kong, the same farmer could earn about a hundred times more. Most in Bao'an had family members across the border and relied on them for income. Villagers would sing a local folk song: "A year of hard work is not as good as 8 cents across the street," a reference to the cost of sending a letter to relatives in Hong Kong, asking for money. Some, trying to skirt import restrictions, wore multiple layers when traveling—sometimes up to ten shirts and eight pairs of pants even in the summer—to distribute to their impoverished families on the mainland. Even the garbage floating across the border from Hong Kong became treasure worth collecting and keeping.

In the late 1960s the Cultural Revolution, in which suspected capitalists and intellectuals were purged, sped up the exodus. Those branded "counterrevolutionaries"—physicists, poets, and others—were publicly criticized, exiled, and "reeducated," and urban youths were sent to the countryside to learn from the proletariat. Others were executed. Hong Kong offered a way out.

Without papers, undocumented migrants could not present themselves to Chinese immigration officials, who let out only those like Chu after determining that they had no production capacity. These desperate refugees took wooden boats or made their own out of rubber. Some climbed across barbed-wire fences lining the borders. So many swam across the Shenzhen River that they became known as "Freedom Swimmers," braving fields of sharp oysters, police patrols ordered to shoot uncooperative fugitives, and the strong currents. The journey could take anywhere from four to eight hours, depending on the tide. As early as 1917, Chairman Mao encouraged Chinese people to exercise, writing that those "whose skin is flabby are soft and dull in will."[8] Some learned to swim, a sport of symbolic importance to Mao. Soon after launching the Cultural Revolution, he swam in the Yangtze River near Wuhan in 1966, hoping to prove his status as the paramount leader and showcase his prowess. Masses of people were now using far more strength to flee his China.

Hong Kong soon became a promised land for critics who did not or could not conform to the Communist Party's rule. The British territory started to develop an identity as one with unmistakable cultural and historical ties to the mainland, but shaped by opposition to the one-party state across the border. Each wave of migrants brought with them scars of mistreatment and starvation. They looked to Hong Kong as a new land in which to rebuild their lives, daring to dream of ample meals, a living wage, and a family of their own, unconstrained by the Chinese Communist Party.

———

VILLAGES WERE EMPTYING OUT, AND CHU FOUND FAMILIAR FACES FROM Zhuwu when he arrived in Hong Kong. One helped him secure a job at a tailor in Kowloon. He joined the masses hustling to make a living among the patchwork of stores and apartments. Chu hoped to learn the trade, one day sewing suits and stitching buttons himself. Instead, he was relegated to menial and demeaning labor. He cooked for his boss and slogged through heaps of laundry while making a pittance. Tired of unending tasks and verbal abuse, Chu quit and took up shining shoes. He set up his perch on Nam Cheong Street, a thoroughfare of the textile industry lined with fabric shops and weaving studios. During the day, Chu knelt before businessmen, polishing their dress shoes. At night, he slept on the street.

Hong Kong was full of people like him, trying to navigate a new world with a dark side entirely unfamiliar after life in the country. Newcomers were struck by the brothels and nightclubs, a window into the powerful organized-crime societies known as triads that ran them. Even among the outcasts, Chu was unwelcome. Other young men smoked and drank, but he couldn't choke down even a drag from a cigarette, and he never developed a taste for alcohol. Triads didn't bother recruiting him to join their ranks. Instead, they extorted him for protection money. When he came up short, they dragged him to a nearby house and smacked him with a rattan cane, not unlike the one he'd used to beat landlords back in his village. Another time, they pounded his foot with a mallet.

Chu bounced from low-paying job to low-paying job. When he was sixteen and working at a corner store, an old man started chatting with him. "Kid, you look like a decent person; you don't want to live your life like this, do you?" The man brought Chu to True Light Middle School, where he started to work as a janitor and studied English at night.

On Sundays between 10 and 10:30 a.m., the school's principal knocked on Chu's door and asked him to attend the Hong Kong Baptist Church with him. This felt like a different city, up on Caine Road in the Mid-Levels district of Hong Kong Island. The altitude of the neighborhood reflected the relative social class of its residents—the wealthiest in multimillion-dollar mansions sitting near Victoria Peak, and the next strata right in the Mid-Levels. The congregants wore stiff suits and fancy dresses. The singing intimidated him. Chu felt out of place. When a guest preacher arrived in late 1959 to share how he became Christian, Chu attended only because he didn't want to be stuck doing more work. As the preacher spoke, a revelation came in a single line: "Jesus answered, 'I am the way and the truth and the life.'" Chu had spent the past years wandering around Hong Kong, aimless and alone. The church presented a path, an escape from the poverty and isolation that had defined so much of his life. "At that gospel meeting, I made the decision" to believe, he said.

He threw himself into the church, attending services, learning to sing, and memorizing Bible passages. Chu felt himself becoming more optimistic, more enthusiastic about learning, and more amiable. When there was a call to ministry, he resolved to answer it. He had a community, stability. Chu hoped to bring that to the people he knew: the shoe shiners on Nam Cheong Street, the homeless and orphaned he had slept with in alleyways for years. "My life has been changed, and I want theirs to be changed."

Chu's enthusiasm quickly ran up against reality. He had only finished elementary school; to be accepted into a seminary he needed at least the equivalent of a high school education, known as secondary school in Hong Kong. He was over the age of admission, so he found a principal to teach him privately. Although he could read, writing was a struggle. The cost of tuition left him hungry, too weak to walk. "Lord, this is your calling," he prayed. "No matter how difficult it is, I will go on." Chu finished secondary school within three years. He felt like he had more within him, and more to give God. He continued to a private college, which supported him with a bursary. Chu worked part-time as a primary-school teacher. He was eventually accepted to a Baptist theological seminary in Taipei in 1969. Chiang Kai-shek's Republic of China was under martial law, making it difficult to enter. He scrambled to get the necessary paperwork and arrived to class a week late. His Mandarin was imperfect. He knew no one. Again, he found himself alone.

As he struggled to keep up, Chu asked a young woman a year ahead of him if he could borrow her notes. Dorothy Leung was smart, and it didn't hurt, he thought, that she was the most beautiful girl in the seminary. She admired his resilience and saw common threads in their stories. When Dorothy and her brother were babies, their mother brought them to visit family across the Taiwan Strait. The Chinese civil war broke out, and Dorothy's mother was separated from her husband on the mainland—the couple divided by the creation of two Chinas—and trapped in Chiang's Republic of China. She felt that she had no option but to give Dorothy and her brother up to a classmate, a young widow who had just lost her husband. The widow wanted only her brother at first. "I was a giveaway," Dorothy said. Yet eventually the widow took both children in and loved them so fiercely that Dorothy sometimes believed that this woman was her actual mother. Most of all, she sacrificed everything for their education, going hungry so the children wouldn't have to work. Dorothy saw in Chu a kindred spirit who understood the complexities of family.

Her affection grew. Sometimes Dorothy played the piano to accompany Chu's hymns. The two didn't want to draw the attention of their classmates, so they left campus separately, then reconvened at the post office in Taipei station before heading out on dates. Still, she had her hesitations. Dorothy had always dreamed of making enough money to one day support her adoptive mother, but here she was, falling in love with an orphan with nothing to his name. Chu started visiting Dorothy's adoptive mother often. Eventually, she gave the couple her blessing, although she knew it would take Dorothy to Hong Kong, away from Taiwan and from her.

They married in 1972, the year Chu graduated. Dorothy wore a white veil studded with dainty flowers over her curled black hair. Chu stood a head taller than her. With those vows, she dedicated herself to Chu and a life of service, wedding both the man and the Church.

When he returned to Hong Kong that year, Chu started a two-year term as the assistant to the dean of the Hong Kong Baptist Theological Seminary. The seminary promised a room for him and Dorothy. They opened the door to their new quarters and discovered it was a cluttered old utility closet. They slept on desks in the seminary classrooms until the closet was cleared out.

Only a year after arriving, Dorothy's adoptive mother died of a stroke in Taiwan, without her children by her side. Dorothy lost her chance to say goodbye. Part of her wondered if her adoptive mother had left her life of suffering to rest, now that Dorothy had someone to care for her.

Chu was working at the seminary in 1973 when Dorothy felt suddenly sick. He brought her to the hospital and was told that she had likely contracted hepatitis. She stayed overnight for treatment. When Chu returned the following morning, the doctor told him that Dorothy wasn't ill; she was pregnant. Their first son, Daniel, was born eight months later.

The birth of their first child brought more pain than joy. Chu felt guilty that he couldn't provide more for his family, and knew his wife was struggling. Dorothy felt unprepared to be a mother and trapped by the demands of caring for a baby. She found herself overwhelmed. Chu promised that they would be fine despite his meager wages and their spartan quarters. Dorothy put her faith in him.

Within a year, Chu took up a pastorship in the easternmost neighborhood on Hong Kong Island. Dorothy continued to work, writing scripts for a gospel radio broadcast, a job that her teacher at the seminary in Taiwan had arranged. The family moved into the church's dormitory—just two rooms, but theirs. Several years later, in 1978, their second son, Samuel, was born. He had a wide smile, ears too large for his face, and a tuft of black hair that protruded from his head in a soft triangle. Dorothy finally began to "sense the joy of life." She wrote articles about Samuel for a local newspaper, sharing how as a two-year-old he pestered her to send him to school like his older brother. Samuel imitated his parents' bedtime ritual, holding up a book in bed although he couldn't understand a word. His antics made her laugh.

Chu relished this simple life and the opportunity to serve his community. He still did not have much, but he had a family. He was no longer alone.

CHAPTER 2

GOLDEN AGE

C HU'S SONS WERE BORN AS THE CITY WAS ON THE CUSP OF A RENAIS-
sance, entering the decade that would give birth to the Hong Kong
of popular imagination. Over the next ten years, Hong Kong would
cement its status as an edgy city of staggering wealth and infinite possibility—as its future paradoxically hung in the balance.

The British had modeled the governance of Hong Kong roughly after
their own system, with English-law courts and an efficient, politically
neutral civil service, but without any democratic participation. The British governor, appointed by the Crown, held the most power, governing
together with an Executive Council—akin to a cabinet—and a Legislative Council. He appointed most members on both councils. They
decided on behalf of the population how public funds would be spent
and what laws would be passed. Without messy elections and with a
government primarily interested in trade and economic growth, Hong
Kong became a bright spot for investment. Free-market capitalism was
allowed to rule alongside the governor.

By the latter half of the 1970s, the economy was expanding dis-
proportionately to the territory's size. Factories began to give way to
skyscrapers and bank towers. Boutiques, discotheques, and fast-food
restaurants seemed to multiply across the city. Hong Kong became an
exporter of pop culture, rare in a region where so much was borrowed,
co-opted, and inherited from the West. The songs of Cantopop divas
spilled from red and silver taxis, awash in a multicolor glow from the
canopy of neon lights overhead. Films from Hong Kong about hardened

triads and heroic cops, kung fu masters and iniquitous henchmen, enraptured audiences in the city's cinemas and those across Asia. A new crop of stars and directors, many of whom eventually made their way to Hollywood, provided daily fodder for tabloids. Families were hooked, crowding around boxy television sets to catch a glimpse of their favorite stars. Episodes of *Below the Lion Rock* were especially popular, dramatizing the mettle and tenacity of everyday residents pulling themselves, and in turn their city, out of poverty.

Those hour-long episodes were not just aspirational. Every day, more than a million commuters suited up, grabbing oversized briefcases and tiny purses before riding the new modern subway system to their office jobs in high-rise towers. There were still huge income disparities, and many continued to toil in numbing factory jobs—but earning more for producing toys, transistor radios, and clothes. Hong Kong now had money and wanted more of everything.

The influx of cash pushed the city ever upward and minted a new tycoon class. Towers were built by an army of workers acrobatically traversing enormous bamboo scaffolding. The growing middle class found themselves literally moving up in the world: parking their sedans in multistory car parks before taking elevators up to their modern apartments. The businessmen who held the land beneath them would soon emerge as kingmakers.

Hong Kong's new fortunes would have been impossible without changes underway on the mainland. After Mao Zedong's death, in 1976, Deng Xiaoping won out over other likely successors and rose to become China's paramount leader in 1978. Deng inherited a country disenchanted with Communism after the purges of the Cultural Revolution, which ensnared Deng himself before his rehabilitation and ascent. Under Deng, the Communist country began a tentative experiment in modernizing its economy. The idea was for China to learn from the superior technology and modernity of the outside world, to "perfect" socialism by opening up on its own terms. For decades, residents watched as their neighbor across the Pearl River Delta reached higher and higher into the clouds while they remained on flat land. Embarrassingly for the Communist Party, people were still fleeing for Hong Kong in the late 1970s as they did during the Cultural Revolution.

It was up to the party secretary of Guangdong, Xi Zhongxun, to help stem the outflow. The Communist revolutionary was purged during the Cultural Revolution, his family shunned, ostracized, and abused. His son, Xi Jinping, barely a teenager, was paraded before the crowd as an enemy of the revolution and exiled for seven years to the rural countryside. Xi Zhongxun didn't see his son again until 1972, after the youth had been drained from his face. When Xi Zhongxun was rehabilitated six years later, he was put in charge of managing the southern state's affairs.

Touring Guangdong, Xi was stunned to see how far the People's Republic had fallen behind in those years. He was horrified by the fugitives he saw returning cuffed from the border, arrested after trying to flee. Xi came up with a solution: he tightened border controls and ordered the construction of more correctional facilities for the foiled escapees. Those caught trying to flee, especially repeat offenders, would be harshly punished. Xi's more essential contribution, and one that made him a progressive within the party, was his realization that economics underpinned the migration. Xi came up with a blueprint that included special economic zones where foreign investment was permitted and central planning abandoned, hoping that people soon wouldn't have a reason to leave. It was a two-part strategy of "treating the symptoms" and "getting to the root" by improving people's lives.

It was a strategy that would benefit and forever alter lives on both sides of the border. The cities where the special zones would be established—Shenzhen, Zhuhai, Xiamen—were deliberately chosen for their proximity to capital-rich Hong Kong. Overnight, slogans of Chu's childhood whipping up rancor against American capitalists were gone, replaced on factory floors with banners like "Time is money, efficiency is life" to remind workers of their new priorities.

If Guangzhou and Shenzhen were becoming the world's factory in the 1980s, Hong Kong was the shop window. Western capital, hungry to invest in the emerging Chinese economy for the first time after Deng's reforms, found a home in the British colony, light on regulation and taxation. Foreign banks quickly moved in, decorating the skyline with their logos.

The triads that once extorted Chu boomed amid this new wealth. Criminals with nicknames like "Big Spender" and "Teeth Dog" undertook brazen robberies, holding up banks and gold shops.[1] The stickups sometimes ended in shoot-outs with police, gunfire echoing down the urban canyons, leaving residents and hapless tourists in shock. Exotic sports cars became a favorite status symbol of the newly wealthy. On the streets that wound dizzyingly around Hong Kong's hills and peaks, illegal street racing flourished. Triad gangs like Sun Yee On, 14K, and Wo Shing Wo burrowed so deeply into the Royal Hong Kong Police Force that they created their own lists of corrupt officers to be promoted through the ranks, ensuring their survival and hold on power.

The import controls on the mainland created difficulties in moving items into China but didn't curb the growing appetite for consumer goods there: cars, Italian leather products, meat, luxury watches. Triad members captained "dai fei" speedboats, armored supercharged vessels that were powered by rows of outboard engines, the newest innovation in the territory's long history of maritime smuggling and piracy.[2] The boats roared northward under the cover of darkness. At times they found themselves outrunning a new, specially formed maritime police unit as they wove through Mirs Bay. Other crimes were without dramatic flair but indicative of the corrosive side effects of the new rush of money. Hong Kong's chief police superintendent, the London-born Peter Fitzroy Godber, was himself on the take, stashing away millions in bribes before being caught and convicted.

Just after acquiring Hong Kong in 1842, the British foreign secretary Lord Palmerston famously described the new colony as a "barren island with hardly a house on it." A century later, after World War II, a visiting American journalist described Hong Kong as a "dying city." Even then, these were not particularly accurate descriptors. Hong Kong and its people were too often underestimated. Some four decades after Chu arrived penniless, Hong Kong was messy, gritty, loud, dense—and thriving.

A deadline was looming. In 1997 Britain's ninety-nine-year lease on the New Territories, won during the second opium war, was set to expire. It was a time of decolonization globally, where new nations were being created and groups of people were defining themselves for the first time. That would not be Hong Kong's fate. A full decade before the British could even think about what to do with its prized colony, Beijing used its growing legitimacy to block any pathway toward self-determination for Hong Kong's people.

The People's Republic of China took a seat at the United Nations in 1971, after a majority of member states voted for it over Chiang's Republic of China as the true representative of the country. Mao's China was growing in international legitimacy, and most nations rightfully believed that Chiang's government couldn't still claim to represent 14 million Chinese on the island and also 700 million on the mainland. The US pushed for dual representation—two seats for the two Chinas—but its proposal was voted down.[3] The ROC, now commonly known as Taiwan, lost its membership in the UN and all its affiliated bodies. That exclusion continues to this day, despite Taiwan's efforts to seek representation.

With the People's Republic in and Taiwan out, Beijing got to work on an issue core to its interests: the future of two key colonial territories, British Hong Kong and Portuguese-governed Macau.

The UN had established a special committee devoted exclusively to decolonization, working on the principle that all countries have the right to self-determination. This committee created a list of colonial territories, acknowledging under international law that those places were ruled over by a different people who did not share their culture, identity, or language.

Beijing objected to Hong Kong and Macau's inclusion. The two, Chinese ambassador Huang Hua wrote, "are part of Chinese territory occupied by the British and Portuguese authorities."[4] The settlement of what happened to both was "entirely within China's sovereign right." With little debate or discussion, the committee's 1972 report parroted his recommendation wholesale. The report then passed easily at the General Assembly in a procedural vote. Other, much smaller territories such as Guam, the British Virgin Islands, and Tokelau, a remote group of three atolls in the southern Pacific Ocean with just over 1,500 people, would remain, but not Hong Kong.

It was a casual act of bureaucracy on an issue obscure at the time, but one with consequences for generations. The UN representatives effectively denied some five million people a voice in their own future. There would be no referendums, no local vote when two titans of history in foreign capitals set out to determine which path Hong Kong would take: a continuation of British administration or a return to China.

CHAPTER 3

UNCHANGED

I N THE OFFICIAL PHOTOS, SHE SEEMED TO HOLD THE ROOM, OVERSHAD-owing the aging Chinese leader with a receding hairline and a relaxed, toothy grin. His faded gray Mao suit was too big, crumpling around his shoulders while she sat stiff, pearls around her neck. But in Beijing in September 1982, it was Deng Xiaoping who held all the cards against British prime minister Margaret Thatcher.

Deng, the architect of China's new "reformed" socialist one-party state courting the world, wanted Hong Kong back at virtually any cost—even if it took a military invasion. Getting all of Hong Kong under Chinese rule was a way to "respect history and reality," to recover from the shame of the Qing Dynasty rulers who signed the territory away to British imperialists. Hong Kong, to Deng and the party, was theirs. China's century of humiliation would end when Deng secured Hong Kong's triumphant return to the motherland.

Deng had come up with an idea of what this return would look like with Taiwan in mind. Four years prior, Beijing had fully normalized relations with Washington and persuaded the US to cut long-standing military ties with Taiwan, a process that began with President Richard Nixon's watershed trip to the People's Republic of China in 1972. Washington had its own strategic interests, hoping that Beijing could counter political and military threats from the Soviet Union amid the Cold War. The US thus agreed to "acknowledge" Beijing's position that there was only one China, with Taiwan a part of it, but amid vehement condemnation from Taipei said that it continued to have an interest in a "peaceful

solution" to the competing sovereignty claims. With the British willing to negotiate over Hong Kong, Deng believed he had an answer to
both territorial problems: an arrangement called "one country, two
systems": the territory could keep its own autonomous systems, but
would be under Beijing's sovereignty. If it worked in Hong Kong, perhaps Taiwan could be won over, too.

Thatcher, the daughter of a grocery-store owner and herself a
free-market evangelist who championed "popular capitalism," had
ideas of her own. The question of Hong Kong came at a high point in
Thatcher's storied career. Buoyed by her country's military victory in the
Falklands in June 1982, just before first negotiations with the Chinese
began, Thatcher vowed she wouldn't easily give up the colony. Her Foreign Office advisers were sure that Deng would not budge on regaining
full control of Hong Kong, but it was a "difficult transition" for her to
accept their fatalism.[1] Charles Powell, her private secretary and among
her most trusted advisers on foreign affairs, explained her thinking: "If
you've just won a war 8,000 miles away to regain British sovereignty in
a small place, you're not particularly keen within a year to be handing it
back in quite another place."[2] Thatcher wanted to hold on to Hong Kong
Island, the city's financial center and seat of government, as well as Kowloon, densely populated and buzzed by jumbo jets. She was committed
to international treaties signed after the opium wars, which stated that
Hong Kong Island and Kowloon belonged to the British "in perpetuity,"
and she believed that they should be changed only by agreement.

On September 24, 1982, the two met inside the Great Hall of the People in Beijing. Deng and Thatcher sat across from each other in over-
stuffed red chairs laid with white lace antimacassars, their note takers
scribbling frantically behind them. They were in some ways mirror
images, steadfast but diametrically opposed in their beliefs. It became
clear that Deng would accept nothing less than a full exit of the British
colonial rulers, despite Thatcher's suggestions of other arrangements.
There was no room for discussion. Thatcher sat up stiffer, a black handbag placed next to her crossed legs. Deng, the diminutive former soldier,
at one point said the Chinese "could walk in and take Hong Kong later
today if they wanted to," Thatcher wrote in her memoirs. She responded

that she could not stop them but that "the world would then see what followed a change from British to Chinese rule."[3]

The two sides did manage to agree on a joint statement. The talks, they said, were held in a "friendly atmosphere." Further discussions would be held "with the common aim of maintaining the prosperity and stability of Hong Kong." Thatcher and her coterie exited, chatting and smiling as news cameras flashed. What happened next became an omen for an already anxious city.

Walking down the narrow concrete steps out of the hall, one of Thatcher's heels caught, and she tumbled, handbag still hanging from her left arm. Almost in tandem, the Hong Kong stock market—a closely watched indicator of popular sentiment in the absence of democracy—fell too. It reflected fears that the handover would mark the decline of Hong Kong, eroding institutions like the legal system, the free market, and the civil service that had come to be a source of pride. So many people in Hong Kong, like Chu, had fled the cruelty of the Chinese Communist Party and saw the British as relatively benevolent rulers who delivered economic prosperity and stability. One unofficial survey by a research firm that year found 85 percent of the population wanted a continuation of British administration.[4]

When she returned to Britain, having been the first prime minister to visit Communist China, Thatcher continued to float workarounds. Could they move Hong Kong toward some form of self-governance or try to set up a joint lease of the New Territories? To all these suggestions, her conservative listeners from the diplomatic corps and the defense forces bristled. They believed that Hong Kong could not be militarily defended, unlike the Falklands, and that the Chinese would not budge on their position.[5] So on March 7, 1983, Thatcher offered her first compromise. She wrote to the Chinese government that if an agreement acceptable to Hong Kong, London, and Beijing was reached, she "would be prepared" to recommend that China resume sovereignty over the whole of Hong Kong.

Beijing continued to set the terms, insisting that an agreement had to be reached by September 1984 or it would simply declare its own Hong Kong policy.[6] Over the next year, the two sides held almost two dozen talks. The British thought they had employed a number of "finesses" to overcome many areas of disagreement with the Chinese. All Beijing saw was capitulation—that the Western power and its supposedly uncompromising leader had given in.[7]

———

THE FINAL DRAFT OF THE SINO-BRITISH JOINT DECLARATION, INITIALED on September 26, 1984, was brief. But it held within it the promise that life in Hong Kong would be the same for the better part of the next century. The "current social and economic system in Hong Kong will remain unchanged, and so will the life style," the draft said. Rights and freedoms "including those of the person, of speech, of the press, of assembly, of association" and movement will be "ensured by law." Hong Kong would once again be under the Chinese—but with a "high degree of autonomy," controlling its own internal affairs. The city's common-law courts, complete with British colonial barristers' robes and perukes, would carry on. So too would its status as a free port, a separate customs territory, and its freely convertible currency.

This arrangement, the agreement promised, would hold for fifty years after the handover, which was set for July 1, 1997.

Congratulations poured in from all over the world, praising the agreement as a diplomatic victory at a time when the world was in the throes of the Cold War. The Joint Declaration seemed to prove that there could be a middle way between two opposing systems. The Hong Kong stock market was bullish the rest of the year, performing better than any other major exchange. Clauses that there would be local elections and laws would be "basically unchanged" were enough to convince many that Hong Kong would have a democratic future. Absent in the draft, though, were the mechanics of actual governance under the Chinese, including when local elections would be held and for what positions. The declaration was a Rorschach test. People saw in it what they wanted.

One memorandum in the Joint Declaration was less ambiguous. Keen to protect its own domestic policy interests, London insisted on adding to the document that Hong Kong people could no longer claim themselves to be British dependents after the 1997 handover. Anyone who had previously held that status could apply for a travel document—what would be later known as the British National (Overseas) passport—which did not grant residency rights in the United Kingdom.

Thatcher signed the document in Beijing on December 19, 1984. She then flew to Hong Kong to present the declaration to the nervous population it would affect most. The reception was frosty. A young reporter put a question to her: "Prime Minister, on Wednesday, you signed an agreement with China promising to deliver over 5 million people into the hands of a communist dictatorship. Is this morally defensible, or is it really true that in international politics the highest form of morality is one's own national interest?" Thatcher claimed that everyone in Hong Kong was hailing the Joint Declaration and, in a slightly cold manner, suggested that the reporter, Emily Lau, might be "the solitary exception." The visit lasted only a matter of hours. Thatcher boarded her flight en route to a snowy Washington, DC, where President Ronald Reagan was waiting to explain the details of his futuristic missile-defense program that the press was calling "Star Wars."

Even as Hong Kong prospered as a center for trade and commerce, and even in the years where China seemed a benevolent new sovereign, Thatcher herself was dissatisfied with the agreement. "Did she, did any of us believe in our hearts that 50 years from 1997, [Hong Kong] was actually going to remain unchanged?" reflected Charles Powell, her foreign policy adviser, in 2022. "Nothing else in the world was going to remain unchanged" over the next five decades.[8] Thatcher calculated that China was likely to stay weak, dependent on the Western world for trade, capital, and legitimacy. She was also convinced, given developments in the Soviet Union, that Communism in China would collapse, leaving Hong Kong a model for what China could be.[9] Deng believed the opposite. He saw Hong Kong strengthening the socialist state and picked fifty years as the duration of the agreement, hoping that China would reach the status of an advanced economy by then. In those fifty years, "there was also a need for a stable Taiwan," Deng said.[10] After that period, he anticipated that there would be even less reason for change, with China so integrated into the world economy and Taiwan sold on the merits of the agreement.

Things did change, quickly. It took only half that time for China to overtake Japan as the world's second-largest economy. But Thatcher—perhaps even Deng—was wrong about the rest. China's system endured and hardened, even as it rose economically. In just over two decades a powerful Beijing under a leader perhaps more significant than Mao would pervert Deng's vision of "one country, two systems" and destabilize the Taiwan Strait in his pursuit to unify China under his singular leadership and vision.

———

As negotiations on the Joint Declaration rattled Hong Kong, Chu made a home for himself and his family in Chai Wan, Hong Kong Island's easternmost coastal settlement. It was then a wild land, emblematic of the inequality that defined the territory. There were no men in tailored suits with briefcases, no women carrying luxury handbags. Residents still hunched over factory lines, many unable to read or write. He had work to do that went beyond evangelizing. Chu's vision as a pastor was always more about bettering his community.

An inland bay surrounded by hills on three sides, the area had been attractive to settlers as early as the Ming Dynasty. The first residents fished and planted crops. Passing ships stopped to refill supplies. The inlet provided in other ways as well; it was filled with coral and seashells, raw materials used to make ceramics. Trees grew in abundance on the hills. Firewood was so plentiful that it became the area's namesake: Chai Wan translates to "Firewood Bay." Average families—the Nams, the Luks—later moved into the area, settling small villages that bore their surnames.

After World War II, streams of immigrants fleeing China helped spur the area's resurgence. The influx brought with it a host of new problems. Housing was inadequate, a legacy of the Japanese invasion. Many people still lived on wooden boats that settled in the stinking mud when the tide was out. Shacks made of repurposed wood and scraps of corrugated metal teetered on stilts above the filthy bay. Basic amenities were nonexistent. A latticework of elevated paths wound through the ever-shifting and expanding warren of homes and shops.

A disaster at one such informal site was foundational to Chai Wan's development. On Christmas Day 1953, a rolling fire consumed the sprawling slum at Shek Kip Mei, leaving fifty thousand people homeless. Pushed to finally address the housing crisis, between 1957 and 1966 the British colonial government constructed the Chai Wan Resettlement Estate, which included a twenty-seven-block public-housing project to shelter refugees from the fire. The accommodations were spartan. Small workshops and factories located in the surrounding area were moved into the complex. A community began to grow around the factory estates built on old Nam and Luk land, providing services to laborers who toiled all day on luxuries like cars and air conditioners they could not themselves afford.[11]

Chu first visited the neighborhood in the 1970s. He traveled with another pastor from the Baptist Church's seminary. In polished dress shoes and a necktie, Chu walked around the wooden shacks and observed the fishermen balancing daintily on their tiny boats. He looked out to the typhoon shelter, an artificial cove to protect boats against severe storms, and wondered if it could really keep those living on the vessels safe. Chu had heard people use Chai Wan as a curse because of the huge number of cemeteries in the area; telling someone to "go to Chai Wan!" was like telling them to go off to their death. This was nothing like the middle-class church where he'd first discovered Jesus, full of men in fine clothes armed with degrees and textbook expertise. Chu felt almost immediately as if he belonged. He and Dorothy moved their family inside the church, which had tiny living quarters behind the chapel.

By the early 1980s, the rush of development began to reach Chai Wan, changing the neighborhood as it had the rest of Hong Kong but at a different pace. An apartment complex with more than 6,500 units rose on land reclaimed from the ocean. The Chai Wan Mass Transit Railway (MTR) station opened in 1985, connecting the neighborhood to the rest of Hong Kong Island and bringing modernity to the eastern district. Chai Wan was growing faster than officials could provide for. There were only three government-run clinics to cater to half a million residents, and not one hospital. The reverend heard horrific stories of bloody car accidents. Some victims had severed limbs, others ruptured their arteries, but all met the same fate: death in the back of an ambulance, the grieving driver stuck in cross-island traffic. Chu intuited that his community faced an acute health-care crisis, even compared to other poor parts of Hong Kong. He wanted evidence to prove it, and he found a willing ally.

Chu's humble church drew crowds from beyond the neighborhood, including eager university students. He was the attraction. Students were intrigued by his approach and drawn to an interpretation of religion that included social activism. One, a bright sociology student named Chan Kin-man, reached out after being moved by a sermon.[12] Chu put him to work quietly collecting health data from nurses and doctors that backed up the anecdotes he heard from residents.

Armed with this proof, Chu started building public support for a hospital. He held a residents' meeting in Chai Wan, where he began collecting signatures. He set up a committee and engaged with the British government. Reporters badgered him with questions. Some church leaders disparaged Chu behind his back and called him a jerk to his face for stepping out from the pulpit into activism. Lobbying was not a natural predisposition for Chu. He was overwrought. What would the government think of him? Who was he to pressure them to do anything? He turned, as he so often did, to the Bible and found his answer in the Gospel of Luke: "The Spirit of the Lord is on me, because he has anointed me to proclaim good news to the poor. He has sent me to proclaim freedom for the prisoners and recovery of sight for the blind, to set the oppressed free."

Dorothy knew that her husband was busy and anxious, so she took on more work at the Chai Wan Baptist Church. She volunteered to perform the administrative tasks and handle matters he could not. Dorothy had another part-time job as a religious director at a nearby school, and she worked to balance the two. She would not get involved in politics but pledged to support her husband. As church workers, "We serve," she said.

Chu's first victory came a few months later, when a new emergency room was set up at a Chai Wan government clinic. Colonial government officials gave the green light to begin work on the thousand-bed Eastern District Hospital soon after. When it opened in October 1993, they invited Chu to the ribbon-cutting ceremony.

———

For Chu, the experience was proof that democratic action could get results. It was the will of the people, alongside lobbying and a small opening in Hong Kong's governance, that got the hospital built—part of a transition happening not just within Chu and Hong Kong's nascent civil society but also in the city's collective psyche. All over Hong Kong, new movements were emerging, demanding housing rights, workers' rights, trade unionization, and political reform, dovetailing with the rise of a new middle class.

The British colonial government was beginning to experiment with granting Hong Kong limited democratic rights, hoping to set it up for the self-governance promised in the Joint Declaration. Until then, the British had largely ignored or willfully avoided Hong Kong's democratic development. Generous observers might say that Britain hoped it would help safeguard Hong Kong's autonomy by encouraging political participation; others, more cynical, might argue that such behavior was palatable only when another sovereign, China, was about to come to power. The fact remained that soon the British would leave, and administration would be largely handed over to Hong Kong's people. Promising young women with names like Regina Ip and Carrie Lam were rising through the civil service, moving through the prestigious ranks of the Administrative Service, until then dominated by their largely male, white, and British colleagues.

In 1982 the colonial government held two District Board elections for the first time, introducing voting for local-level administrators. These were not particularly glamorous roles, more about managing residents' water-supply issues and complaints about public facilities than debating high-level policy. A majority of the seats on the District Boards were still appointed, with only about a third elected. Still, they represented the first direct electoral contest in Hong Kong. The elections empowered civil society, which could now secure commitments from prospective administrators and then hold them to account. It was a platform for Chu to raise support for the Chai Wan hospital. Nearly every candidate supported the project.

There were more fundamental matters that were still in flux, too. The Joint Declaration set up only the framework for Hong Kong's governance, not the specifics. Those would be detailed in the Basic Law, a mini-constitution for the territory. China insisted that the British stay out of this process and in 1985 set up the Basic Law Drafting Committee, appearing to create some space for Hong Kong people to have a say in their governance like they now could in local affairs. This say turned out to be negligible, and Beijing dictated the terms of the little that did exist. The appointed committee, which reported to Beijing's National People's Congress, was stuffed with officials aligned with China's interests. A majority, thirty-six members on the fifty-nine-person committee, were from the mainland itself. The twenty-three members from Hong Kong were mostly pro-Beijing figures or tycoons. There were a handful of exceptions; two in particular were emerging as cornerstones of what would become Hong Kong's pro-democracy movement.

In many ways, the two were opposites: Martin Lee, a poised British-educated barrister who spoke perfect Queen's English, and Szeto Wah, an anticolonial, leftist union leader who in his youth recruited for the Chinese Communist Party before becoming a teacher. They and a small group of progressives started to form the vanguard of the city's civil society, founding members and tireless advocates of the kind of government that they believed they were promised by both the British and the Chinese in the 1984 agreement. With the die not yet cast on how Hong Kong's governance would look, they campaigned for direct elections for the Hong Kong government, proposing that representatives to the Legislative Council be based on one person, one vote.

Chu was part of these efforts, invited by Lee and Szeto to represent activist religious leaders in an organization that was pushing for greater democratic rights. The success of the hospital had raised his profile. He formed deep relationships with the two men, comrades despite their wildly different paths. Chu felt his calling grow beyond the immediacy of his neighborhood. Just as he pushed himself to continue on to the seminary in Taiwan, he again believed that he had more to give. Chu saw harmony between his work as a Christian reverend and promoting democracy. Democracy could compel the state to care for the most needy and vulnerable. There was dignity in believing in your God-given potential and power to make a difference in your community—this, too, was foundational to democracy. It allowed you to have your say, no matter who you were, how much land you owned, or how much rice you had to eat.

CHAPTER 4

ALLIANCE

WITH THE WORLD'S EYES ON BEIJING IN APRIL 1989—THE MONTH the first students marched to Tiananmen Square in unexampled defiance of the Chinese Communist Party—it was easy to miss the political awakening happening in tandem some 1,220 miles away, in Hong Kong. Yet the party itself was watching these developments in its soon-to-be-unified territory. The party would never forget.

The events of those early days are well-documented: Deng's celebrated opening and reform had created a new slate of problems. Inequality was growing, inflation was rampant, and corruption was pervasive. Economic changes were not accompanied by political liberalization. Communist leaders instead held firm to the one-party system, pushing out liberal reformers who dared to ask for more and had supported earlier protests. One in particular, Hu Yaobang—blunt, outspoken, and among the first Chinese officials to shed a Mao suit for a Western one—was deeply respected by students who wanted political change. On April 15, 1989, Hu died of a heart attack, his death tipping the first domino in a series of events would forever change China and Hong Kong.

On the eve of Hu's funeral, students marched to the square, demanding that his legacy be honored by accelerating the types of reforms he championed. Their grief at Hu's passing swelled, and they began to speak of democracy, a free press, and universal rights—changes that would have a revolutionary impact on party rule. Leaders began to emerge from the masses. One of the first was the cocksure Wu'er Kaixi, a twenty-one-year-old ethnic Uyghur from Beijing Normal University.[1] The party quickly branded the students as antigovernment conspirators trying to "plunge the whole country into chaos and sabotage the political situation of stability and unity."[2] Angered, more and more students joined, reaching a million people at the height of the protests.

The profound uprising in China came at a time when Hong Kong's identity was still fluid and as a new generation of local leaders like Chu were coming into their own. This confluence—and the way the protests in China would eventually end—gave birth to Hong Kong's own pro-democracy movement. It would turn a people dismissed as apolitical, stereotyped (as economic migrants often are) as concerned only about their own financial well-being, into dedicated followers of collective action.

The students in Beijing saw the people of Hong Kong as their brothers and sisters, common descendants of the modern Chinese nation. On May 1 the Beijing university students issued a public letter that was also broadcast over radio to "compatriots in Hong Kong," explaining their aim to accelerate political change in China: "We hope that the development of democracy and the reform of economic institutions on the motherland can have certain progress before Hong Kong returns . . . let's unite and push forward."[3]

The call to arms helped further galvanize people in Hong Kong, already captivated by events in Beijing. The city's economic ascent over the last decade meant that almost every household owned a television set. Families were now glued to it. Hong Kong media coverage of the developments resembled America's twenty-four-hour live news cycle, revolutionized by CNN when it launched in 1980. Hong Kong residents followed every twist and turn: the student walkouts, the hunger strikes, Mikhail Gorbachev's state visit, the breakdown of talks between protesters and party leaders—and the chilling declaration on May 19 that marked the beginning of the end.

Chinese premier Li Peng on that Friday had gathered party apparatchiks for a major announcement. Reading a prepared script, his dark, pronounced eyebrows accentuating his oversized glasses, Li Peng characterized the students as influenced by "very, very few people" who hoped to create turmoil and overthrow the Communist Party. He denounced the protesters and called for a return to calm. Martial law, he said, would begin in Beijing the next morning at 10 a.m. Chinese president Yang Shangkun announced at the same time to rousing applause that troops would be sent to the capital.

Hong Kong's weather aligned with the sentiment of the city that night. The first tropical storm of the year, Typhoon Brenda, made landfall on May 19, intensifying as the hours passed. As the winds picked up and rain moved northwest, millions were stuck in their apartments, watching the Chinese leaders speak. The Hong Kong Observatory raised the T8 signal—the highest storm warning—at 5:15 a.m. on May 20.

Pro-democracy leaders in Hong Kong, led by the leftist union leader Szeto Wah and barrister Martin Lee, voted to formally lead a series of protests over the next days at Victoria Park. They hoped that the rest of Hong Kong would join them.

———

REVEREND CHU AND DOROTHY STOOD UNDER THE RAIN AT VICTORIA PARK that afternoon, their clothes and shoes waterlogged. They sought out Szeto, who had packed a towel and an extra set of underwear so he wouldn't fall ill.[4]

Skipping the rally was never an option for the organizers, but others harangued Szeto ahead of it, asking if it would still go ahead under the conditions. He dismissed their concerns. Szeto rightly felt that his city was boiling, incensed by Li Peng's declaration. *Don't worry*, he urged; *they'll come.* By the time both Chu and Szeto turned up, hours before the march was due to start at 3 p.m., thousands had already gathered, awaiting instructions. One man took to a raised stage and shouted, "Li Peng, step down!" The crowd repeated after him. The slogan, already popular in Beijing, began to echo through Hong Kong's streets.

The crowd marched to the Xinhua News Agency and sat in front of its glass doors. China used the state media offices as its de facto diplomatic mission because the British didn't permit formal representation to be established out of fear of Chinese interference. The newspaper offices' staff, though ostensibly pro-Beijing, waved messages and banners of support from their windows. If the typhoon was a test from God, Szeto thought, Hong Kong had passed. Standing in front of the newspaper offices, he and other organizers made a spontaneous decision: they would hold another rally the next day, May 21.

That afternoon, Hong Kong residents streamed into Chater Garden, stepping over puddles and drains still choked from the storm. The manicured plaza sat under the shadow of the Legislative Council building, which housed the city's parliament, built in the early 1900s by the same architects who'd designed the principal facade of Buckingham Palace. It could not hold the crowd, and they spilled onto surrounding roads, snaking through central Hong Kong. Teachers, priests, children, the elderly, movie stars, business tycoons—all were there. The Royal Hong Kong Police Force had deployed only fifty officers, who were briefed to expect about eight thousand demonstrators.[5] The crowd grew to almost a million, a sixth of the population of the British colony.

Organizers were overwhelmed. They tried to keep the crowd flowing to avoid chaos. The sea of humanity needed a direction. Banners held high read: "What is happening in Peking now will happen in Hong Kong" and "Long live democracy!"[6] Shopkeepers handed out sweet buns and water bottles, passing along the supplies with clockwork efficiency as the masses moved past. Housewives and shop owners emerged from their homes, donating packets of food. Drivers rolled down their car windows and stuck their arms out, waving Hong Kong currency notes as donations. It could have been anarchy, but it was so orderly that there was no need for any policing. Chu and Dorothy had Daniel and Samuel with them, just sixteen and eleven years old. Samuel was too short to see above the crowd or make out much more than a wall of legs and feet splashing through the water pooled on the roads. The boys stuck close to their parents' sides and never once complained. Chu insisted on bringing his children, no matter the weather or duration of the march, hoping to imprint the profound importance of this movement. He was not an anomaly. Families like his, across socioeconomic divides, were mobilized and turned up, the fear of a crackdown or anarchy entirely absent.

After negotiations with the British government, guards at the Happy Valley Racecourse, among the city's most glamorous sites and a testament to its enduring love for gambling, opened their gates to the protesters. They filled the vast horseracing track in minutes. Crowds held up a large banner, a slogan painted in black: "Li Peng, Li Peng, we will not accept your tyranny." The march lasted eight hours and was the biggest political protest by Hong Kong people that had ever occurred. One foreign journalist wrote some days later: "The tumultuous events across the border have given the colony a political voice and propriety which was, in Beijing or, for that matter, London, never thought to exist."[7]

That evening saw the formation of a new organization, the Hong Kong Alliance in Support of Patriotic Democratic Movements of China. The May 21 rally was its debut, turning Lee, Szeto, and others into household names as representatives of this burgeoning democratic consciousness.[8] For the next thirty years, the Hong Kong Alliance, as it was commonly known, would stand as a pillar of the city's pro-democracy movement, enduring long after hopes of a democratic China were quashed and standing as testament to everything that "one country, two systems" had promised.

The crowd eventually dispersed, but not for long. They were back at the racecourse the next Saturday for a music marathon that stretched into twelve hours. Onstage that day were the biggest stars in the region, lending support and fund-raising for the students in Beijing. They'd swapped sequined dresses and velvet jackets for identical white T-shirts with "Concert for Democracy in China" across them. The petite Anita Mui, effortlessly stylish in light wash jeans with a black belt, took to the stage to perform a fiercely patriotic song co-opted by student dissidents across China: "If it's to be so, grieve not, the flag of our Republic has our blood-stained glory." The 500,000-strong crowd sang, some with tears in their eyes.[9] Chow Yun-fat, still years away from his Hollywood breakthrough, delivered a message of solidarity. Action star Jackie Chan serenaded the crowd as they waved squares of yellow fabric, a color that would become emblematic of Hong Kong's democratic aspirations, as in the US women's suffrage movement in the late nineteenth century and the 1986 People Power Revolution against Ferdinand Marcos in the Philippines. A New York Times reporter asked one concertgoer the perfunctory question of why they had turned up. The attendee looked slightly confused. "Can't you see?" they said. "We are Chinese."[10] The concert raised more than $2 million in support of the protests.

Outside observers were taken aback. A Western diplomat blithely said that "Hong Kong reserves its gambling instincts for the stock market and the mah jong table" rather than "sticking their necks out for a very iffy cause."[11] Still, the momentum continued. The day after the concert—May 28, another Sunday—more showed up to yet another march, answering the call of Beijing students to hold solidarity rallies around the world. The final participant estimate was over 1.5 million. It would hold the record as the largest march in Hong Kong's history until another seismic event, three decades on.

———

CHU STOOD AT THE CENTER OF TIANANMEN SQUARE IN THE MUGGY 90 degree May heat, squinting under the glare of the sun. He had missed the enormous march in Hong Kong on May 28, having arrived in Beijing that day to witness the demonstrations there for himself. Chu looked around, trying to take in the enormity of it all.

A fresh portrait of Mao Zedong hung above the Gate of Heavenly Peace, replaced after young people pelted an earlier version of the enormous painting with pigment-filled eggs, staining the leader's suit with flecks of red, black, and blue. Mao's portrait still bore its slight smile as it gazed down at the tens of thousands of students chanting and singing below. Chu wrinkled his nose at the stench of decomposing garbage and a sour odor from thousands of young, sweaty bodies. It looked to him like a small city, complete with a printing office, a broadcast station, clinics, and a pharmacy.[12] All those present had their assigned duties, offering full-service bureaucracy within the perimeters of the vast square. This was a self-contained world of some several thousand people, mostly students, cut off from the rest of Beijing and somehow enduring despite a lack of municipal services like trash collection and running water. The young people ran on hope and their own ingenuity, blissfully or willfully unaware of the unfolding dynamics within the Chinese Communist Party.

The reverend came with some cash donations from concerned Christians in Hong Kong. Others Hong Kong residents had previously brought over supplies like tents. Volunteers from the Alliance followed Chu a couple days later, bringing with them more than a million Hong Kong dollars, roughly $302,000 US in today's money.

The goodwill was excessive. Chu found a movement flush with resources and materials, but deeply divided on what to do next. The students didn't need the money; they needed direction. More and more were falling ill from the heat, lack of nutrition, and poor hygiene. Student leaders, having nurtured these democratic aspirations and raised expectations, now found themselves struggling to manage the thousands of lives collected at Tiananmen Square who looked to them for guidance. The enthusiasm of the first heady weeks was waning, and the crowds were dwindling. Morale was dropping. It felt like one heavy downpour could clear out the square.

The day before Chu's arrival, student leaders including Wu'er Kaixi proposed that protesters end their occupation, which had gone on almost uninterrupted since April. It would have been the bloodless conclusion to a story that had captivated the world. But it was not what everyone wanted. Even as soldiers from the People's Liberation Army in green fatigues remained deployed on the outskirts of Beijing and some students went back to their respective campuses, young people kept arriving from provinces all across China. These newcomers wanted to preserve the community they had traveled to experience.

Whatever their private views, the student leaders decided to postpone withdrawing from the square until at least June 20, when the standing committee of the National People's Congress, China's legislature, was due to meet.

———

CHU NEVER GOT A PROPER NIGHT'S SLEEP DURING HIS TIME IN BEIJING. He arrived, checked into the Beijing Hotel, and did not return until he was due to check out. He walked and walked, circling the perimeter of the enormous square that covered a hundred acres. Chu spoke to anyone he could, asking, "What do you want for China?" He also spent some time at Tsinghua and Peking Universities, which Beijing's elite students had turned into staging grounds for demonstrations and rallies. Chu wanted to bring the information back to Hong Kong and strategize with other civic-minded religious leaders on how best to lend support. He slept in the streets among the students. Chu felt that they had achieved so much but needed a plan so their movement could endure. Home in Chai Wan, his younger son, Samuel, was glued to live broadcasts from the square. He missed his father and tried without success to catch a glimpse of him amid the throng.

Just as the mood at the square had dipped, stench and fatigue too much to bear, the Goddess of Democracy arrived. Three-wheeled carts carried parts of her base, torso, and head, ferrying the statue slowly down Chang'an Avenue with an entourage fit for an emperor. Firecrackers lit up the sky. Martial law was still in place, but few took it seriously. They watched in defiance of the government curfew as the students who molded her set up a scaffold structure around the sculpture. These sculptors, drawn from art institutes, worked through the night assembling the white plaster and Styrofoam. The quick-setting plaster caked their hands like crusty white gloves. By daybreak, she was almost ready.

Coincidentally, the thirty-three-foot statue bore a striking resemblance to the Statue of Liberty: a woman in flowing robes with a torch held solidly in her in two hands, arms stretching to the sky. She faced toward Mao's portrait, staring him down in a brazen symbol of the students' challenge to China's one-party dictatorship. The statue, built over four days, was a moving culmination to the months-long movement. "Today, here in the People's Square, the people's goddess stands tall and announces to the whole world: a consciousness of democracy has awakened among the Chinese people! The new era has begun!" the art students declared. "We have still another hope: Chinese people, arise! Erect the statue of the Goddess of Democracy in your millions of hearts!"[13]

The square was electrified, alive again with musical performances, jubilation, and, indeed, hope. This new atmosphere of defiance proved fleeting. Party leaders intensified their condemnation of the students.

The statue, they said, was an affront to China's dignity, a clear violation of the law, a "serious distortion of freedom and democracy." By day, the mood remained light, the square filled with songs, cheers, and impassioned speeches. By night, the crowd was tense. The army was taking up positions closer and closer to Tiananmen Square. Under cover of darkness in the early hours of June 3, a contingent of unarmed soldiers tried to jog into the square along Chang'an Avenue from the east but were turned away by jeering crowds near the Beijing Hotel. Using buses and trucks as barricades, they screamed: "What are you doing?" "Are you the people?"[14] The soldiers were thwarted, but it would not hold. Hong Kong journalists at the square captured the deteriorating atmosphere, broadcasting updates back to a city hanging on every development.

Earlier that day, Chu finally returned to the Beijing Hotel to retrieve his bags. He was due back in Hong Kong to officiate the wedding of a young journalist he'd met five years earlier. There was one last conversation he needed to have in the square. Chu sought out Wu'er Kaixi, floppy hair framing the twenty-one-year-old's handsome, dimpled face. He told him that the students, in so many ways, had won. The world now cared about China's democratic aspirations, Chu said. The students had ignited something within Chinese people all over the world, including and perhaps especially in Hong Kong. Now they could work together to build something better.

Chu hesitated before adding another thought, one that had been weighing on his mind. The army, he told Wu'er Kaixi, was closing in. You, just students, have so much, but you have no means to fight back. "You should plan carefully," he advised. "What happens when the venue is cleared?" With those words, he returned home.

The following afternoon, the reverend stood in front of the long mirror hanging inside his wooden closet and tightened a maroon tie around his slim neck. He combed his bangs, which fell in wisps across the right side of his forehead. He and Dorothy boarded the MTR at Chai Wan and traveled across the city to a small church. There, Chu officiated as the young journalist, Connie Lo, and her fiancé exchanged vows. He pronounced them husband and wife before God. Connie was a picture-perfect bride, holding a bouquet of red roses dotted with delicate white baby's breath.

Later that evening at a seafood restaurant on the edge of a public-housing estate, wedding guests took their seats at one of the forty tables set up for the banquet, where groups of twelve were arranged around a lazy Susan in the center of each table. A few chairs were empty. At the last minute, some people couldn't make it, still covering the protests in Beijing. The restaurant was adorned with red banners and flowers symbolizing wealth and luck. Dishes of abalone and fish emerged from the kitchen, but no one was particularly interested in the food. The newlyweds and their guests were distracted. At the center of almost all the tables were radios, delivering crackling live broadcasts from Tiananmen Square.

The army, they heard, had started to move in their tanks and convoys from every direction, converging on Tiananmen.[15] The guests listened to harried reporters at the square announcing that students and their supporters were trying to push back the soldiers with anything they had: disabled cars, barricades, their own bodies. It sounded like havoc. *Please don't shoot*, Chu prayed. He asked God to keep the students safe. He wished he had misheard when the crackly radio delivered the "pop, pop, pop" of live fire. But it was unmistakable.

Chu and Dorothy returned home around 10 p.m. and found Daniel and Samuel huddled around the television, their frames cast in the glow from the screen. The boys were not usually allowed to watch TV on their own at night, and certainly not before the next morning's Sunday service. The couple sat down beside them, the gravity of what they were watching sinking in.

The massacre was now in full view, broadcast across Hong Kong and the world. As people tried to stop the armored vehicles, they chugged forward unyieldingly and pulverized bodies. The tanks then moved toward the Goddess of Democracy. She fell, reduced to rubble like everything else—the pharmacies, the printing office, the tents that Hong Kong people donated. The injured were everywhere, loaded onto wooden carts. Some were carried on people's backs or on doors fashioned into stretchers. The feed was blurry, but Chu could clearly make out blood staining white T-shirts. Corpses were placed outside Beijing's hospitals, the men who transported them frantic.

At 4 a.m. on the morning of June 4, the square went dark as the electricity was cut. The broadcast continued with nothing decipherable but rounds of machine-gun fire. The square was cleared by 5:40 a.m.

Chu's body shook. The whole family was in tears—silent. "What can I do?" he prayed silently. "In the face of such a cruel scene, such a murderous situation, God, what can I do?" The answer did not come. There was only despair.

———

THIS VISCERAL REACTION REVERBERATED ACROSS HONG KONG. PEOPLE wailed in sorrow; others struggled to breathe. Two decades later, many still choked up when recounting their experience of that night, remembering an acute sense of powerlessness.[16] The city experienced a collective nervous breakdown.

The events of June 4, 1989, triggered Hong Kong's own paranoia about the Chinese Communist Party and misgivings about its future. The carefully manufactured illusion of the 1984 Joint Declaration came crashing down the moment that the People's Liberation Army (PLA) soldiers fired their first shots. No longer could Hong Kong people be placated by Thatcher, middle-aged white British men, or Chinese officials promising that the Joint Declaration would preserve their rights and deliver autonomy. Hong Kong's people felt shaken and betrayed. How could they trust a government that would gun down its own people? How could such monsters be allowed to govern them? Why did the British sell them out?

Martin Lee, the barrister and pro-democracy leader, spoke to the fear: "Never before has any government in the world seen fit to order its own troops to kill its own people when they were not armed and not in rebellion of any kind, in its own capital city. To hand over five and a half million peace-loving people of Hong Kong to such a regime in 1997, I suppose, is like handing over five and a half million Jews to Nazi Germany during the Second World War, when they were born in a British territory."[17]

It was an event as profound in Hong Kong as in China itself, delivered to the city without the constraints of censorship present on the mainland. Hong Kong, connected and relatively wealthy, watched on their televisions and listened on their radios. The students had made them proud to be Chinese, without caveat. It was once a label they looked down on, preferring "Hong Kong Chinese" for the perceived superiority: the suits, the English language, the cosmopolitan culture. The students' goals were earnest; they'd tried everything from negotiation to hunger strikes to peaceful rallies and still lost against the force of the regime.

Yet there was also a realization across Hong Kong. Now that the hopes of the students on the mainland had been so definitively crushed, it was an obligation—a calling—to continue the fight in their still relatively free city.

The Hong Kong Alliance channeled the collective desperation and anguish into action. June 4 was a Sunday, and a march had already been scheduled. The Alliance adjusted the theme. Rather than support the students, who by now were scattered, in hiding, or dead, they instead gathered to denounce the murderous regime.

Chu, again with his sons and Dorothy in tow, headed west across the island after morning service at the Chai Wan Baptist Church. He was only half-listening when a lecturer from a Hong Kong university tapped his arm and asked, "Where's God if there is one? Why does God allow so many innocent people to suffer?" Chu pointed to the crowd around them and said God was there, in all of them working to support justice. He believed that. Although he was full of sorrow, Chu's faith never wavered.

Marchers shuffled along from the Happy Valley Racecourse, filling every street and alley as they made their way toward central Hong Kong. Subdued emotion turned to raw anger when they passed the Xinhua newspaper offices.[18] Along the route, it seemed like the whole city was enveloped in the condemnation and sorrow: the photocopying shop that filled its windows with images of bodies and bicycles heaped together in a grotesque tangle at Tiananmen Square, the dozens of volunteers lined up outside blood banks, the hundreds swarming Chinese banks to withdraw their deposits in protest and panic.

Even the Chinese state newspapers were unvarnished in their horror. *Ta Kung Pao*, a Chinese state-owned paper that would later evolve into Beijing's attack dog in Hong Kong, declared on its front page: "History will always remember this day, the citizens witnessed the tragic situation . . . [and] were full of questions about who was the sinner of the people."

Replica statues of the Goddess of Democracy began to appear across university campuses. Every June 4 after 1989, the Hong Kong Alliance commemorated the victims with a candlelight vigil in Victoria Park. Some went far beyond that—proving their support with a covert operation that would change the lives of China's most-wanted dissidents. Hong Kong became more than a place where slogans were chanted and money was raised. The plans set in motion in the aftermath of June 4 in Hong Kong created an early model for the mettle it takes to avoid the clutches of an authoritarian state. Chu would soon find the answer to his desperate question, the one he'd asked God as he watched the massacre unfold: "What can I do?"

CHAPTER 5

REFUGE

I N THE BEGINNING, IT WAS KNOWN SIMPLY AS "THE UNDERGROUND PAS-
sage," whispered between the few involved. None of the organizers
can quite agree on the origins of codename Yellowbird. Some said it
was inspired by the nineteenth-century Haitian folk song "Choucoune,"
eventually popularized in English as "Yellowbird" by the smooth har-
monic stylings of the American quartet the Mills Brothers. Others
quoted a Chinese proverb: *The mantis stalks the cicada, unaware of the
yellow bird behind.* Szeto Wah gave yet another explanation in his post-
humously published memoirs, citing an ancient Chinese poem in which
a young man used his sword to free a yellow sparrow trapped in a net.[1]
Whatever the inspiration behind the name, it reflected the immense
courage of ordinary people in times of crisis, turning regular civilians
into clandestine operatives and desk-bound bureaucrats into masters of
le Carré–style spycraft.

After the security forces opened fire on the protesters in Beijing, there were hundreds, perhaps thousands, of "cicadas," Chinese
activists and intellectuals who escaped and were being relentlessly
pursued. Their choice was to flee or disappear into China's Communist Party–controlled legal system. Wu'er Kaixi, Chai Ling, Zhou
Fengsuo, Feng Congde, and Li Lu were labeled as instigators, not
just figureheads, of a mass movement. Their false confessions and
denouncement as enemies of the state would be scripted even before
officers fastened cuffs on their wrists. From the moment their names

appeared on the list of twenty-one most-wanted Tiananmen leaders, they were guilty.

The Yellowbirds were members of a Hong Kong–based operation that came together to save these people. Who or how many was never fully documented, obscured by a deliberately nebulous structure and code names like Tiger and Brother Six. At great risk and with unwavering moral conviction, this group—hardened triad members, diplomats, businessmen, British government officials, activists, and one Baptist reverend who just years earlier was hesitant to lobby for a hospital—worked together to spirit away the most-wanted and more to Hong Kong and then on to refuge abroad.

Those they rescued, about three hundred in all, set out in new lives. Some remained prominent activists; others left politics behind. Li Lu, the first saved by Operation Yellowbird, founded a successful venture capital firm with investments from the likes of billionaire Warren Buffett. Bob Fu, one of the last to leave Hong Kong, became a Christian pastor in Texas and evolved into a prominent supporter of US president Donald J. Trump, attending the January 6, 2021, insurrection. All owed the freedom—their ability to determine their paths—to the Hong Kong operation.

———

SZETO WAH GAVE CHU AN ADDRESS, BUT NOT MUCH MORE. HE TOLD CHU to help "them" but never said who "they" were. Approaching the entrance of the Hong Kong Hotel in late June, just over two weeks after the massacre in Beijing, Chu quickly looked over his shoulder to make sure he hadn't been followed. He walked down the long corridor, slipped past the slightly ajar door, and went into a room. It took a moment to adjust to the dimness. The curtains were tightly drawn. The hotel advertised itself on matchbooks as "overlooking the world's most magnificent harbor," but the two men Chu had come to meet weren't interested in the view. They'd picked it because of its numerous entrances and exits that linked to the busy streets of Tsim Sha Tsui. If they needed to escape, they could blend into crowds of shoppers.

The precautions were not without reason. Chu had defined himself a few ways before: orphan, reverend, father, and activist. But he never imagined himself as a clandestine operative, about to enter the high-stakes world of covert cross-border rescues.

The operation started with pleas from the dissidents themselves. They'd bolted from the square without money, clothes, or much else. What they had were stacks of business cards. Over those months at Tiananmen, they'd stuffed their pockets with the contacts of everyone from BBC journalists to filmmakers like John Sham, who organized the twelve-hour concert in Hong Kong with Anita Mui and Jackie Chan. Drawing random cards from their pile, they desperately called the numbers beginning in 852, the Hong Kong area code.

Those they reached in Hong Kong marshaled the resources of unlikely allies. The triads, Chu heard—the same organized-crime groups that used to bully him in his youth—had long-standing and deep ties with Hong Kong's film industry. The Sun Yee On had directors and actors among their ranks, and other triad groups extorted film crews for protection money.[2] There was little time to consider the implications of partnering. Even seconds made a difference when China's sprawling security apparatus was hunting you down. Triad bosses quickly agreed to direct their seasoned smugglers and their sophisticated boats away from jewelry and watches, and instead ferry wanted dissidents across the Pearl River Delta.

Arriving in Hong Kong was only the first step. Organizers knew it would be unwise for the wanted students to stay permanently, given that the colony would be handed back to China within the decade. They hoped to find sympathetic Western nations to take them in, but it was more difficult than they'd imagined. The United States was interested only in helping top leaders of the movement. Australian and Canadian diplomats demurred, concerned with red tape and negotiations with their immigration authorities. Only one didn't hesitate. *Bring the students to me*, Jean-Pierre Montagne, the French deputy consul-general in Hong Kong, said. He didn't even bother to ask Paris. *It was like taking a pee*, Montagne later explained. There wasn't any time to ask permission.[3]

Days after Montagne's commitment, Wu'er Kaixi arrived at the diplomat's stately mansion up on Victoria Peak, his yellow-colored athletic
tracksuit smelling like seawater and his feet cut from the oyster bed he
had dashed across to reach his rescue boat. A "dai fei" speedboat, captained by a man with thick gold rings on each of his ten fingers, had
rushed him from Zhuhai to a quiet dock in Hong Kong. It went so fast
that "it was like flying," Wu'er Kaixi said.[4] Montagne opened his house
to him, offered him halal food and a warm bath, then got to work preparing travel documents bearing a fake name that allowed him to travel
onward to Paris.

The two men Chu met in the hotel explained where things stood. The
rescues had begun, and about ten high-profile leaders had been saved
in that way. But the operation was growing quickly, with dozens more
arriving each day. Most did not share the name recognition of Wu'er
Kaixi and wouldn't be whisked away to foreign capitals with the same
urgency. The two men gave Chu his instructions: to persuade Western
consulates to take more students in. And while these political refugees
waited in Hong Kong, they wanted Chu to look after their needs, from
providing safe houses to calming their jittery nerves.

The two men provided no details about what their own roles were in
the rescue operation. Chu knew not to ask. Operation Yellowbird was
intentionally designed to be siloed: if any organizer were arrested, it
would not compromise the whole mission.

The responsibilities weighed heavily on Chu. He was not psychologi-
cally prepared for this. The fate of so many young people was now in his
hands. His concerns weren't for his own safety. He was simply worried
that he couldn't accomplish what was being asked of him. The full-time
pastor was also trying to placate the fears of distraught congregants
worried about what Beijing might do next. Still, he said yes.

———

THERE WAS SOME DISCONNECT BETWEEN THE REALPOLITIK ADOPTED BY
Western leaders after Tiananmen and the exceptional humanitarian
care they showed to some of the most-wanted dissidents. President
George H. W. Bush, a former envoy to Beijing, immediately suspended

high-level meetings with the Chinese, but less than two weeks after June 4, he privately wrote a letter to Deng requesting he receive secret emissaries from the US government. Bush did not want the massacre to define their relationship. Deng agreed. He met the envoys in the Great Hall of the People, chastised the American media and politicians for "rumor mongering," and denied there was ever a bloodbath. The army, Deng said, had simply put an end to "rebellion," lawfully. The Americans, National Security Advisor Brent Scowcroft among them, did not push back. They told Deng that Bush was a "true friend" and reminded him of the $10 billion in trade between the two countries.[5] The trip was not made public until five months later.

Margaret Thatcher took a similar approach. On June 5 she spoke over the phone with Bush. Thatcher agreed with the president that channels of communication with China should be kept open and "like him . . . did not want to go too far in castigating the Chinese leadership or taking measures against them."[6] Tiananmen Square had just barely been cleared, but both Washington and London were eager to move on. Britain resumed talks over the Hong Kong handover by the end of July.

Yet these same governments were marshaling the full capabilities of their diplomats, secret services, and security forces, going far outside protocol in a bid to save lives. Bush authorized the US embassy in Beijing to offer protection to one of Beijing's most wanted, the astrophysicist Fang Lizhi and his wife. The Chinese Communist Party had identified Fang, who had captivated students with his lectures on human rights and democracy, as one of the biggest "black hands" of the movement. US ambassador to China James Lilley, a former CIA operative, hid the Fangs amid stacks of books before setting them up in the embassy's medical ward. Only a few dedicated staff were allowed to care for them, offering reading materials, a microwave, fresh clothes, and a sun lamp.[7] They lived in the compound for more than a year until the US negotiated their safe release to Britain. Every rule in the book was broken for the Fangs. It is technically not possible to request asylum at a US embassy or consulate, only within the country. "How do you explain that?" asked Ray Burghardt, an American diplomat in Beijing in 1989, who helped protect the Fangs. "It is a sort of fascinating example of the

tension that always exists in American foreign policy; between the real-
ist strategic approach and the need to continue to uphold and to demonstrate our values."[8]

Similarly, although London was unwilling to repatriate Chinese
dissidents over concerns that it might affect the handover, the British
government in Hong Kong was actively providing assistance to Operation Yellowbird. Soon after the meeting at the Hong Kong Hotel, Chu
began liaising with a British diplomat with a penchant for bow ties
who served as deputy political adviser to the governor in Hong Kong.
In that role, the diplomat managed Hong Kong's external relations,
including with the mainland. By July, the political adviser and his
office were helping Chu devise covert plans to streamline the process
and minimize the trauma of the arriving refugees. The immigration
department wanted to verify who these people were, a review process that could take up to a month and keep them in detention in the
interim. Chu appealed for generosity—it sounded to him like a prison
sentence. Chu and the officials agreed that rescuers would deliver
dissidents on a Monday, giving the British government in Hong Kong
five full working days to verify their identities, grant them temporary
protected status, and release them. By Saturday, they could be moved
wherever Operation Yellowbird organizers saw fit.

Securing an exit from Hong Kong took weeks, sometimes months,
demanding a kind of patience unreasonable to expect from young men
and women who had just fled an atrocity. While government officials
worked to process their papers, Chu enlisted a dried-seafood trader
known as Tiger to help protect and look after these young people. Tiger
had unwittingly been drawn into Operation Yellowbird when he housed
fleeing students at his warehouse among packets of dried scallops and
pungent fish parts.[9] He later wanted to do more and approached Chu,
who asked him to identify and rent safe houses for the arrivals. Tiger
scoured the New Territories for suitably secure sites, ranging from condominiums with private security to simple walk-up houses in precolo-
nial villages that housed Hong Kong's indigenous settlers.

Once they were in his care, Chu had strict rules for the dissidents,
harsher than those he imposed on his children. They were not to leave

their homes on their own, the security risk too high. They were also not to date, for it could complicate plans to transport them out of Hong Kong if new couples insisted on being resettled together. Everyone had suffered enough heartbreak already. Tiger tried to cheer them up with Egg McMuffins, trips to the beach, kite-flying excursions, and even outings to Ocean Park, the city's biggest amusement park, for those who could not be easily identified. In the evenings the fugitives cooked regional dishes from their Chinese provinces, pitting rice against noodles and spicy against sour. On rare occasions, Tiger brought beer to accompany the meals. They played poker. A Hong Kong volunteer who was helping at the safe house fell in love with a Chinese student leader. They exchanged sweet nothings while they took out the trash. Tiger knew, but he didn't tell Chu.

The dissidents were still on edge. They had lost everything—even control of their own destiny. Some grew angry when friends left before them. Others groused at their onward location. It seemed like everyone wanted to go to America, flipping CCP propaganda on its head: if Beijing hated the US, then it was probably a good place. Chu eventually got his in at the US consulate through Joseph Bracken, a young American program officer who was familiar with the labyrinthine, politically charged world of immigration because of his work on refugee resettlement. Bracken did not look down on Chu's halting English or his confusion at the US immigration system, full of acronyms and complex forms. By October, the Tiananmen dissidents were arriving in groups of ten to states such as California, on student visas, on business visas, or through a rarely used system called special humanitarian parole status.

That same month, Chu touched down in Paris, feeling both exhausted and buoyant. Leading members of the Hong Kong Alliance joined him, descending on the city that had given their compatriots from the mainland safe haven. They were joined by supporters from Toronto, Vancouver, San Francisco, Boston, and New York for the inaugural conference of the Federation for a Democratic China. Despite what had occurred at Tiananmen, there was an excitement among the group about the possibility of a broad, global coalition advocating for democracy in China and Hong Kong. The crackdown had laid bare the callousness of the Chinese Communist Party. They hoped the crushed movement could be resurrected from abroad with an active diaspora. Agitating for change overseas, they believed, would eventually bring an end to one-party rule. Great risks had been taken to get the Chinese dissidents somewhere safe. The hope was that they would now carry on the fight.

Among those gathered in Paris was a man named Andrew, a tall pharmacist who had moved from Hong Kong to California to study and never returned home. When Yellowbird organizers needed help in the US, Andrew volunteered. He did whatever was needed with prompt professionalism, guiding new arrivals through the immigration process, finding them houses to rent, and helping them pass the state driving exam. Over dinner at a Chinese restaurant after a day of meetings and speeches, Chu and Andrew began chatting. Andrew struck Chu as caring and reliable. They spoke only for a few hours, but Chu felt that he could trust Andrew with the most sensitive of tasks. In short order, Chu would test the merit of his instincts.

———

In those early months of Operation Yellowbird, Chu loaded up on insurance: accident insurance, disability insurance, life insurance—he bought them all. An amateur in this world, he tried to create a kind of guarantee for Dorothy and his kids in case anything went wrong. His contacts in the political adviser's office told him to avoid the industrial Sai Wan pier on the western side of the island from Chai Wan, where cargo ships and sand carriers frequently docked. *Once they drag you into those waters*, they told Chu, *no one will know.*

Anxiety was palpable all through Hong Kong, even among those who had nothing to do with sensitive operations. In the wake of Tiananmen, calls for the British to grant all Hong Kong people the right of abode in the United Kingdom grew louder. Hopeful migrants were flocking to the Australian consulate or taking advantage of Canada's relatively open immigration policy to settle in Vancouver and Toronto. Britain held firm that right to abode was "unrealistic" but eventually agreed to issue passports to fifty thousand people, including some at risk of persecution after the handover. Chu qualified, but not the rest of his family.

One other pathway out was available to the Chus. When Dorothy was a student at the Taiwan seminary, her biological mother got in touch, hoping to reconcile with the daughter she had abandoned. Dorothy ignored her at first. She wanted nothing to do with her. Eventually, moved by her faith and a realization of what that generation had endured, Dorothy started to engage. It began a long process of healing that led to Dorothy discovering a potential lifeline for her children.

Her mother had by then remarried and had other children. The youngest married an American GI. By the early 1990s, Dorothy's aging mother had settled in the United States. It meant that Dorothy herself qualified for US residence. Using that family link and Chu's new contacts at the US consulate, Chu got to work accelerating another guarantee, one with a more permanent effect than a life-insurance policy.

In August 1990, Reverend Chu said goodbye to his wife, Samuel, and Daniel at the Kai Tak International Airport. He was stoic. Samuel carried a Walkman in his hands, loaded with a cassette tape of his favorite singer, Leslie Cheung. He had been playing the same song on repeat, about farewells and a lost childhood romance.

Chu and Dorothy had decided that their family would be safer overseas in America. He was, of course, the main target. But the reverend felt it important to stay to comfort his community. Daniel was almost ready for college, and wanted to study abroad. Finishing his last year of high school in the US would help with the transition. That was the easiest part to figure out. But Samuel was just twelve. They agreed that Dorothy would accompany their younger son. She had always been the main caregiver, managing everything from Bible study to doctors' appointments. Dorothy set about preparing herself to live and raise Samuel without Chu, halfway around the world. She spent a year learning how to drive, at first by following a familiar route from the church where they lived to a school where she worked, and back again. She was terrified every time she got behind the wheel but knew she had to push through. South Pasadena, unlike Hong Kong, did not have any subways.

The family had their own apartment at first, but Dorothy was traveling back and forth to Hong Kong and needed someone to look after Samuel when she was gone. They eventually moved in with Dorothy's mother. Dorothy told Samuel she was family, but he barely knew her and they couldn't communicate. Dorothy's mother spoke no Cantonese or English, only Japanese and Mandarin. She was also in her late eighties. Dorothy was sometimes away even when in California, working part-time at a nearby church. Samuel struggled with the isolation and unfamiliarity. He had already moved schools four times in Hong Kong. Taken from the father he adored and a childhood crush, Samuel spent his days sobbing. Chu visited, but each time he left, Samuel felt more devastated than before. Dorothy asked what Samuel missed about Hong Kong; he felt as if he had neither the words nor the permission to answer fully. "I was broken over so much," he said. Chu, his son noticed, lived his life publicly, reciting stories to rooms full of people, but was deeply private around his family and kept his emotions to himself. Samuel also learned to swallow his feelings.

Two years later, Chu fell ill with pneumonia and tuberculosis. Dorothy told Samuel that she had to return to Hong Kong to care for his father. There were obligations beyond Chu. With him ill, the Chai Wan church wanted Dorothy to take over as a preacher. Samuel promised it was totally fine: *I'll be OK*. His parents had raised him in an environment where there was "always a higher calling and a greater cause." Because of her mother's age, Dorothy placed Samuel in the care of Andrew, the pharmacist Chu had met over dinner in Paris years earlier. After helping Chu sponsor Chinese dissidents, he had become a close family friend. Andrew became Samuel's legal guardian. Dorothy never fully got over the guilt. Her younger son was barely a teenager. How could she leave him so far away? "I know it wasn't fair to him," she said, but told herself it was the best arrangement. They were blessed, Dorothy believed, to have so much support. Samuel thought Andrew was calm and kind, and slowly opened up to him, but didn't like explaining their circumstances. He avoided anything at school that required parental-consent forms. It was easier that way.

As the handover neared, the British government urged Chu to make plans for himself. His safety, they told him, could not be guaranteed under the Chinese. The reverend figured that it was also an opportunity for a break. In 1997, seven years after seeing off his family to California, Chu made a solo journey to the United States, arriving in Morningside Heights on the West Side of Manhattan in mid-June as a visiting scholar at Columbia University.

Daniel, his elder son, was working at a social-service agency in Michigan, and Samuel was at the University of California, San Diego, majoring in political science. Dorothy remained in Hong Kong, helping to look after the church. Chu had to be independent as well. The lanky pastor wandered the cacophonous streets of New York. He found some moments of peace at Riverside Park near his campus, a small sanctuary of green nestled by the Hudson River. He prayed at the gothic cathedral on its fringes, Riverside Church, kneeling before a statue of Jesus Christ in a small room only big enough for one. Chu felt less at home in his accommodations, the International House student dormitory. Lettuce from the salad bar "and other raw things" did not appeal to him, nor did pizza or bitter American coffee. He longed for cooked meals: braised pork over fluffy grains of white rice or a warm bowl of soup with a tangle of egg noodles and floating dumplings. Chu found himself succumbing to a deep loneliness, a feeling that he thought he'd said good-bye to when he met Dorothy as a student in Taiwan. Dorothy knew he was miserable. She wrote letters and phoned Chu often. The expensive international calls added up quickly. She braced herself before opening the phone bill when it arrived in the mailbox.

Chu felt like he was in temporary exile, a fate he had helped so many others achieve. From the United States, he watched the live broadcast of the handover ceremony on July 1, 1997. Guards lowered the British flag in Hong Kong for the last time, "God Save the Queen" fading out into the rainy night. The camera panned for a moment to Prince Charles, looking guileless and uncomfortable. Then within seconds, the distinct trumpet call broke the silence. The "March of the Volunteers" accompanied the red flag with its yellow stars as it rose higher on a steel flagpole. Hong Kong now belonged to the People's Republic of China.

While in the US, Chu kept in touch with Szeto Wah and his pro-democracy colleagues, who were assessing whether it was safe for him to return. None of the worst-case scenarios they predicted came true. Chinese dissidents were still living in the territory. The *Apple Daily* newspaper still ran scathing commentary against the Chinese Communist Party. Even some of the British police officers who had helped with Operation Yellowbird were still on the force. Chu tested the waters with a trip home that Christmas. It was uneventful. He returned permanently the next year. Chu went right back to the church, continued his activism, and worked on health-care projects. Life, he thought, really did seem unchanged.

CHAPTER 6

BORROWED TIME

THE MUGGY SUMMER—THE WARMEST JUNE ON RECORD—WAS GIVING way to a wet fall when Finn Lau Cho-dik started at Funful English Primary School in September 1999. He loved kindergarten and proudly displayed his graduation certificate, bound in a pastel-pink frame, in his bedroom. But Finn was apprehensive about what came next. Primary school seemed to have so many books. When they were all neatly packed into his backpack, it seemed to the six-year-old that it weighed as much as he.

Finn was the first to be picked up on his bus route. He had awoken before dawn and was still groggy as he greeted the driver. The white minibus traveled for more than an hour into the upper-middle-class district of Kowloon Tong, where Lion Rock, just north, peeked out behind the condominiums. The granite peak, shaped like a crouching lion, symbolized the spirit of Hong Kong: the resilience that transformed the territory from postwar ruin into an economic powerhouse. It was an appropriate marker for the aspirational neighborhood. The tree-lined roads were wider, without the high-rises packed into nearby Mongkok. Expansive villas, obscured by flowering bougainvillea trees, and coiled barbed wire lining high walls hinted at the wealth of the residents. Alongside them were some of the best schools in Hong Kong.

Kowloon Tong bore the same moneyed feel as in the early days of its development in the 1920s, built for an emerging middle class that wanted to live like suburbanites.[1] Every morning, thousands of children like Finn descended on the neighborhood, some making similarly long commutes. Parents who couldn't afford to live here justified the inconvenience and steep tuition by telling themselves this was the first step to their child's success in Hong Kong's hypercompetitive, exam-obsessed education system. The names of the streets in the district—drawn from British counties and university towns such as Oxford and Cambridge—added to the sense that children were getting a superior, anglicized education.

Funful was one of the schools in Kowloon Tong that offered most of their classes in English rather than Cantonese. The Laus pulled together what they had to enroll Finn, determined to make it work. Other parents after the handover forced their children to perfect their Mandarin, hoping to prepare them for future opportunities on the mainland. But the Laus were deeply suspicious of China. They stubbornly held on to their British National (Overseas) passports, although these did not offer residency in the United Kingdom, and they refused to apply for Hong Kong ones. Finn's parents wanted him to benefit from what they believed was the most valuable legacy of the British: English. He would grow up mastering a language they still struggled with. Funful's garish red gate, set between two towers designed to look like giant Lego pieces, would be Finn's entry into a life different from theirs.

In his first months of primary school, Finn was beloved by his teachers. He had perfect penmanship and was always on time with his homework. Finn developed a reputation for exceptional politeness, an impression he'd continue to give well into adulthood. Still, he sometimes struggled to focus on studies, tripping over multiplication and even English. He stared at the C- grade for the English spelling and vocabulary section on his report card, and promised himself that he would work harder.

There was one subject that felt a little more intuitive. General Studies, as Finn was taught it in 1999, was conceptualized in the final years of British rule as an introduction to social studies. The guidelines on civic education were specific to Hong Kong's arrangement: to help students understand the "importance of democracy, liberty, equality, human rights and the rule of law" but also their relationship with China.[2] Textbooks discussed the Basic Law and how the government worked. To Finn, it was the only subject that taught him the stories of his home. He began to possess the vocabulary to explain why Hong Kong was so different from anywhere else.

One afternoon, several weeks into the start of primary school, Finn sat hunched over his General Studies textbook. He read along as the teacher spoke. Her high ponytail swishing, she began to teach the basics of Hong Kong's political system. She made the class recite in unison: "one country, two systems" and "fifty years without change."

Finn wrote out a simple calculation in his textbook. He was six, and it was two years into the handover. In 2047 he would be fifty-four. That wasn't too far off from the age of his grandmother who died of cancer, missing his kindergarten graduation ceremony the year before. Finn raised his hand. "What happens after fifty years?" he asked. Would Hong Kong die too? he wondered.

His teacher couldn't really answer. No one in Hong Kong could.

———

Even at that young age, Finn felt a deep connection to his city. Unlike the vast majority of people in Hong Kong, his paternal family did not have any traceable ties to the mainland. Their ancestors were among the Hakka Chinese who lived on the land when the British took over the New Territories in April 1899. The Laus were indigenous to Hong Kong. It was a point of pride. Australian journalist Richard Hughes wrote in 1960 that Hong Kong was a "borrowed place," a nod to the economic migration that defined the territory. But for the Laus, this land contained the blood and bones of their ancestors, buried in the hills.

Finn grew up deep within Sai Kung, a verdant peninsula on the rugged eastern coast of Hong Kong. His village, Ng Fai Tin, was one of the hundreds inhabited by families who traced their lineage back to a single ancestor. During the annual grave-sweeping festival, Finn and his clan trekked deep into the hills around the village—not the well-trodden hiking routes frequented by tourists or expats changing it up from weekend boozy brunches—to commemorate their forebears, laying offerings of white lime and joss sticks. Rural Hong Kong was tucked away as an anachronism of the rapidly modernizing city, beyond the high-rises, new shopping malls, and subway lines.

Finn's father, Tsz-yin, had nine elder siblings. All lived in Ng Fai Tin. The village was a small enclave at the foothills of a 1,128-foot-high mountain. The homes were almost identical, each a three-story walk-up either in modest white or brown, topped with a terracotta roof. The Laus would always have claim to this land, protected under law.

A new moneyed class began to arrive in Ng Fai Tin to escape the dense city. Local TV stars and expatriates moved into new townhouses and bungalows looking out on the ocean. Finn's family home lay in the shadow of these new developments, a cluttered single-story dwelling hidden in a depression between shrubbery and a patch of stagnant marshland. It barely looked like a home because that was not its original purpose. It was built to keep pigs raised by his great-grandmother. When the farmlands and animals were gone, Finn's grandfather converted the pigsty, erecting walls to make two bedrooms. He affixed a corrugated metal roof at the end of the house to create a small, sheltered patio, and he covered the home with tarps on both ends. He passed it down to Tsz-yin, born in 1969.

Even before spending time in wealthy Kowloon Tong, Finn knew that his family was poor. When he was six, his parents sold the small flower shop they'd run in another part of the city, giving up the one asset in their name. Finn felt as if he'd lost a second home. Before they turned over the keys, Finn claimed all the stuffed toys he had stashed in a back room. He walked out of the shop for the final time struggling to hold them all. A series of unfortunate accidents exacerbated the Laus's problems. One afternoon in 1999, the same year Finn started school, Tsz-yin swerved to avoid another car and hit a motorcyclist. He saw no physical injuries on the driver but called an ambulance and waited until it arrived. The man thanked him, and Tsz-yin drove home, relieved that it wasn't worse. Months later, Tsz-yin received a letter from the motorcyclist asking him for damages, claiming severe mental trauma from the accident. Tsz-yin turned to his insurance company. Having filed the necessary paperwork after the accident, he was sure they could bear the cost. As it turned out, his broker, a friend, had never submitted the claim.

The Laus fell into debt at a time when Hong Kong's economy was contracting. They lost their car. Finn began to spend more time on minibuses. The small green-and-white vehicles were infrequent and sometimes dirty. The drivers were notoriously harried, careening around corners and past slower cars. But even these occasionally white-knuckle rides were a luxury. Finn and his mother saved on transport by making the trip to nearby Tseung Kwan O, the mall-dense neighborhood with the closest markets and grocery stores, only twice a week. They carried as much as possible, lugging bags of supplies and stretching them out over the next days.

His parents' hardship was made worse by their lack of education. The childhood sweethearts stopped studying at seventeen and married shortly after. When asked at school, Finn could not easily explain what his father did. Other parents were lawyers, doctors, or accountants, but without a degree, Tsz-yin jumped from gig to gig. He found work as a cook in a dim sum restaurant and then as a security guard when the restaurant closed. He dabbled in construction too, installing automatic doors on the platforms of Hong Kong's ever-expanding MTR subway network. Briefly, he managed a cleaning company. Finn rarely saw his father. Tsz-yin made the decision that his absence was a necessary trade-off for the education he was trying to provide his son.

The Laus had only Finn; they were unable to afford another child. There were no other children in his village either. His cousins, much older, had moved to more urban parts of Hong Kong. Finn grew up with the companionship of Goby, a black-and-tan village dog named after a species of bug-eyed, snaggle-toothed fish. Ng Fai Tin had hills and fields of wild overgrowth but no playgrounds with colorful slides or plastic rocking horses. Finn longed for the conveniences his peers enjoyed in public housing or brand-new condominiums. He spent hours on his own outside the stuffy confines of his home, staring at the sky. Clouds shape-shifted over the horizon. Sometimes they unleashed a torrent of rain that was deafening under the house's metal roof. It would be cool to predict the weather, Finn thought. He enjoyed knowing things before others did. Finn, as children do, stubbornly settled on a dream: he would become a meteorologist.

The pain of isolation, ironically, grew with the dawn of the internet. Hong Kong was among the first places in the world to launch broadband services in 1998, but that connection never reached Ng Fai Tin.[3] Every time Finn wanted to use the internet, he had to plug a telephone cable into the clunky computer, asking for permission from his parents. Phone calls would disrupt service. Finn spent hours playing *Little Fighter*, an offline PC game released in 1995. Rudolph was his go-to character, a ninja in a blue kimono whose skills included cloning himself or transforming into his enemy.

As he made his way through primary school, Finn retained the curiosity that led him to question his General Studies teacher but lost his outspokenness. He grew introverted, speaking so softly that people strained to hear him. The long bus rides from Ng Fai Tin to Kowloon Tong and back again became time to observe his evolving city or lose himself in his Gameboy.

The animated conversation around him on one such bus ride tore him away from his thoughts. It was July 2, 2003—a Wednesday. Students were just a few weeks out from summer vacation, but few discussed travel plans or upcoming beach trips. The bus driver, his colleagues, and his classmates were all chatting in awe of the number of people at the previous day's protest.

———

It should have been obvious that Article 23 of the Basic Law would emerge as the first major point of tension within the "one country, two systems" arrangement. The history of the clause was inextricably tied with Beijing's innate suspicion of Hong Kong, especially in the wake of Tiananmen. The crisis it created would be the first major blunder of the naive new Hong Kong government, but such mistakes would be repeated by later bureaucrats and tycoons playacting as politicians while serving Beijing's interests.

Work on the Basic Law was suspended for six weeks after June 4, 1989. Three months after it resumed, Szeto Wah and Martin Lee were expelled from the committee for their role at the forefront of the protests. Beijing said they were "counterrevolutionaries." Chinese officials who dominated the committee then worked to finalize the mini-constitution. Many articles followed from the Joint Declaration: the autonomous legal system, the stipulation that Beijing controlled only Hong Kong's foreign and military affairs. But two in particular, articles 23 and 45, were left vague. They pitted two opposing desires against each other—Hong Kong's for democracy and the Communist Party's for control—and would come to define the crux of the city's political struggles over the next three decades.

Article 23 required Hong Kong to pass national security legislation. The wording of this clause was tightened after the Tiananmen protests to add the vague crime of "subversion" against the Central Government in Beijing. It was one of the earliest indications that Beijing didn't quite trust Hong Kong and knew its propensity to carry on the democratic fight. Still, the article said Hong Kong should pass such laws "on its own," autonomously. Alongside it was Article 45, which promised that the chief executive be selected "by election or through consultations held locally." The "ultimate aim," according to Article 45, was the selection of the chief executive "by universal suffrage."

Similar wording was used to describe the seats on the Legislative Council. Theoretically, it promised that Hong Kong—even if not in the early handover years, or even within the first decade of its establishment—would one day be able to fully elect its own government.

Apart from this major ambiguity and although it would shift over time, the structure of Hong Kong's government was largely set by 2003. The chief executive ran the city with a cabinet known as the Executive Council that advised him on policy decisions. The Legislative Council, a unicameral legislature, passed laws and contained a mixture of seats. Some, called geographic constituencies, were directly elected. Others, known as functional constituencies, represented specific industries, such as real estate and construction, catering, and textiles and garment manufacturing. Only those working in the sector were eligible to cast ballots for those representatives. Originally introduced by the colonial government under corporatist motivation, the arrangement placed tremendous voting power in the hands of a few individuals and entities. Given Beijing's co-optation of big businesses and industry, results in these races almost always favored candidates sympathetic to mainland interests. Beijing used these seats as a check against those that were directly elected, and functional-constituency lawmakers wielded disproportionate power in the lawmaking process.

A third, less powerful pillar was the District Councils, renamed from the District Boards the British government set up in 1982 when it first introduced local elections, around the time that Chu was lobbying for the hospital. Members still handled local issues like trash collection and traffic in neighborhoods across the city. Initially, some district councilors were appointed by the chief executive, curbing the influence of popular pro-democracy parties. In 2013 appointed seats were abolished, creating the only direct elections that provided a rare window into the true political leanings of Hong Kong residents.

Because universal suffrage was the "ultimate aim" rather than an immediate setup, Hong Kong's first chief executive, Tung Chee-hwa, was selected by a four-hundred-member committee packed with Beijing loyalists. Tung, jowly with close-cropped salt-and-pepper hair, seemed to have the right mix of "east and west," the enduring Hong Kong trope. Observers outside the city fawned over the fact that he was British-educated and a fan of the San Francisco 49ers from his years in the United States yet also seemed to be deeply trusted by President Jiang Zemin.[4]

Not all, though, were convinced by the mild-mannered Tung. In the halls of Hong Kong's high-society social clubs, rumors, first denied and then later confirmed by Tung, swirled among businessmen about China bailing out his family's shipping empire during financial struggles in the 1980s, which some believed made him beholden to Beijing. He stunned a US congressional delegation in early 1997 when he told them that advocating for independence for Tibet or Taiwan would not be tolerated in Hong Kong under Chinese rule. The pro-democracy camp saw him as little more than Beijing's proxy. Lee told the outgoing British government that Tung was not simply ultraconservative but actually "a dictator."[5]

Lacking the legitimacy of a popular leader, Tung tried to bolster his appeal with economic promises and infrastructure projects. The geopolitical climate made it easy. Ties between the US and China were warming, and Hong Kong was set up precisely to reap the benefits. President Bill Clinton was the first to arrive at the new Hong Kong International Airport when it opened in July 1998 as the biggest passenger terminal in the world. Clinton, also the first sitting US president to visit Hong Kong, arrived hand in hand with Hillary Clinton and was greeted by a troop of lion dancers on the tarmac.[6] The president was at the end of a nine-day trip to China, the beginning of a policy of "constructive engagement" with Beijing. The cheery mood would prove fleeting. A set of external shocks—the dot.com bubble that burst in late 2000s and the 9/11 attacks on the World Trade Center—rocked the globalized city. Economic growth slowed, pushing unemployment to 7.3 percent in 2002.

Tung's government proved more attuned to Beijing's desires than Hong Kong's sentiments. Just over six months after a meeting between the justice secretary and Chinese premier Li Peng—still remembered in Hong Kong for his role in ordering the Tiananmen crackdown—the Hong Kong government released its *Proposals to Implement Article 23 of the Basic Law* on September 24, 2002.

The government claimed that the proposals were the start of a consultation process but treated them like a blueprint. They also went far beyond the Basic Law requirements. The government argued that police investigating Article 23 crimes should have emergency entry, search, and seizure powers without a warrant. Any organization that was banned in China should also be banned in Hong Kong, particularly chilling for the Falun Gong religious group. The proposals suggested that the crimes could also be extraterritorial, applying to any Hong Kong residents who committed them anywhere in the world, once they returned.

It looked to many that after the first years of largely benign rule, Beijing was ushering in a more authoritarian legal regime. The Hong Kong government dismissed those concerns. Implementing this law, it said, was not just a legal and constitutional obligation but a "moral" duty as well.[7]

———

ARTICLE 23'S STRONGEST LOCAL BACKER WAS HONG KONG'S SECRETARY OF security, Regina Ip. Ip was twenty-five, a master's graduate from the University of Glasgow, when she joined the civil service as an admin-istrative officer in 1975. As soon as the flag of the People's Republic of China was raised over the territory, Ip deftly switched her allegiance to the new ruling power. In 1998 she was appointed secretary of security under the Tung administration, the first woman to hold the post.

Ip used the September 11 attacks and catastrophic bombings in Bali, Indonesia, the following year to bolster her argument for Article 23. Hong Kong was peaceful, but the attacks provided an opening. They were, Ip said, "stark reminders that deep down, none of us can really question why security matters." No conflict was too far afield or too obscure for Ip as she searched for justification for the laws. She pointed to armed uprisings in Fiji, to secessionist attempts in Indonesia's Aceh Province, and to the Kurdish rebels in Turkey. At a university talk on the bill, Ip pushed back on the broader idea that democracy could protect civil liberties in Hong Kong. "Hitler was returned by universal suffrage and he killed seven million Jews," she said.[8]

In February 2003 the government put forward the Article 23 propos-als, sending them directly to the legislature, confident that they would pass with backing from the two main pro-government parties: the Dem-ocratic Alliance for the Betterment and Progress of Hong Kong (DAB) and the pro-business Liberal Party. They did not need the people's support.

That month, Hong Kong recorded its first case of severe acute respi-ratory virus (SARS). By the end of April, the virus had spread to some 1,700 people, racing through cramped, poorly ventilated apartments. SARS killed 299, including nurses and doctors, and it tanked the econ-omy. Schools shut for seven weeks, confining Finn and all other children to their homes.

Hong Kong people saw themselves, a small territory at China's door-step, as victims of China's SARS cover-up. The virus originated in pub-lic markets in Guangdong months before Beijing alerted global health authorities. Hong Kong dealt with the virus with comparable openness, its rambunctious press dogged in its reporting. The risks of superimposing a system where compliance was prized over openness were never clearer. Still, the government pushed on.

Just as the Hong Kong Alliance had been birthed after June 4, a new coalition of activist groups coalesced to challenge Article 23 and rally popular support. The Civil Human Rights Front began as an organization with thirty groups but would grow as opposition mounted. It was a diverse and loose coalition consisting of pro-democracy parties, labor unions, religious organizations, and LGBTQ+ advocacy groups. Each had its own specific concerns about the proposals. Journalists were apprehensive that reporting might land them afoul of vaguely defined "offenses relating to the disclosure of state secrets." Librarians who toiled in university stacks feared that they could be found to be handling seditious publications. The Catholic Church and other denominations worried that their links to underground churches on the mainland would put them at risk.

The Civil Human Rights Front made an appeal for people to turn out in the streets on the sixth anniversary of the handover. It was their chance, the front said, to prove that the city would not be silent.

The morning of July 1 began with Tung and Chinese president Wen Jiabao belting out the "March of the Volunteers" at the Golden Bauhinia Square. President Wen, there to celebrate the handover anniversary, called for understanding, trust, and solidarity, "confidence, courage and action."[9] By the afternoon, some 500,000 people had turned up at Victoria Park, just a mile away from the golden Bauhinia statue that more closely resembled an ostentatious cabbage than the flower that served as the city's emblem. They marched through the streets, singing "We Shall Overcome" in Cantonese. "Power to the people!" they chanted. Many who attended were doubtful that their presence would change anything. Martin Lee stood on a stool near the park, shaking hands with demonstrators and collecting money for pro-democracy politicians. Chu and Dorothy were among the crowd. The marchers returned home without any violence or vandalism.

The unraveling began that evening. A shaken Tung issued a statement, promising to listen to the people. He then proposed changes to the most contentious aspects of the proposed legislation, such as police search powers, but pushed for the rest to go ahead. It was not enough. The weakened government lost support from the Liberal Party. Tung no longer had the numbers to pass the bill. On July 7 he announced a deferment on the second reading. Ip left her post later in the month. Tung himself resigned in 2005 halfway through his second term, claiming that his health had deteriorated, although he would remain an active public presence for more than a decade.

Activists celebrated their first post-handover victory—unthinkable just months earlier. It opened Hong Kong's eyes and imagination to what could be achieved through protest. From that year, July 1 became an annual carnival of dissent, marked by processions of varying sizes depending on the political atmosphere. Concern was now grounded locally rather than in the faraway dream of democracy in China. With Article 23 forced into retreat, the focus turned to Article 45, working to achieve that "ultimate aim" of democracy.

———

NEITHER FINN NOR HIS PARENTS WENT TO THE PROTESTS IN 2003. THEY were forced to save money in any way they could, including on weekend transport. Finn later couldn't help feeling he had missed out.

In 2006 Finn graduated primary school after another set of education reforms. Hong Kong scrapped national examinations for twelve-year-olds. Instead, grades from the last two years of primary school would determine their secondary schools. Rather than ease pressure on students, it turned those final years into a hellish exercise in curating young résumés. It wasn't enough to get good grades. Wealthy parents rushed to sign their tone-deaf children up for violin lessons; others enrolled their hopelessly undersized kids to train like NBA stars. Students were made to believe that their secondary school would determine their lives: where they went to college, their job, even what kind of socioeconomic class they'd marry into. It all boiled down to those two years.

To his parents' disappointment, Finn ended up in a second-tier school that taught classes in Cantonese. The expensive English-language primary education they could barely afford now seemed like a waste. But Finn excelled immediately. He was at the top of his class in the first year. Grades mattered less to the thirteen-year-old than the relationship he'd begun to develop. Finn and Stephy were both Scorpios, their birthdays just nine days apart. It helped that she was also a top student, so the two were frequently paired by teachers for assignments. They developed a little routine, speaking on MSN Messenger, Finn still enduring sluggish dial-up speeds to chat long into the night.

The next year, Stephy told Finn she was moving to a better secondary school, one that used English as its language of instruction. Finn, both a little competitive and more than a little smitten, decided he would change schools to be with her. He reasoned that if he was again one of the top students, the school would easily accept him. At the end of that year's exams, Finn ranked fourth. His transfer was rejected.

In explaining his desire to switch schools, Finn told his parents he wanted to better his English, making no mention of Stephy. His mother searched for other English-language schools in Kowloon Tong that might be open to him. He had lost his interest in the whole process by then but was too embarrassed to own up about the romance. Finn begrudgingly sat for more admissions tests and eventually earned a place at a neighboring school, just across the road from Stephy's.

Finn struggled to fit into preexisting cliques at the new school. His nightly ritual of speaking to Stephy became a source of comfort. Eventually, he built up confidence to suggest she be his girlfriend, officially. Stephy disappeared from MSN Messenger before he had the chance to ask. Lacking distractions, Finn dedicated himself to school but struggled. Physics, chemistry, biology—he was overwhelmed. Finn used his summers to catch up on schoolwork, still wedded to his dream of becoming a meteorologist.

In the final year of his secondary school education, Finn applied to the University of Hong Kong. He chose Earth Sciences as his major, the pathway to a career at the Hong Kong Observatory. Confident that he would get in, he selected random backup options with little thought. Finn fell short of the grades required by just one mark. He stared at his acceptance letter from the City University of Hong Kong, in the BSc

Surveying program. Finn didn't even know what surveying was. He felt that he hadn't done justice to his parents' sacrifices. Finn started looking into universities in the United Kingdom and Australia, dreaming of a different future. Again, a budding romance would determine his path.

Finn had begun dating someone new in the penultimate year of secondary school. It was his first real relationship. Theresa was petite and slim, with long, straight hair that reached her hips. They'd alight from the minibus every morning and walk the rest of the way to school with their fingers entwined, a public declaration of love that Stephy never gave him. Theresa had been accepted into a nursing program at a college that excelled in health-care education. She didn't want a long-distance relationship. Finn didn't want to lose her. He enrolled at City University and was scheduled to start in September 2012. The university's campus was on the northern edge of Kowloon Tong. The neighborhood, he thought, had trapped him.

————

THE SUMMER BEFORE FINN STARTED UNIVERSITY CLASSES WAS ANOTHER exceptionally hot one, a balmy stillness permeating the air even after sunset. That July, thousands were again on the streets, resisting a proposal that would erode the education system that he and thousands of others had benefited from.

Hong Kong's curriculum planners, as it turned out, had been true to their goal of developing critical thinkers. For all of its flaws and the obsession with grades and exams, the system helped young people develop a sense of themselves. Teachers drummed into the post-1997 generation that their territory had rule of law, whereas Chinese human-rights activists such as Liu Xiaobo were locked away in solitary confinement without trial. Protests were celebrated in the wake of Article 23 and the law itself debated. In some schools, reading materials included columns from the pro-democracy tabloid *Apple Daily*, alongside the more pro-government *Sing Tao Daily*.

In 2012 Hong Kong's government, under an abrasive and staunchly pro-Beijing chief executive, attempted to implement a plan ten years in the making. Like those designing General Studies in 1996, officials introduced a new subject for both primary and secondary schools imbued with ideology: Moral and Civic Education. The proposed subject would "cultivate students' Chinese identity." What that meant became clear in a curriculum booklet called the "China Model." The text made no mention of the Tiananmen Square crackdown, erased in the document as it was on the mainland. China's ruling party, according to the booklet, was "progressive, selfless and united." Multiparty systems, like those in the United States, were bound to bring disaster and chaos. The director of Hong Kong's National Education Services Center, obtuse about the idea of public messaging, explained the proposals this way: "All education is, to some extent, designed to brainwash."[10]

Whenever Beijing pushed, Hong Kong found a new way to resist. In 1989 there was the Hong Kong Alliance, and then the Civil Human Rights Front in 2003. In 2012, with education now at stake, a new icon emerged. Toothy, bespectacled, and sporting a bowl cut, Joshua Wong Chi-fung was just fifteen when he and other teens founded Scholarism. Joshua and other teens started with simple leaflets handed out at the subway station, the activist version of a lemonade stand. Soon he was giving live interviews with a stirring eloquence in rapid-fire Cantonese. His generation was inheriting the energy of those who came before them. Scholarism joined forces with concerned parents, the pro-democracy teachers' union, the Civil Human Rights Front, and the Hong Kong Federation of Students, a group that had helped organize Hong Kong's Tiananmen response over two decades earlier. Together, they mobilized some ninety thousand protesters to rally against the proposals in late July 2012.

Finn joined the July protests and campaigns that summer, a transitional period before the start of university. He didn't personally know Joshua but found himself in awe of him, three years younger yet already defining a movement. Finn wondered why he had wasted so much time on academics. When university began that September, Finn scoffed at the mandatory two-week orientation. He had no patience for choreographed dances, tug-of-war competitions, or trust falls. In the middle of one of these games, he left, heading to a protest area outside the Central Government Offices.

The complex, home to the offices of the chief executive and the Legislative Council, was designed as a shared space. Architects planning the Central Government Offices in 2002 wanted the buildings to symbolize openness and "effective communication" between the people and their leaders. The two main towers, connected by a walkway, resembled an open door. Architects placed a forecourt at the east entrance of the buildings, a public space that served as a pedestrian entryway. The design was supposed to give the Tamar administrative district "back to the citizens"—they could have some symbolic buildings, even if not an elected government.

In 2012 the open concept proved to do exactly that. Students protesting the national education proposals turned the space by the east entrance into a theater of civic action, with speeches, performances, and a hunger strike. They referred to it first among themselves as a yard. But when calling for a sit-in, Joshua Wong and other members of Scholarism gave it a new name: Civic Square.[11] Their sit-in, he said, would last for as long as the government continued with its proposal.

Finn had gone to Civic Square for a few nights with his friends. Sometimes the crowd was thin, barely enough to fill the thousand-square-foot space. But the night he left the orientation games—September 8, the tenth day of the sit-in—thousands were gathered. There were grandparents, couples with young children, and so many students. In black T-shirts, they camped out on the floor, shouting slogans and raising arms crossed above their heads. Finn took a black ribbon from a volunteer and tied it around his wrist. He'd never attended a June 4 vigil. He wasn't at the 2003 protests. Now, finally, he was at his first protest. Finn was energized. This, he thought, was what it meant to be from Hong Kong.

Just over an hour after Finn arrived, the chief executive, Hong Kong's third since the 1997 handover, called a hasty press conference. The crowd watched what he had to say on a large screen set up at the square. Leung Chun-ying, a surveyor—the same trade Finn was about to study—blamed the previous administration for causing the crisis, then announced he would withdraw the national education plans, leaving the choice up to individual schools. When Leung was finished, people erupted into cheers. Some hugged; some cried. "People power!" they shouted. They had won, again.

That was it? Finn thought to himself. *It was over?* He couldn't shake the feeling that this was just a momentary reprieve.

CHAPTER 7

OCCUPY

I N THE FALL OF 2014, FINN WALKED OUT OF HIS UNIVERSITY CLASSES. So did tens of thousands of other students, some as young as thirteen, and their teachers. Momentum was building that September, about to explode into a hopeful, youthful, almost innocent movement that would define a generation.

The issue this time was more fundamental than education or even national security legislation. Beijing that August had issued a decision that backtracked on the promise so many had held on to in the Basic Law: the "ultimate aim" of universal suffrage.

Joshua Wong's Scholarism and the Hong Kong Federation of Students had called for the weeklong boycott of classes, starting on September 22, a Monday. On the last night of the boycotts, September 26, students took their fight from campuses to the heart of the Admiralty administrative district—Civic Square, where they'd celebrated their victory against the national education proposals two years ago. The area looked a little different. Civic Square was closed off to the public in mid-2014. When it reopened, the space was encircled with a three-meter-high metal fence. It looked like a cage built to protect nothing but the two flagpoles, one with the Chinese flag and one with the flag of Hong Kong. Security cameras lined the perimeter. The public space, the "open door" to the government, had been shut. Yet, in trying to end its capacity for protest, the government served only to elevate Civic Square's symbolic power.

By the time Finn reached Admiralty that evening, thousands of students were gathered. He found a spot to sit on Tim Mei Avenue abutting Civic Square and joined the chanting. Within the hour, Finn grew bored. It felt all too familiar to him, and a little bit useless. So he left, taking the MTR back from Hong Kong Island to the New Territories.

His parents had since moved to a more urban area known as Ma On Shan. The relatively new MTR line built to service that area had a modern feature—twenty-two-inch LCD TVs in every carriage. Finn was watching when he saw Joshua Wong, still with his unmistakable bowl cut, take a mic while up on a small stage and exclaim: "I urge everyone to join us in reclaiming Civic Square!" The camera panned to the gates surrounding the square. The students he'd dismissed as too placid, Finn realized, were now scrambling up the metal fence and hopping over it into Civic Square, in full view of the police, security cameras, and television crews. Many still had their school backpacks strapped on their shoulders.

Finn couldn't look away. Joshua rushed over and joined those breaking in, dozens following behind. Police officers cordoned off the area, pulled Joshua down, and arrested him. In the scuffle his glasses broke, leaving him squinting through his myopia. The crowd kept shouting: "Civic Square is our square!" Frontline officers unleashed streams of pepper spray on the crowd. Someone in the scrum opened an umbrella to protect against the sting. Others followed; the crowd was soon shielded by a wall of umbrellas.

It was too late to go back, Finn thought, but it was a moment he'd hold on to. History was happening—Hong Kong people were escalating—and he was not there. He'd carry that regret with him until he finally found his own place at the center of the action.

––––––

THAT NIGHT, THIRTEEN PEOPLE WERE ARRESTED. POLICE THE NEXT MORNing encircled those who had made it inside Civic Square and detained them too. The scenes of cuffed preteens and young people writhing in pain from the pepper spray brought thousands more rushing to the surrounding streets. The crowd spilled over into Harcourt Road, a major thoroughfare that links Hong Kong Island's commercial and business districts, running past the government headquarters. Finn's parents didn't let him go; they said it wasn't safe. They were right. Tens of thousands were gathered when police officers started suiting up in heavier gear. At 5:58 p.m. on Sunday, September 28, police fired the first of eighty-seven rounds of tear gas they'd dispense that night.

The pops of exploding canisters continued into the early morning. Streams and clouds of asphyxiating gas, illuminated by the yellow glow of streetlamps, wafted over the crowd. Some pinched their noses or covered their eyes in vain. Others coughed so hard they began to retch. Police eventually stopped, and the fumes dissipated. But within hours, tens of thousands more people had arrived. The tear gas birthed a movement into being.

This riot-control weapon had hardly ever been used on these streets before, deployed just once after the handover, in 2005, against South Korean demonstrators trying to disrupt World Trade Organization talks. Earlier upheavals resembled parades more than anger-fueled uprisings. The Lonely Planet travel guide in 2012 cited protests in Hong Kong as a tourist attraction for their "theatrics and eruptions of song, dance and poetry." They followed a certain predictable route, set in 1989 when Reverend Chu marched with Dorothy, Daniel, and Samuel from Victoria Park down to central Hong Kong. Protests were a family affair. They were not meant to end with tear gas.

What had started at the government headquarters in Tamar spread to the bustling shopping district of Causeway Bay and across the harbor to the dense neighborhood of Tsim Sha Tsui on Kowloon's tip. A street occupation began to take hold in Mongkok, its tone mirroring the grittier neighborhood. Their defiant campaign would become known as the Umbrella Movement, named for the only defense that protesters had.

————

THE TEAR GAS WAS A PHYSICAL MANIFESTATION OF ILLIBERAL FORCES THAT had been working quietly and methodically to rein in Hong Kong. Every embarrassment at the hands of the pro-democracy movement strengthened the hand of hawks in Beijing, who argued that Hong Kong had to be dealt with. It took a new leader to put that into motion—one for whom the question of Hong Kong and control over China's vast hinterlands was personal.

In November 2012, just after the defeat of the national education proposals, the Chinese Communist Party named a new general secretary: Xi Jinping. He became president a year later. Xi was the first Chinese leader born after the establishment of the People's Republic, part of a generation scarred by the cruelty of Mao's Cultural Revolution. Xi saw his father, Xi Zhongxun, imprisoned, harassed, and subjected to manual labor. When the elder Xi was rehabilitated and put in charge of Guangdong, tasked to stem the outflow of millions fleeing to Hong Kong, Xi Jinping visited often. He saw his father cement a legacy as a leading reformer under Deng, credited for modernizing China with special economic zones in an ideological departure from socialism. It wasn't clear how those experiences would shape his own leadership until he secured his grip on power.

Without much intel on the guarded man in a deliberately closed system, Western analysts optimistically pegged Xi Jinping as a globalist. They hoped he would continue in the vein of his predecessor, Hu Jintao, who at least partially opened his country to the world when Beijing hosted the 2008 Olympics. In 1985 Xi had even visited Muscatine, Iowa, on an agricultural study mission and befriended small-town Americans. At the time of Xi's ascendance, social media networks such as Twitter, which helped play a part in the Arab Spring, were still banned, but China's own social media use was growing. Notably, the microblog Weibo provided users with a new and slightly less restricted forum to air their grievances. Nicholas Kristof, who became a *New York Times* columnist after winning a Pulitzer for his coverage of the Tiananmen Square crackdown, predicted in 2013 that Xi Jinping would "spearhead a resurgence of economic reform, and probably some political easing as well."[1] Following this thinking, perhaps Xi Jinping would usher in universal suffrage in Hong Kong.

These assumptions would turn out to be among the biggest political misreadings in modern history. If Xi Jinping saw himself inheriting his father's legacy, he also saw himself as a devout nationalist with a historic mission to hold the Chinese Communist Party and the country together, said Joseph Torigian, author of an upcoming biography on Xi Zhongxun.[2] To Xi Jinping, Hong Kong might have symbolized a rejection of the party's supremacy, a territory that, even with unmistakable historical and ethnic ties to China, believed in the superiority of its own systems. China was now ascendant, but Hong Kong was still resisting Beijing's efforts to bring it closer. Xi Jinping was a revolutionary nationalist who had suffered under the system but still emerged believing fervently in it. Hong Kong, a hyper-capitalist financial center that jumped to protest every Beijing-backed move, stood as a mockery to men like him.

In June 2014, Beijing delivered a policy paper on Hong Kong that was an early answer to the question of what kind of leader Xi Jinping would be. The white paper, a 14,500-word document, publicly spelled out caveats to Hong Kong's promise of "autonomy," a reimagining of the arrangement Deng had crafted thirty years earlier for a different, weaker China. With the condescension of an imperial ruler, the white paper asserted that Hong Kong residents were "confused or lopsided" in their understanding of "one country, two systems." The high degree of autonomy that Hong Kong enjoyed, it said, was not inherent. It was granted by Beijing. Hong Kong's power was authorized by the Central Government and subservient to it. The document served to remind everyone who was in charge: Hong Kong would have freedoms only if Beijing decided it should.

The intention of the white paper's authors might have been darker still. Xi, as he ascended through the party ranks by crushing internal opposition, began an ideological flirtation with scholars of China's "New Left." The grouping despised American-style liberalism, promoting a vision of China that blended Marxism, Maoism, and fascism—specifically the ideology of Carl Schmitt, a Nazi legal theorist who believed that the law should be used to further political power. One of these New Left intellectuals, Jiang Shigong, was widely credited with crafting the white paper.[3]

Jiang, a legal scholar, had arrived in Hong Kong from Beijing in 2004 after the Article 23 debacle for a three-year stint at the research department of the Liaison Office of the Central People's Government in Hong Kong. Housed in an imposing gated building on the western part of Hong Kong Island, the Liaison Office replaced the Xinhua News Agency as Beijing's representative office in 2000.[4] Even under Chinese rule, Beijing was not allowed formal representation in Hong Kong and was officially required to keep out of its internal affairs. But for years—long before the white paper—Jiang's division was among the more than twenty departments of the Liaison Office that operated like a shadow government, marshaling support for pro-Beijing lawmakers, controlling newspapers, and cajoling business leaders to back Beijing's agenda.

Jiang, while in Hong Kong, spoke to business leaders, politicians, and community leaders. He collected his notes in a monograph when he returned to Beijing.[5] He came to believe that although "one country, two systems" was a brilliant arrangement, it could not solve a fundamental problem: identity. Hong Kong people should be loyal to China but were not. Some were still nostalgic for the Crown and growing stronger in their sense of self. The way forward was to strip Hong Kong of its local ties and help it rediscover "patriotic warmth" toward the mainland. Jiang agreed with the premise of what Deng and Thatcher signed in 1984 but disagreed with its end goal and the purpose of the fifty-year period. Those five decades were also an opportunity to "witness the arrival and departure of several generations," and for Hong Kong's heart to be returned to China. He argued that "one country, two systems" was a transitional process before China took control of every aspect of life and eradicated local autonomy. Jiang was nakedly parading Beijing's ambitions to be a new world empire, a word he used with positive connotations, fully integrating territories such as Tibet and Hong Kong—and then Taiwan.[6]

Two months after the white paper was published, on August 31, 2014, China's top political body issued an interpretation of the Basic Law that set out how the next chief executive should be elected in 2017. It was a rare direct intervention in Hong Kong's governance. It agreed the chief executive should be selected by universal suffrage, but with a caveat. Hopefuls would have to go through a screening process to win support from an election committee before the general population could vote. The election committee was still dominated by Beijing loyalists.

The decision ensured that a predictable and pliable leader would be elected. This was not democracy; it was a slap in the face.

––––––––

THE DAY AFTER THE WHITE PAPER WAS RELEASED, THE POLITICAL CAR-toonist Harry Harrison sketched two potbellied policemen in his *South China Morning Post* column. "What sort of response do you think Beijing is hoping for its white paper?" one asks. The other replies: "A white flag."[7] Hong Kong was again underestimated. The white paper only served to strengthen an idea that had percolated for over a year, that of civil disobedience as resistance.

After years of government inaction on electoral reform, a relatively unknown law professor at the University of Hong Kong had a thought on how to speed things up. On January 16, 2013, Professor Benny Tai Yiu-ting published an article in the *Hong Kong Economic Journal* titled "Civil Disobedience: The Most Lethal Weapon." Tai's political awakening mirrored the rest of the city; it traced back to the events in Beijing in 1989. While pursuing a master's degree in law at the London School of Economics the next year, he found Christianity and vowed to put his life in God's hands.[8] Tai became active in promoting civic education. He focused his research on the intersection between law and politics, and religion and the law.

Tai's article laid out a seven-step progression of resistance. He believed that the threat of some ten thousand people occupying the streets of central Hong Kong might be enough to sway Beijing. Even if this "lethal" weapon of civil disobedience was never used, Tai argued, it could intimidate Beijing and act as a negotiation tool as mainland officials decided what their interpretation of "universal suffrage" would be.

Tai thought he had considered every aspect of his plan. But when a journalist asked who might join him in leading such a campaign, he was stumped. Tai was a scholar, not a civic organizer. He blurted out the only two names that came to mind. Reverend Chu Yiu-ming was one.

Chu read the *Economic Journal* daily and came across Tai's article. Chu knew Tai well; he had officiated his wedding and was familiar with his work in promoting democracy as a legal scholar. Chu thought the article was too long and read only the headline. Almost seventy, Chu was suffering from a range of ailments. A few years prior, he was preaching at church when he experienced severe stomach pain. Chu was admitted to the Eastern Hospital, benefiting from the facility he helped establish in the 1980s. Nurses rolled him on a stretcher into the emergency ward. The pain was excruciating. Chu couldn't stand. He was hurting too much for any more tests, he told the doctors. They refused to let him leave. Doctors discovered that his intestines were perforated when a CT scan showed that the dye administered before the procedure had leaked into his body. They rushed him into surgery but told him to say his good-byes, not confident he would pull through. He eventually recovered, but without part of his intestines. Chu thought he didn't have much longer. He retired from the Chai Wan Baptist Church two years later, as did Dorothy. They spent more time with Daniel, their elder son, who had moved back to Hong Kong with his wife and two children.

The other name offered up by Tai was Chan Kin-man, the former university student who had helped Chu research and lobby for the Eastern Hospital. Chu called him up. Chan, now a university professor with a wall covered in diplomas from Yale, was in Paris, drinking a coffee. "Did you see our names in the news?" Chu asked. "What should I tell reporters when they ask me about it?"

Chan laughed. "You go ahead and say yes; tell them you'll participate. We'll talk in detail when I'm back."

The answer surprised both men. The stakes were high for Chan too, who alongside his academic work had for decades been working to build China's civil society and to train staff for nongovernmental organizations (NGOs). Like Chu and other pioneers of the Hong Kong democracy movement, Chan believed firmly that the futures of Hong Kong, Taiwan, and China were inextricably linked: fostering democracy on all sides of the Taiwan Strait, across historical and political divides, would secure a more open China. Chan knew that by saying yes, he was entering the spotlight as an organizer standing in direct and public confrontation with Beijing. He'd likely have to give up his work on the mainland.

Just two years earlier, Szeto Wah had died from lung cancer at seventy-nine. Szeto's last words to Chu were to "hold on to the fight."[9] Chu also recalled the days of his youth. Christ came to him then, gave him a community and purpose. He could not now leave his comrades to go it alone. Chu decided it would be his last push. It would begin at a chapel.

The three men gathered on March 27, 2013, in the Kowloon Union Church. The red-brick Anglican church looked like part of an Ivy League campus that had become lodged in the middle of one of Hong Kong's busiest neighborhoods. Tai, Chu, and Chan stood before a cross and took questions from reporters. Chu's silver hair stood out among the two other men's jet-black crops. "We shall be like preachers communicating . . . universal values such as democracy, universal and equal suffrage, justice and righteousness," Tai said. He reiterated his hope that ten thousand people would participate.[10]

The white paper and Beijing's decision that Hong Kong could not entirely choose its leader expedited Tai's plans. Student activists that summer started preparing for their showdown, the class boycott. After the escalation at Civic Square, Tai, on the morning of September 28, 2014, declared that Occupy Central had begun.

Beijing's Liaison Office in Hong Kong tried to brush it off, quipping in response to questions from journalists that "the sun rises as usual."[11] No one—not Tai, not the Liaison Office, not Xi—could control what unfolded over the next months. By the time the last occupiers were cleared out 79 days later, some 1.4 million people—20 percent of Hong Kong's population—would have participated in one form or another, fighting for genuine universal suffrage.

———

FINN JOINED THE PROTESTS OFTEN, MOVING AMONG ACTIONS AT ADMIralty, Causeway Bay, and Mongkok, depending on the needs at each site. He went with friends or sometimes on his own. But there were many who still only had a passing interest in the movement. One was Theresa, his girlfriend. She never enjoyed talking about politics. She begrudgingly went with him to the Admiralty site one time, but only after an argument about how passive she was about Hong Kong's predicament. She remained uninterested.

Others actively despised what the activists were doing. Tommy, years before his last New Year's Eve camping trip on the beach at Tai Long Wan, remembered his father shouting accusations at Joshua Wong on the television, an explosion of emotion rare in his family. They were being paid by the Americans to destroy Hong Kong, Tommy's father told him. Why else would they do this?

Tommy, fifteen at the time, was in secondary school like many of the Umbrella Movement protesters. Influenced by his father's convictions but also apathetic, he visited Admiralty, the main protest site, just once in late October 2014. Even that trip wasn't intentional. He was with a group of friends headed to a nearby shopping mall for dinner. They wanted to check out the scene. He felt like a visitor gawking at animals in a zoo.

Small camping tents of all colors lined the asphalt, like a music festival had taken over the city center. Parts of the road were covered with soft mats, making the ground a little more comfortable. Installations of tiny yellow umbrellas, folded in the style of Japanese origami, hung from pillars and overhead walkways. Under makeshift gazebos, some people held talks; others gathered in groups, playing protest songs on guitars. A popular anthem was 海闊天空 or "Boundless Oceans, Vast Skies," a 1990s ballad from the Cantopop band Beyond. It drove protesters to tears before it reached its chorus, the first line roughly translating to "Forgive me for this life of uninhibited love and indulging in my freedom." On the steps leading up to Hong Kong's Legislative Council, people placed colorful sticky notes with words of encouragement—a "Lennon Wall," named for the one created in Prague after the murder of the Beatles singer. Under a shelter, students had set up a library and a study corner. Some were entirely absorbed in their books, oblivious to the carnival around them.

Tommy tried to understand why they were camped out and he wasn't. Until he was seven, Tommy was raised by his paternal grandparents. His mother was living in China, where she was born, waiting for papers that would allow her to emigrate to Hong Kong. His father couldn't care for Tommy and his sister on his own. Tommy grew up hearing how his grandmother had escaped at nineteen with three others from southern China in the late 1960s. She was a Freedom Swimmer, fleeing Mao's Cultural Revolution. Because she couldn't swim, she told him she used a float to bob her way along the Shenzhen River until she reached the shores of Hong Kong. Some aspects of the story seemed fantastical, but Tommy asked his grandmother—he called her Mama, as his first maternal figure—to repeat it like a bedtime story. He loved how she got carried away with the details. He laughed at the disparaging song she and her friends came up with about Mao Zedong. The melody wasn't catchy, but the lyrics, "Mao Zedong, eat shit and die," were.

Tommy worked hard not to disappoint his grandparents or his parents. When he was ten, he tried to secure a place at a good secondary school, stuffing his schedule with extracurriculars. He joined the Boy Scouts and signed up for basketball and high jump, although he was terrible at both. The only thing he found himself enjoying was art class. When he returned from school around 6 p.m., he'd eat quickly and turn to his piles of homework.

At the time, Tommy's grandfather was in and out of the hospital with pulmonary disease. But the boy kept studying. When others visited the elderly man, he hung back. His grandfather died that year, in 2009, and Tommy performed horribly in his exams. He felt an anger that he couldn't put into words. He started to hate who he had become and began to question the assumptions that governed Hong Kong's education system and the city altogether. He missed his grandfather and hated to see his Mama so lost. It did not matter what secondary school he went to. He decided all that mattered was spending time with the people he loved. Tommy stopped studying, and as he fell behind in academics, teachers wrote him off, and the cycle perpetuated. Because they thought he was stupid, he didn't even try. He focused instead on pursuing a simpler goal: fun. "I gave up," he said. "I wanted to just enjoy everything, YOLO."

Tommy permed his hair and fished around in thrift stores for deals. One of his crowning glories at school was fashioning a dress out of raw chicken for an art project, a play on the Cantonese word for chicken that could also mean prostitute. He told his teacher he was raising the plight of sex workers and made a classmate wear the dress, although it had begun to rot. Another time he dressed as Anna from Disney's *Frozen* for a class project. Tommy saw little in common between himself and the movement leaders. Their meticulous approach to organizing and rules was at odds with his more lax attitude. The crowd at Admiralty seemed far more studious and a little more middle class than he was. Tommy was preoccupied with sneaking into bars and ordering corrosively sweet glasses of Long Island iced tea.

The movement was fraying by the time Tommy visited. Hong Kong residents, even those broadly supportive of the goals of the occupiers, began to resent such a permanent inconvenience to their lives. Infighting plagued the activists. Followers of Joshua Wong and the other student leaders resented Benny Tai, Reverend Chu, Chan Kin-man, and the rest of the older generation, labeling them as conservatives who hadn't done enough in their time to push Beijing to give Hong Kong full autonomy. Others saw Wong and Scholarism as still too tepid in their demands and too controlling. They rejected their "big-stage," top-down leadership at Admiralty and gravitated instead to Mongkok, where there was no hierarchy and a stronger determination to push back against incursions from the police or pro-Beijing sympathizers. "No leaders, only the people" was the slogan of Occupy Mongkok, where social norms and class boundaries dissolved into a unified collective. A certain militancy took hold there. Those days reminded Chu of his visit to Tiananmen Square in 1989, when the students were flush with resources but divided on what to do.

By November, the weather was turning colder, and fewer people wanted to sleep on city streets for a demand neither Beijing nor the Hong Kong government was acquiescing to. Hong Kong's courts granted an injunction, brought by the taxi and minibus industry, to prohibit the

continued occupation of Argyle Street, the main road in Mongkok. Demonstrators were not united in their approach against the police as they
began to enforce the injunction. Some simply sat and refused to leave
until they were beaten. A smaller group waged street battles. Within
hours, the police overran the area, clearing the Mongkok camp. In early
December, after another clash between police and protesters that saw
more than forty hospitalized, Tai, Chan, and Chu said they would surrender themselves to the authorities and urged the students to do the
same. They'd started their movement in the name of love and peace but
feared a Tiananmen-style massacre was about to unfold in Hong Kong.
Chu, close to tears, admitted that an elderly man like him was "unable
to lead all the Occupy protesters home unharmed, and protect young
people from being hit." He felt that he had failed his flock. Police didn't
file charges against the three and let them go.

The Umbrella Movement ended on December 15, 2014, without a government concession. Hong Kong's next leader would not be chosen by
universal suffrage, just like the ones before. Because Hong Kong didn't
want Beijing's white paper or proposal, the method of selecting the chief
executive would be unchanged, voted on by just a small pool of elites.
Beijing had won. But the demonstrators had a last message to convey.
Giant banners, posters, and gold balloon letters strung together on a
gate—they all carried the same slogan: "We Will Be Back." It took only a
day for cleaning crews to remove those, along with everything else that
stood at the site.

———

TOMMY WAS SITTING IN A CHINESE HISTORY CLASS SEVERAL MONTHS
later. Normalcy had returned to Hong Kong, and school was back in session after winter break. In the classroom the lights were turned off to
reduce the glare from the projector. Despite the grainy quality of the
YouTube video, Tommy made out armed soldiers rolling through Beijing's streets in tanks. Trucks were on fire. Young men in white head-
bands carried injured friends on stretchers.

When the video stopped playing, his teacher turned the lights back
on and began discussing the scenes the students had just witnessed,

of the 1989 Tiananmen Square crackdown. He started telling the class how he'd felt when watching those same scenes as a boy—helpless, distraught, like life could be taken anytime by the state, the individual powerless to stop it. The teacher started to cry.

Tommy was taken aback. His history teacher had often scolded him, whether for skipping class or not doing his homework, and cast an intimidating presence, built like an amateur bodybuilder. Yet here he was, standing in front of the whole class openly crying, a display of emotion rare even from Tommy's own parents.

So many questions emerged after that lesson, and Tommy was determined to find answers on his own terms. His school incorporated half an hour each day for quiet reading of English and Chinese newspapers, and Tommy used the time to read political columnists. He bothered his friends who were studying politics, asking them to discuss their lessons. Tommy wanted to learn, not for exams or grades, but for himself. History suddenly didn't seem so far away.

Tommy failed his exams and was forced to repeat the year. He worked part-time at McDonald's, moving between assembling burgers and making cups of coffee. He thought about dropping out of school entirely. Tommy buried his distress in humor, cracking jokes and goofing off, but he was starting to think that a job as a fast-food server was all he could accomplish. Scrolling through Facebook one day in 2016, he came across a video that many of his friends were sharing. It featured Edward Leung Tin-kei, a young candidate for an upcoming by-election to fill a vacated seat in the Legislative Council, representing a new party called Hong Kong Indigenous. Leung, who wore a blue hoodie and khaki pants to debates, described himself as a loser, a nobody, a common teenager. He loved to cycle and play guitar. He smoked almost constantly. Leung spoke of how he was entirely apolitical until the Umbrella Movement. "It was at that moment when I finally saw hope. Indeed, nothing was achieved, but at least our generation has finally understood that we can no longer rely on the existing parties and politicians," he said. "When we are no longer timid, and bravely challenge the regime, no matter how strong our opponents may be, Hong Kong shall truly belong to us, the Hong Kongers."[12]

Leung and Hong Kong Indigenous, formed on the occupied streets of Mongkok in 2014, promoted a political ideology still on the fringe in the city: independence. They were localists. Sometimes, this meant protesting at border towns that many mainland residents visited over the weekend, jeering at them and calling them "locusts." Other times, it meant espousing the words of Edward Said and speaking of a Hong Kong nation, a fully autonomous place—separate from China. Why should the 1972 decision at the United Nations determine Hong Kong's fate? Why was it so radical to dream of an independent Hong Kong? It might have been foolish. It was nearly impossible. But it was the only way, they believed, to leave this authoritarian regime.

It was nativist at worst, and perhaps naive. But at best, the ideology that Hong Kong Indigenous and Leung espoused was the dream of a lost generation. Young people found their identity on the streets in 2014. The regime was now telling them to give up and go home. Some were lost to the point of suicide in the aftermath of the Umbrella Movement. Leung told them to keep believing.

Tommy felt as though Leung was speaking to him personally. Watching the oil drain from fries before salting and shoving them into red McDonald's holders, he had given up on a better life. He believed he had nothing—his city had nothing. Working like this just to afford a cramped public-housing apartment in a suppressed city dominated by tycoons and sycophants was pathetic. Leung spoke of a different world: the right to vote, accountable leaders, freedom. "The possibility he was talking about was amazing," Tommy said. "Maybe we have another choice, another chance."

———

IN EARLY 2019 BENNY TAI, THE LAW PROFESSOR WHO HAD SEEDED THE IDEA of occupation, wrote another article, this one marking the thirtieth anniversary of the Tiananmen Square massacre. Tai characterized the events of June 1989 as the first landmark in Hong Kong's pro-democracy movement, followed by the 2003 Article 23 protests and then the 2014 Umbrella Movement.

"The seeds of democracy have been planted in Hong Kong's soil," Tai wrote. "Is the pace of events quickening? It took fourteen years after Tiananmen for the July 1 rally to happen, and then eleven years after that for the Umbrella Movement to appear. It seems likely that the fourth landmark event will come before so much time goes by again . . . we must do everything we can *now* to prepare ourselves, so we are ready to rise to the challenge of that moment when it arrives."[13]

His prophecy would soon come to pass, with a tragedy that seemed entirely disconnected from politics.

PART TWO

BURN WITH US

CHAPTER 8

THE LEADER WHO KILLED HER CITY

M ARCH 26, 2017, WAS A REMINDER OF EVERYTHING THAT HONG KONG had failed to achieve. That day there was an election, or at least the semblance of one. The process bore some features of a democratic exercise. After the votes were cast, officials unlocked vault-like ballot boxes and emptied their contents onto long sorting tables to be counted. Like magicians selling their illusion to the crowd, they made sure to show the empty containers to journalists and officials who looked on. Yet the boxes contained fewer than twelve hundred ballots, representing the small number of Hong Kong elites who—again—were the only ones out of a population of seven million able to vote on who would serve as the territory's leader for the next five years.

At the end of the night, three candidates who had spent the previous two months campaigning stood onstage awaiting the results. Any anticipation they showed was feigned. Long before the majority of that small group of elites—777 people—ticked the name Carrie Lam Cheng Yuet-ngor, Beijing had already decided that she would be the fourth chief executive of Hong Kong. Lam, a career bureaucrat who had spent decades as a civil servant, bowed before the audience. Smiling tersely, with her hair styled in a short bob, she shook the hands of her opponents and nodded in a show of humility as cameras flashed.

Flanked by her husband and one of her two sons, Lam gave a victory speech that alluded to the political upheaval of the past few years. "My priority will be to heal the divide and to ease the frustration—and to unite our society to move forward," she said. She would strive to uphold the values of "inclusiveness, freedoms of the press and of speech, respect for human rights, and systems which have taken generations to establish, such as the independent judiciary, rule of law, and clean government."[1]

Lam was reserved and collegial on election night. She played the role of gracious victor who had prevailed over her opponents in a competitive race. Two months after her win, on the morning of July 1, 2017, Lam's mood had shifted to positively giddy. Dressed in a pale-pink cheongsam and a long white jacket, her hair teased slightly higher than usual, and a wide grin spread across her face, Lam entered the convention center along Victoria Harbor, clapping as she walked. The hall was filled with officials from Hong Kong and the mainland, most in dark suits adorned with Chinese flag pins. To her right was Xi Jinping, China's leader, in the city for her inauguration and to mark the twentieth anniversary of the handover. He walked ahead of Lam, in line with their respective positions of power. The two were a study in contrasts: Lam's disposition cheery and light, Xi's heavy and inscrutable.

Xi's outward mien matched the dark speech he gave later that morning. Standing in front of the Hong Kong and Chinese flags, the latter always larger than the former, Xi warned that "any attempt to endanger China's sovereignty and security, challenge the power of the Central Government" or "use Hong Kong to carry out infiltration and sabotage against the mainland is an act that crosses the red line."[2] China analysts pored over Xi's thirty-minute speech, attempting to decode not just the contents but everything from his facial expression to how he walked as he descended from the stage.

What might happen if China perceived Hong Kong had crossed the "redline" would become clearer over the next years, when the frustrations of a long-suppressed territory at the periphery of this powerful yet insecure authoritarian state collided with the ambitions of its paramount leader. Lam kick-started this unraveling. Since 1997, pundits and journalists had made a parlor game of foretelling the death of Hong Kong, bracing for the definitive moment when the freewheeling territory could no longer claim to be autonomous. Some predicted it would come if China's rule over Hong Kong materialized as military force, laying waste to the concept of "one country, two systems." Lam said she wanted Hong Kong people to "be happy and possess hope" after her time in office.[3] Instead, history would judge Lam as the leader who killed her city without needing any soldiers or tanks.

———

THERE WAS ONLY ONCE IN HER THIRTEEN YEARS AT AN ELITE CATHOLIC girls' school that Lam failed to rank at the top of her class, a shortfall she vowed to never repeat.[4] After graduating, she enrolled at the University of Hong Kong, where she was well-liked and politically active in the student union. She marched with fellow university students to the British governor's residence, Government House, in 1978 to protest the expulsion of four secondary school students from a local school for "leftist" pro-Chinese activities. Lam became interested in assisting the needy, drawn in by a popular TV drama she watched growing up that followed the lives of social workers.[5] She briefly toyed with joining the field.

Lam was later tasked by the student union president with planning a trip to Tsinghua University in Beijing. The University of Hong Kong students were eager to glimpse how life was changing under Deng's fledgling reforms. Mainland officials were skeptical of the visitors' intentions. Fastidious and detail oriented, Lam excelled at finding a middle ground.[6] The students met a liberal journalist and writer, Xie Wanying, better known by her pen name, Bing Xin. Xie was persecuted under the Cultural Revolution and sent away to the remote countryside. She resumed writing after Mao's death. Lam's takeaway was not the cruelty or the lost years but that Xie had a steadfast sense of duty to her country.

This period, under British governor Murray MacLehose, marked an opening within Hong Kong's civil society. There was an optimism on campus about the future and how it could be shaped for and by Hong Kong people. Lee Wing-tat and Sin Chung-kai, two other undergrads who were part of the student union with Lam, became prominent and long-standing members of the pro-democracy movement. Lam charted a different path. When she graduated in 1980 with a degree in sociology, she joined the government, entering the Medical and Health Services Department. One of her first projects involved the construction of a new medical facility in Chai Wan—the Eastern District Hospital, Chu's hard-fought achievement.[7] To him, the hospital proved the value of civil society. For Lam, it hardened a belief that the best way to help people was to work within the system rather than against it.

Within a few years, the government rewarded Lam by funding her studies at Cambridge University in England. While riding her bike in the university town one day, she was struck by a car and admitted to a hospital for treatment. A local newspaper covered the story. It made the rounds among other Hong Kong students at the university. A small group visited Lam in the hospital to wish her a swift recovery. One was Lam Siu-por, a soft-spoken and slightly awkward PhD student studying advanced mathematics.[8] The two hit it off. They married in 1984.

Lam's professional career continued to flourish. The Fulbright program awarded her a prestigious fellowship, allowing her to go on an exchange to the Environmental Protection Agency in Washington, DC. In 1993, back in Hong Kong, Lam landed at the Finance Bureau. She quickly showed a disdain for the waste and inefficiency of fellow bureaucrats and was impressive in her deft handling of numbers. Her recall of dates and facts showcased a memory that seemed to border on photographic. Critics saw Lam as a feckless bookkeeper with little interest in anything beyond the bottom line.

The handover came and went. Although she was working for new bosses, Lam's hard-driving approach remained unchanged. One noticeable difference, a friend noted, was that she began swapping out the power suits popularized by Thatcher in favor of traditional Chinese cheongsams. She "embraces this very valueless mindset," the friend said Lam's of ability to serve those in power without question, "which is actually a colonial legacy."[9]

When Lam was appointed director of social welfare in 2000, it was a chance to return to an area that she had admired during her youth. Gone, however, was any sign of idealism that imbued her earlier views. Before taking the job, Lam bemoaned that those in the field were too sentimental and complained of the inability of social workers and NGOs to take blunt criticism. Lam described her own working approach as one of compartmentalization, where cold pragmatism always trumped emotions. "At a personal level," she said, "while at times my heart urges sympathy, my intellect tells me to press on with a change."[10] The uneasy relationship came to a head in the spring of 2003, when Lam slashed welfare without consulting social-service groups. She said she had "no emotion" toward money and wanted only to put it to good use. In response, a thousand protesters took to the streets in early March; some called on Lam to resign. She flatly refused.

Lam displayed a rare flash of savvy in retail politics during the SARS crisis later that year. She gathered three other high-ranking civil servants and quickly started a fund soliciting donations to help children whose parents had died from the disease. It pulled in tens of millions of Hong Kong dollars. Lam visited the orphaned children in the hospital and recounted to the press the horrific stories she had heard. At least temporarily, she had softened her outward image.

Lam left the civil service in 2007, until then the only career she knew. Her new job was hardly a radical departure. She joined the administration of Chief Executive Donald Tsang as the secretary for development. It was a newly created position, one closely watched in a city where real estate developers held unparalleled power. Soon into the new role, Lam got her first taste of what it meant to be the face of an unpopular government plan.

That spring, the Hong Kong government was preparing to close Queen's Pier, which was marked for demolition. It jutted into Victoria Harbor and had been a landing for visiting royals including Queen Elizabeth II; her son, the Prince of Wales; and his wife, Princess Diana. After the British sailed away, it became a beloved public space in a place that had few such luxuries. The decades-old structure reflected the rhythms of the city. In the mornings, elderly residents gathered to practice Tai Chi; during the day, workers used it as a spot to eat lunch and for a momentary escape from the office. At night, people of all ages stared across the harbor toward the skyline of Kowloon. Domestic workers enjoying their day off crowded the pier each Sunday. The romanticization of the aging structure wasn't enough to save it. The government prioritized plans to modernize the waterfront and decided the pier was in the way. It had to go.

The revitalization projects became a microcosm of Hong Kong's political system as a whole: the demands of Hong Kong people ignored in favor of a few wealthy developers. Those opposed to the projects also saw a fight for identity. Keeping those local landmarks was a way to reinforce Hong Kong's sense of itself.

Lam had little time for nostalgia. The vestiges of old Hong Kong held scant interest for her. She saw them as impediments to a sleeker, faster, more efficient city. Lam visited the pier to debate demonstrators gathered there, some of whom had gone on a hunger strike. Eddie Chu Hoi-dick, a twenty-nine-year-old activist who had studied in Iran and worked as a journalist in the Middle East, led the demonstrators in discussions with Lam. She answered their questions for hours, wearing a short-sleeved pink polo in the sweltering weather and holding firm to the government's position. Chu found the substance of Lam's arguments weak but admitted that her appearance among the people was remarkable. Lam managed to quell tensions somewhat, making it easier for police to remove the group from the pier days later. Many in the public were impressed by Lam's even-keeled performance and her willingness to descend from the halls of government to meet the public face-to-face. The media dubbed her the "good fighter."[11] Her new nickname would soon be tested.

Four years after the Queen's Pier was finally demolished, Lam was named the city's number-two official, commanding the civil service in which she had dutifully served. Lam was generally well-liked among the public, but less so by Leung Chun-ying, the chief executive. The two had a fractious relationship that at times devolved into pettiness. Lam privately professed a dislike of the color orange because Leung used it during his election campaign. When her popularity ranking dipped during the 2012 national education protests, a tearful Lam said in an emotional TV interview that she had "gambled her integrity and credibility on the government."[12] It would become one of her favored tropes: lamenting how much she had selflessly sacrificed for Hong Kong without being recognized for it.

As the Umbrella Movement pressed on in autumn 2014, Lam was asked to meet with students to discuss their demands. It was a reprise of the role she played as peacemaker at Queen's Pier. She was a softer face than her boss, Leung, who was nicknamed "The Wolf" and struck an uncompromising line with protesters. Lam led four other government officials in debating student leaders on October 21, 2014, live on TV. The activists were slightly disheveled after spending weeks on the streets. They dressed in black shirts emblazoned with "Freedom Now" in a bright-green font. Hong Kong residents watched for two hours as the two sides pitched different visions for how the city should be governed. Lam grew frustrated by the students' absolutism. She stressed pragmatism and at one point chastised them like a disappointed mother. "I hope you have the courage and wisdom to think of a way out of the current situation," she said.[13] The talks ended without a breakthrough. Lam's popularity dipped.

With the streets cleared of demonstrators and Leung's first term ending, Lam, almost sixty, told friends that she was preparing to retire. She wanted to split her time between Hong Kong and Cambridge, where her retired husband lived. Her two sons were grown; the younger had just graduated from Cambridge too, and the elder was working in Beijing. She inquired with friends about possible opportunities volunteering or working with civil society. Lam would have gracefully slid into her older years with the reputation of a consummate civil servant who had risen to the second-highest position in government. These plans were jettisoned in December 2016, when Leung abruptly announced that he would not run for a second term. Like Tung before him, he insisted his reasons were personal, but it was obvious that he was the latest chief executive to fall short in Beijing's eyes. Almost immediately following Leung's announcement, Lam said she would consider the job. She declared her candidacy the following month.

Lam was far from natural on the campaign trail. She fumbled when attempting to use a subway pass. She admitted that she struggled to find where to purchase toilet paper after spending so many years in the bubble of government life, with staff attending to her every need. None of that—not Lam's cringe-worthy attempts at public stumping or her charismatic opponent, who was favored by almost twenty points in the polls—mattered. A devout Catholic, she believed that God had called on her to serve Hong Kong. Her fortunes were the product of a less divine force.

Privately, Beijing had been working for months to ensure her win. The "invisible hand" of the Liaison Office warned off other hopeful candidates, making certain they wouldn't get far enough to challenge her.[14] As soon as Lam's candidacy was announced, mainland officials instructed state media to devote more space to coverage of her. Beijing's proxies in Hong Kong inserted themselves further as the election day drew near. They instructed members of the election committee to cast ballots for Lam and summoned some of those who wouldn't to Shenzhen, where high-ranking officials intimidated them into explanations.

Lam still seemed convinced by the fiction of a fair fight. "I know perception is important," she said in an interview with the BBC after her win, "but to say that I am just a puppet, I won this election because of pro-Beijing forces, is sort of a failure to acknowledge what I have done in Hong Kong over the past 36 years for the people."

The interviewer asked Lam about a comment she had made as chief secretary in 2015 that a place was reserved for her in heaven. "What makes you so confident that you are on the side of the angels?" the journalist asked. "Because I do good things," Lam shot back.[15]

For the ferociously competitive and incredibly self-righteous Lam, the title of chief executive was vindication for a life obsessively focused on ascension. Her colleagues couldn't stand her for most of her career. She made them look bad by keeping punishing hours and being a constant micromanager. Working harder than anyone else and adeptly balancing the demands of developers, democracy activists, and local politicians had helped her rise over them. Lam had reached the pinnacle of Hong Kong's government. It was almost like she was top girl again.

Lam moved into Government House, the first woman to lead the city dating back through British rule, and threw herself into the job. It wasn't the history of the building, the honor of sitting as a Chinese woman where British men once had, or the manicured estate with an ornate koi pond that impressed her. Lam told a reporter the best part about living in the stately white mansion was never having to leave the office.[16]

———

IN THE MONTHS BEFORE LAM WAS SWORN IN, SHE MET FREQUENTLY WITH the US consul-general in Hong Kong, Kurt Tong.[17] Tong had relatively free rein on Hong Kong policy. State Department bureaucrats checked in on the Hong Kong file now and then, but saw it as largely peripheral, even in the context of relations with China. It was an odd assessment. Beijing had undermined the Basic Law by denying full universal suffrage. More alarmingly, Chinese agents had started to more openly operate in Hong Kong, breaching the legal firewall between the two territories. In early 2017, Xiao Jianhua, a Chinese Canadian billionaire, was abducted from the Four Seasons Hotel in Hong Kong. Plainclothes Chinese officers hustled him out of the luxury property in a wheelchair, his head covered by a blanket. He reappeared only in 2022, in Shanghai, where he was sentenced to thirteen years in jail after pleading guilty to bribery and other crimes.[18] His followed a string of disappearances two years earlier. Five Hong Kong staffers from Causeway Bay Books and publisher Mighty Current mysteriously went missing from Hong Kong and Thailand.[19] The bookstore was popular for carrying gossipy books on Communist Party elites that were banned in China. The five similarly resurfaced in custody on the mainland.

In Washington, this was noted with concern but not huge alarm. It was "bad for morale" and an unfortunate incident, but probably not something that would happen frequently. Hong Kong, per Washington's assessment, was still a remarkably autonomous place and would remain that way for the foreseeable future. It was "ridiculous," one senior US diplomat on Hong Kong told a journalist, to think that Hong Kong would become just another Chinese city.

That view largely held even after the election of Donald J. Trump. Trump fundamentally overturned the nature, tone, and respectability of American politics. Washington operated under new rules, including those governing its relationship with China. Trump accused China of "raping" the US and vowed to start an economic war with the country.

But if Hong Kong was viewed with suspicion in Washington, it was largely within the perimeters of tariffs and trade. The "one country, two systems" arrangement meant Hong Kong was treated separately from China on economic and trade issues, spelled out in congressional legislation known as the Hong Kong Policy Act. In the early days of the Trump administration, there was suspicion that China could avoid US economic pressure through Hong Kong's free markets. Still, it was a fringe concern. "Hong Kong was kind of a sideshow in the broader confrontation and in our rectification of U.S. policy toward China," said Matt Pottinger, Trump's deputy national security advisor and a key architect of his China policy.[20]

Seeing little direction from Washington, Tong developed his own approach. He wanted to emphasize to the Hong Kong government, more than legislators back home, the values that made the city a desirable outpost for American activity: rule of law, good governance, with "some democracy thrown in, a little bit." He thought this approach would be better than chiding Hong Kong for the bad. He had grand ideas too on how to strengthen the relationship. Tong wanted to introduce a visa waiver for Hong Kong travelers entering the US. He suggested setting up preclearance for US customs at a new Hong Kong airport terminal that was in the planning stages. These were encapsulated in a simple if slightly cheesy slogan: "U.S. Loves Hong Kong."

Lam was an active part of Tong's strategy. She had visited Washington the previous year as chief secretary and impressed those she'd met.[21] Tong pitched her on a US tour that included stops at universities. He discussed getting her some face time with the new president, who he guessed would be keen to meet even amid the China rhetoric. Trump liked Hong Kong. He had visited the city in 1993 and said it was the only other city in the world that impressed him other than his own New York. Hong Kong billionaires helped save Trump from bankruptcy by investing in one of his Manhattan properties the next year.[22]

Lam lost interest soon after she was sworn in. She dismissed Washington as insincere and taking too long to deliver. Tong sensed she had turned her focus up north. Lam was fixated on collecting a list of accolades, like a report card filled with top marks, to present to Beijing. Her aim was securing something her predecessors never could: serving two full consecutive five-year terms as chief executive.

———

LAM'S TERM BEGAN WITH THE ARREST OF THREE MEN. A DAY AFTER SHE was elected, police abruptly called up Benny Tai, Chan Kin-man, and Reverend Chu, telling them to report to the nearest station to face charges for their roles in the Umbrella Movement—more than two years after they'd tried to turn themselves in.

Later in 2017, four lawmakers voted into the Legislative Council in the previous year's elections were disqualified for turning their oaths into political statements. Among them was Nathan Law, a student leader close to Joshua Wong whose stature after the 2014 protests saw him elected as the youngest lawmaker in Hong Kong's history.

Special efforts were dedicated to localists. Edward Leung, the pro-independence candidate who had inspired Tommy, was awaiting a sentence for his role in riots back in 2016 between police and localist followers trying to stop authorities from clearing out street food sellers in Mongkok. The clashes were known as the Fishball Riots, named for the squishy white balls the vendors hawked. Authorities also prevented Eddie Chu Hoi-dick, the activist who faced Lam at Queen's Pier, from running to represent a rural village of just a hundred constituents. His infraction wasn't even supporting independence but saying that Hong Kongers should be free to advocate for it.

The repression extended not just to promoters of the independence ideology but also to those who gave them even a modest platform, in this case a wooden stage on the second floor of a colonial building housing the Foreign Correspondents Club (FCC) of Hong Kong. In August 2018 the FCC hosted Andy Chan, a founder of the Hong Kong National Party and an independence advocate. Authorities outlawed the party the next month. In October, immigration authorities denied a routine visa renewal to Victor Mallett, the Asia editor of the *Financial Times*, who hosted the discussion with Chan. It marked the first ban of a political organization and the first expulsion of a foreign correspondent since 1997.

Beijing, enabled by Lam's administration, was chipping away at Hong Kong's autonomy. At the same time, Lam was putting a friendlier face on government, a departure from the cutting smugness that had come to define her predecessor. In March 2018, Lam accepted an invitation to the Hong Kong Democratic Party's annual gala. Not only did she attend, which Leung Chun-ying had refused to do; she also donated nearly $4,000 to the party's coffers.[23] She sat next to the party's chairman, Wu Chi-wai, and clinked glasses as they toasted the party and celebrated its place in Hong Kong politics. On Instagram, she shared a photo of the event with the hashtag "Great reconciliation." Lam also abolished the Central Policy Unit, an internal government think tank that had become mired in allegations of opacity and cronyism and was closely associated with Leung.[24] In its place she started a policy-coordination group filled with overachieving young recruits who were tasked with finding fresh ideas to tackle the city's issues.

Lam's biggest achievement came in the autumn of 2018, when the West Kowloon rail terminal opened, connecting Hong Kong to the mainland by high-speed rail. Inside the ribbed, clamshell-shaped station was an unprecedented arrangement. A thick line made from black and yellow tiles demarcated two different areas within the premises: the "mainland port" and the "Hong Kong port." The entire station was, of course, within Hong Kong territory. Within this arbitrarily defined "mainland port," though, passengers were subject to Chinese laws, enforced by Chinese authorities. Pro-democracy parties had tried to stop the proposition, which they said was unconstitutional. Only small pockets of people answered their calls to protest. Officials dodged any possible disruptions of the ceremony marking the deal by holding it in the middle of the night without alerting the media.[25] Thanks to Lam, it was the first time that mainland police were allowed to legally operate within the city.

The next month, Lam was in Xi Jinping's presence once again for the opening ceremony of the Hong Kong–Zhuhai–Macau bridge, a $20 billion megaproject connecting the two autonomous territories with the mainland. The bridge, the world's longest sea crossing at thirty-four miles, looked from the sky like a great umbilical cord tethering Hong

Kong to its motherland. Xi's mood was light and cheery. He and Lam stood side by side, chatting like old friends, her cheeks as flushed as her pink Mandarin-collar jacket. There was much to celebrate. Just fifteen months into her term, the accolades were remarkable. Democracy advocates were subdued. The border between the two territories was dissolving.

Lam closely monitored the turnout of protests like the annual June 4 vigil and the July 1 march. She studied the numbers of people who showed up in opposition to the West Kowloon railway. The diminished crowds were encouraging. Things were looking "pretty good and rational," she said.[26] She calculated that people were growing tired. Lam was also encouraged by her popularity ratings. So when her colleagues in the city's main pro-Beijing party, the DAB, came to her with news of a grieving mother struggling to find justice for the murder of her daughter Poon Hiu-wing, Lam had an answer.

Poon had taken a Valentine's Day trip to Taiwan with her boyfriend, Chan Tong-kai, in 2018. As the trip was ending, the two started to argue in their hotel room. Poon, who was twenty, told Chan that she was pregnant but that the unborn child was not his. It belonged, she said, to an ex-boyfriend. She showed Chan a video on her mobile phone of her having sex with another man. Enraged, Chan attacked Poon, killing her after a violent struggle. He then went to bed. The following morning, he lugged out of the hotel a bright-pink suitcase the two had purchased at a night market. Chan took a train to the northern outskirts of Taipei, where he dumped Poon's body out of the luggage and coolly flew back to Hong Kong as scheduled. One of the first things he did when he arrived was use Poon's bank card to take money from her accounts. Police, alerted to Poon's disappearance by her family, questioned Chan about the withdrawals. During the interrogation he confessed to murdering Poon.[27] Taiwanese police found her corpse decomposing near a clump of bushes by a train station. The pink suitcase was ditched behind a department store.

A confessed murderer was now sitting in jail, his victim identified. It should have been an open-and-shut case, but for a catch. Hong Kong, a special administrative region under China, and Taiwan, a self-ruling island that did not want to be a part of China, had no extradition arrangement. Chan could be tried only for the crime he committed in Hong Kong—using Poon's bank card.

Without instruction from Beijing, Lam, in consultation with trusted advisers, came up with an idea. Hong Kong couldn't just make a law for Taiwan because Beijing considers Taiwan part of China. So her administration, she decided, would change the law to allow extraditions to Taiwan—but also China, Macau, and, for good measure, anywhere else with which Hong Kong didn't have an existing extradition treaty. It was a perfect plan, the ever-overachieving Lam believed, solving more than just the problem of Poon's murder. Shadowy Chinese agents would no longer need to sneak into Hong Kong and quietly remove wanted billionaires from their hotel rooms. This would be her ultimate gift to Beijing.

Instead, it became the catalyst that Benny Tai had prophesied.

CHAPTER 9

GWYNETH

GWYNETH HO KWAI-LAM QUICKLY REALIZED SHE HAD WOKEN HER roommate, Kathryn Lam.[1] Gwyneth was hungry and hoping for some company on a grocery run when she knocked on the other girl's door. When Kathryn emerged, groggy and a little out of it, Gwyneth saw that the blinds behind her were pulled down and all the lights were off. She apologized repeatedly and, with a quick half-bow, turned to leave.

Random responses on the student questionnaire had brought the two young women together in a brick dormitory complex with floor-to-ceiling windows, tucked in a corner of the University of Aarhus, one of Denmark's oldest universities. Gwyneth was a journalist from Hong Kong, and Kathryn, whose father was from Malaysia, grew up in Seattle. Both were excited to room with another Asian woman. Kathryn, though, was a little intimidated by Gwyneth, whose photo she had seen on a WhatsApp groupchat for their master's program. Standing in front of her, Gwyneth was even more stunning in her structured blue jumpsuit. A headband held her long, jet-black hair in place. Kathryn was half-awake, and her hair was a mess. She wondered if all women from Hong Kong were so elegant. Gwyneth was only four years older than her, at twenty-eight, but seemed so much more mature.

Kathryn pushed through her jet lag and took up Gwyneth's invitation to stock their fridge. The two strolled to the closest Lidl hyper-mart, past the oak trees in the university's park and a family of waddling ducks. It was the fall of 2018. They were starting the Erasmus Mundus Journalism program, a two-year degree with a first compulsory year at Aarhus and then a second at another university in Europe. Gwyneth had started researching the program many years earlier. She told Kathryn that she planned to spend her second year at the University of Amsterdam, studying the intersection of journalism and politics. In between, she'd spend her summers back in Hong Kong reporting for an outlet called *Stand News*, under an editor she looked up to as a model for her own journalism. Gwyneth had things mapped out. In contrast, Kathryn knew that she wanted to have a positive impact in the world but was still finding her path.

When they reached the entry of the Lidl, Gwyneth almost squealed in excitement. She gawked at the selection: rows and rows of boxes, cans, and bags of food. The cheese was a fraction of the cost in Hong Kong, she told Kathryn, as she giddily picked up fat chunks of brie. Kathryn laughed, less impressed by affordable dairy products. Gwyneth explained that her parents managed a Japanese restaurant and that she loved to cook. In food, the two found their common language. They had their first breakfast together the next morning, a neatly arranged spread of bread dusted with poppy seeds, bright red strawberries, raspberry jam, yogurt, and scrambled eggs. Trips to the grocery store became the highlight of their week, offering new ingredients to experiment with. They developed a ritual of buying a special treat in addition to pantry staples, usually a new type of cream liqueur, Gwyneth's favorite. Kathryn didn't share her sweet tooth but always gave in.

In class, Gwyneth made an impression too. They were barely past the stage of perfunctory introductions when she raised her hand and challenged her professor, who was lecturing about globalization and the world order. Other students took note, talking among themselves about how Gwyneth seemed so worldly and bold. Kathryn was one of the few who knew how often Gwyneth overslept and was nearly late to class. She always made sure that Gwyneth ate breakfast before she left.

Kathryn and Gwyneth grew close to a few other female students in their late twenties. Together they were an eclectic mix, hailing from Venezuela, Ukraine, Belgium, and a handful of other countries. Kathryn was the only American in the group and had grown disillusioned with

her country. The election of Trump felt particularly bleak, a reaffirma-
tion of the deep racism and bigotry that still plagued the US. Gwyneth and the others were less pessimistic. They often mused about the
meaning of democracy, and although she acknowledged the bad, Gwyneth saw America as a "super democracy" with freedoms like an unconstrained media.[2] At least Americans could choose their own leader,
however bad that person was. Hong Kong could not.

Their group had long cerebral debates about the state of the world
in the confines of their small apartments, fueled by glasses of wine and
cans of cheap beer. Gwyneth shared her perspective, shaped by her
undergraduate life at Beijing's Tsinghua University—Xi Jinping's alma
mater but also one of the campuses at the forefront of the June 4, 1989,
protests. Before university, she didn't read newspapers or attend vigils.
She was convinced when a senior at Tsinghua told her that the June 4
massacre was the inevitable consequence of the students' naïveté and
the government's inexperience. A YouTube clip changed her mind.
Clicking around the platform, she came across a stand-up routine where
Dayo Wong, a Hong Kong comedian, pointed out how the People's Liberation Army in 1989 didn't have tear gas or water hoses, just guns.

"What do they do if there's a fire?" the comedian asked. He acted out
a scene where Chinese guards would ask where the fire is, then whip
out their machine guns. "Say, where's the fire? Boom, boom, boom," he
mimicked.

Gwyneth called it her moment of awakening. No one is killed because
there is "no other choice," she wrote.

Those discussions and evolutions were happening in a different
China. Gwyneth had studied there from 2008 to 2012. She told her
classmates in Europe about a cautious but still vibrant society with
active civil groups hosting seminars and workshops. Chinese citizens
online moved faster than the censors—it wasn't hard for her to jump
the Great Firewall and access YouTube and other banned sites. Xi Jinping changed that—Gwyneth called him a master of dark arts, like
Voldemort. She always made her views known and clear, whether on
Xi or anything else, even among students from the mainland. It wasn't
so much that she sought out arguments, just that she never accepted

something disagreeable without questioning it. Her thought process was like a researcher's, dissecting and piecing together every bit of information to try to make sense of her own experiences, her own city, and how it all fit together.

Gwyneth and Kathryn cooked elaborate meals in their tiny kitchen, stuffing as many people as they could in the narrow corridor or in their bedrooms. Gwyneth didn't know what a s'more, the staple of American summer camps and bonfires, was until Kathryn showed her. She toasted her first marshmallow that winter, watching the white puff turn into a golden caramelized crisp. Once that fall, they made banana fritters. Gwyneth did the frying. She wasn't afraid of the splatter from the hot oil. It seemed she had little regard for her own safety. Gwyneth was careless with knives. Her fingers were often decorated with Band-Aids in a variety of shades and sizes. She never bothered to buy new utensils and cooked with pots and pans that had their plastic handles falling off. She was self-deprecating and blamed herself whenever a mishap happened: "I'm so clumsy, so forgetful, so messy." At times, she acted only on impulse. Once out on a walk with friends, someone plucked a mushroom off the ground. Gwyneth popped it into her mouth like a hungry toddler, oblivious to the fact that it might be poisonous.[3]

The international group of students took turns hosting parties. The Indian students threw a Diwali celebration, the Brazilians had a Latin night, and a group of Danes organized a Christmas gathering. Gwyneth and Kathryn were competitive. They wanted a party to outdo all others. During Lunar New Year in 2019, they hosted a dinner for the whole cohort to welcome the Year of the Pig. It took weeks to plan, involving frequent trips to the library to print off posters and fake money. Gwyneth ran the card table like a dealer in a Macau casino pit and organized a calligraphy booth. They handmade all the noodles they served, drying them on empty wine bottles and then cutting them. The two turned a common room into a night market, laughing and drinking into the early hours.

Even though the two grew close, Gwyneth was always slightly guarded, fearful of appearing overly emotional. The exception was when she drank. A glass of wine or a few bottles of beer accompanied dinner almost every night as the master's students embraced Denmark's heavy drinking culture. Kathryn had never had an older sister but imagined if she did, it would be like her friendship with Gwyneth—warm and fun, but within the limits of the barriers that siblings sometimes put up in front of each other.

Gwyneth told Kathryn she was a political reporter back in Hong Kong and had first worked for an outlet called *House News*, which was online and styled after the *Huffington Post*. It had a clear allegiance to the pro-democracy movement. *House News* closed under political pressure just a few months before the Umbrella Movement began in September 2014. Gwyneth, part of a small team of employees that felt more like a family than colleagues, found out with the rest of the public when she read a farewell letter posted on the outlet's website. She hadn't finished the note before she started crying. She cried also when she described the publication's closing to other people, when she rode the bus, and when she was alone at night. Gwyneth felt that her contributions had helped build something that was then "smashed into ruins by just one finger of tyranny."

After *House News* shut down, Gwyneth and most of the team moved to the *Dash*, a news site affiliated with Joshua Wong's Scholarism. Gwyneth used her access to produce reports detailing factionalism in the 2014 movement, including dissatisfaction with Joshua's leadership. Traditionalists in Hong Kong's media dismissed these journalists as less ethical because they were embedded with the activists, an unfair charge. Gwyneth was a reporter first and clear-eyed about the shortcomings of the movement. But how could anyone, especially a young Hong Kong journalist in the streets among the occupiers, be unmoved and emotionless? Gwyneth produced meticulous, long articles (brevity was never her forte) but was also deeply affected by the trajectory of her city.

The *House News* editors eventually regrouped and launched *Stand News* in December 2014. Gwyneth joined the outlet but also wanted to go to Europe to pursue a master's degree in English, hoping that it would help her unpack the role of journalism in her evolving city.

On the streets and in the years that followed, she grew close to many of the activists she interviewed. When the Umbrella Movement fizzled, she watched as many paid the price for their roles. Gwyneth felt a deep sense of guilt. Why was she so limited in her ability to influence anything from her perch as a journalist? Why was she free, and not these people who put themselves on the front lines for Hong Kong? Gwyneth told herself that if she wanted to remain a reporter, she had to continue her education to get better at her job. She wanted to keep working until the day she was eventually locked up, like the Chinese journalists turned political prisoners on the mainland. Only then would it justify her decision not to do more. In those months in Aarhus, when she was alone in her room and thought no one was awake to hear her, Gwyneth sobbed. Nothing brought about that despair, that sense of worthlessness, more than her feelings about Hong Kong and her role—limited, insufficient—in it.

Kathryn heard the cries more than Gwyneth realized. She didn't try to check up on her; it felt like intruding. But she did know how to cheer her friend up. The two loved karaoke and knew every lyric to every song sung by Mika, the British pop singer with a sweeping vocal range. The uplifting beats turned Gwyneth into a different version of herself, unlocking the part of her that idolized pop stars, burst into song, and lost herself in dance. Her favorite Mika song was "Staring at the Sun." Kathryn and Gwyneth sang the French version and then the English, and then back to the French, for hours on end.

Gwyneth and her classmates finished their final exams in April 2019. They celebrated in typical university style, cracking their first drinks in the late afternoon after they handed in their final papers. Gwyneth had also finished one of her last features on Ukraine for a Hong Kong outlet after five months of work. She had gone on a reporting trip there that past December and developed a strong interest in the country. Gwyneth saw commonality between the search for identity in Ukraine and in Hong Kong; both were bordered by powerful authoritarian states that sought their subservience. Gwyneth was emotionally exhausted, as she always was after submitting a long piece. The process for her was always fraught with self-doubt.

After hours of drinking, the group moved from a dorm room to the common room to continue the celebrations. As always, there was karaoke. Gwyneth was distracted and oddly not into the music. She was engaged instead in deep discussion with a Ukrainian classmate. They looked like war veterans trading stories on democracy and sovereignty. Friends tried to steer her toward the music, but it didn't work. Gwyneth eventually said she was tired, excused herself, and went back to her and Kathryn's suite.

Kathryn followed a few hours later. When she reached the lobby of the dorm, she heard wailing coming from somewhere down the hall. It was so loud that Kathryn could hear it even before she walked through the building's entrance. The cries were punctuated with deep gasps, like the person was struggling to breathe. She reached the front door and saw it was wide open. Gwyneth's keys were still hanging from the lock. Clothes were strewn in the entryway. On the bathroom floor, Gwyneth lay in a crumpled heap, wearing her pajamas. Her body was limp, convulsing as she wailed.

Maybe in the time she'd walked home, Gwyneth had been followed and attacked, Kathryn thought. She rushed to her side, panicking. Kathryn sat on the cold bathroom tiles next to Gwyneth and wrapped her arms around her friend. Neither of them was the hugging type, but Kathryn didn't know what else to do. She knew Gwyneth had been crying that whole year, but not like this.

The two sat next to each other for hours. Gwyneth's head was bowed, her long hair falling over her face. Both were drunk. Through the sobs Kathryn made out bits and pieces. Gwyneth had not been attacked. Physically, there was nothing wrong with her. She spoke with an almost manic urgency about something very dark settling over her city. She spoke of friends being thrown in jail one by one. The state apparatus was piercing them, yet she was here and could do nothing. Here she was, able to travel, live her life, achieve, while they were behind bars.

Kathryn couldn't understand many of the names or references but picked up the sentiment. There was a sense of self-sacrifice in her friend's voice that unsettled Kathryn and made her a little afraid for Gwyneth. It should be me, Gwyneth repeated; it should be me, not them.

The two never discussed the incident. Two months later, on June 6, 2019, they took the ferry from Aarhus to Copenhagen, to catch their flights back home for the summer. Gwyneth had her internship lined up in Hong Kong and was looking forward to being back at *Stand News*. Before Gwyneth boarded the shuttle to the airport, Kathryn gave her friend a hug. Watching her leave, Kathryn had an odd sense that she might never see Gwyneth—her roommate, her friend, the closest she ever had to an older sister—again.

CHAPTER 10

EVIL LAW

THE HONG KONG GOVERNMENT'S CAMPAIGN FOR AMENDMENTS TO ITS extradition laws similarly began with tears. On February 12, 2019, almost a year to the date of Poon Hiu-wing's murder, two of Beijing's most ardent loyalists in Hong Kong called a press conference. Seated between the two lawmakers was Poon's mother, making her first public appearance, in a black cap, sunglasses, and a blue surgical mask to protect her privacy. Between weeping gasps, she managed to speak: "Although my daughter has been dead for almost a year, my husband and I still can't accept this fact."

The legislators soon took over the press conference, which they titled "Seeking Justice." The only way to comfort this broken woman, they said, was to amend Hong Kong's laws and allow for extraditions not only to Taiwan but also to mainland China. To underscore their apolitical motive, the lawmakers used the word *justice* fourteen times among them.[1] Other parts of the government followed, all with similar messaging: the laws had to be amended to allow "murderers, rapists, etc." to be transferred to the People's Republic of China, and elsewhere, to face the consequences of their crimes.[2]

Carrie Lam soon publicly joined the push. People should not be too concerned about the bill, she said. There was no ulterior motive for her government; it just could not ignore this tragic case. "The parents of the victim have not stopped writing letters to the government. There were five addressed to me," she said. "If you have read these letters . . . you would also feel that we must try to help them." Journalists asked if there would be a public consultation. Lam focused on one of her pet peeves, inefficiency. Having a consultation would slow down the process. Lam had read her brief. She believed she knew better than doubters, dismissing worries as "almost imaginative and overly anxious."[3] The government, she pledged, would amend the extradition laws within that legislative year, ending in July 2019.

It was a short timetable for such a consequential piece of legislation. The amendments covered forty-six offenses, ranging from murder, rape, and kidnapping to white-collar crimes such as bribery, corruption, fraud, and tax evasion. These were forty-six possible covers under which the mainland could summon a political enemy back to its jurisdiction. Hong Kong did not have democracy, but it did have courts that were globally recognized and trusted, still bearing the ceremonial pomp of the British system. The city was a global center for arbitration and commercial law, teeming with international lawyers making millions in billable hours. The changes would allow the unelected chief executive, with a stroke of a pen, to authorize the removal of criminals from Hong Kong and throw them into the quicksand of China's legal system. It went further than even the Article 23 national security proposals in 2003.

An incident just a few weeks prior to the proposals underscored the kind of "justice" China subscribed to. In December 2018, Canadian nationals Michael Spavor and Michael Kovrig were taken into custody in China, in naked retribution for the arrest of Huawei executive Meng Wanzhou in Canada. They were denied access to their consular representatives and lawyers, and before they were even charged, they underwent an incarceration of 557 days in a facility where the lights were kept on for twenty-four hours each day.[4] China had a conviction rate of more than 99 percent.

Lam might have been genuinely moved by the desperation of Poon Hiu-wing's mother, but critics believed she was co-opting her grief. They started to call the extradition bill the "evil law."

––––––

SOME OF THE EARLIEST OPPOSITION TO THE LEGISLATION CAME FROM AN unlikely source: wealthy businessmen, many of them connected to pro-Beijing political parties. They were not concerned about being caught up in a protest; "human rights" was to them an annoying phrase bandied about by their pro-democracy colleagues. Many of their families, though, had made their fortunes on the mainland, primarily in manufacturing and real estate. When they built their businesses, corruption was endemic. Bribing officials to secure land or permits was an operational cost as much as staffing and sourcing raw materials. The proposals in the legislation were ambiguous. There was no guarantee that the law, when passed, could not be used retroactively. The businessmen were afraid that their past transgressions could be wielded against them by disgruntled partners or mainland officials. In the future, it could give people on the mainland leverage, opening them up to the possibility of blackmail or extortion.

Joseph Lau, a billionaire property developer with a voracious appetite for fine wine, high-end art, and enormous diamonds, served as an example of the conundrum. He was found guilty of bribery and money laundering in Macau in 2014. Without an extradition agreement, Lau continued to live freely in Hong Kong, a short ferry ride from the city where he was facing a five-year prison term. Lau believed if the extradition bill passed, he would be sent to jail.

Apprehensive businessmen and lawmakers loyal to Beijing began to meet privately with John Lee Ka-chiu, the secretary for security. He was the chief executive's right hand in handling this latest metastasizing crisis. They urged Lee to hold off. If it was really about Poon, surely there were other ways forward. One businessman asked why a one-off agreement could not be signed with Taiwan. Lee didn't seem to have an answer. He told the group that it was his job to "clean the mess up." The proposals, he argued, were logical. "Why do we have extradition with America and England but not the motherland?" he snapped—a curious way to describe the mainland. In a separate meeting, another pro-Beijing lawmaker told Lee that he would be driving a stake into the heart of Hong Kong. "We have compromised the legislature, we have compromised the executive, and only the judiciary is yet to be compromised—but this is what you are doing now," the lawmaker charged.

Their discord achieved some results. The Hong Kong government removed nine white-collar crimes from the bill, including those related to tax and bankruptcy. On March 29, 2019, the government confidently brought forward the Fugitive Offenders and Mutual Legal Assistance in Criminal Matters Legislation (Amendment) Bill 2019. Lam and her executive council laid down a legislative time line. But by then, the concerns of the business community had dovetailed with mobilization from Hong Kong's traditional pro-democracy groups in an unlikely kinship. The Civil Human Rights Front, reprising its 2003 role, called for a march to the government headquarters on March 31.

Standing at the front of the crowd that day with an oversized black banner were veterans of the pro-democracy camp.[5] In a green T-shirt and a backpack, looking more like a friendly, aging neighbor than a loquacious multimillionaire, was Jimmy Lai, the entrepreneur who had founded the pro-democracy tabloid *Apple Daily*. Jimmy Sham, the excitable convenor of the Civil Human Rights Front and a longtime LGBTQ+ activist, shouted into the mic. In front of him were other pro-democracy lawmakers, including Claudia Mo, a former journalist who had covered the Tiananmen Square massacre. Next to Mo was Lam Wing-kee, one of the Causeway Bay booksellers detained on the mainland in 2015. Standing much farther behind in the procession, among the twelve thousand mostly veteran activists and older residents, was a visual arts student with a mop of permed hair: nineteen-year-old Tommy.

Tommy was in his first year at Hong Kong Baptist University, pursuing an associate degree in visual arts. He'd dropped out in his last year of secondary school and went full-time at McDonald's, working ten-hour shifts. For his final art project in school, Tommy made a video of himself hunched over a desk in his school uniform, hugging trophies and scribbling in a notebook while scenes changed behind him: students playing basketball, family members gathered at a wedding banquet, young couples on the beach. He wanted to tell the story of how students abandon happiness to get decent grades and chase jobs with large paychecks. He hoped that more would think about what they had given up to get to where they were, and ask themselves if it was worth it.

He studied for university entrance exams on his own, eventually eking out grades good enough for tertiary education. His course was designed as a stepping-stone to a full bachelor's program. Tommy didn't mind that he had failed in the Hong Kong dream of achieving a place at university. It was enough for him to pursue art in some capacity. Art—drawing, creating, making videos, painting—filled him with a sense of direction. It was the one undertaking he effortlessly excelled at and was motivated enough to pursue on his own without the prodding of his parents or teachers. Between studying and his grease-stained job, painting and sketching served as his anchor.

In the winter of 2018, Tommy traveled to the mainland to attend the Shanghai Biennale. He found the city manicured and plastic, but the exhibition opened his eyes to the subliminal, sometimes cheeky, and deeply political messages that art could hold. Art would never make him rich, he realized, but was a medium through which to try to correct broken systems or at least to expose someone to a truth. Art, he came to believe, could flourish only in a free society.

Tommy urged his new friends at the visual arts program to attend the rally on March 31. "You guys have to care," Tommy told them. "What will Hong Kong become if we don't show up?" They, like most youths then, were fatalistic. After the collapse of the Umbrella Movement, many resigned themselves to China's dominance, pushed politics aside, and enjoyed the simpler things in life, flocking to hot-pot outlets for meals and taking weekend trips to Shenzhen. They had little interest in spending their Sunday on the streets. Tommy told them it wasn't about what they wanted to do—it was their duty. He managed to convince only a few.

The rally felt more like an amiable gathering than a protest. Their small group shuffled down from Wan Chai to Admiralty, the government district, repeating slogans in unison. This was standard fare for Hong Kong demonstrations, and the rally on March 31 was authorized by the police. CHRF had a permit, so police officers protected them from oncoming vehicles and directed traffic, keeping the crowd along their approved route with a cordon of blue and white tape. After a few hours, the march ended with speeches from the pro-democracy activists, and the crowd dispersed. His friends started haggling over where they should have dinner. His frustration suddenly gave way to a moment of inspiration. Tommy excused himself for a few minutes, racing off down the street.

One of his course instructors had asked the class a few weeks earlier to use their bodies to create an art piece. Standing in the middle of the crowded central district, Tommy held up his iPhone in a jammed corridor between a shopping mall and an outdoor escalator connected to a pedestrian bridge and began filming. After sixteen seconds, he inhaled deeply, filling his lungs, then let out a loud, primal scream. He wanted to convey the desperation and anger he often felt. He continued to film, holding his phone perfectly still as he bellowed. Some people glanced back, startled; others looked past and pretended they didn't notice him. Within seconds, life on the street continued as though nothing had happened.

Tommy called his project "The Power of a Voice." It was a bit obvious, the premise idealistic. In Hong Kong, there were millions, each with a voice of their own. If they all spoke up, "it can change anything. I believed that." Tommy knew that twelve thousand was too small of a showing to move the government. It was his way, he thought, of passing on an urgent message: you must show up; you must fight back.

―――――

For Western diplomats, Hong Kong was generally a predictable, sociable posting. A tour in Hong Kong was a reward for tumultuous years in places like Myanmar and Pakistan. Working in the city meant multimillion-dollar apartments on roads snaking up toward the Peak, dinners at Michelin-starred restaurants, prestigious international schools for one's children, and a domestic helper to help co-parent. At foreign chambers of commerce, keeping members happy took little effort. Business was Hong Kong's raison d'être. But in spring 2019, these officials were frantically meeting with every government representative they could, hoping their influence could stave off disaster. The extradition bill was starting to be seen internationally as a continuation of illiberal behavior accelerating under Xi Jinping.

Trump's foreign-policy inner circle had caught wind of the extradition bill. Their interest was piqued in part by the pro-democracy camp's own efforts. In late March, three Hong Kong pro-democracy lawmakers traveled to Washington to meet with Vice President Mike Pence and Deputy National Security Advisor Matt Pottinger. Pottinger, pessimistic that China would act with restraint, told the lawmakers that he could push within the administration for sanctions, which might give Beijing pause. The Hong Kong advocates did not want it to come to that, conscious of the unintended damage to their city they might cause.[6] Still, returning from the US, they carried Pottinger's threat: if Washington considered the territory insufficiently autonomous, Hong Kong's special treatment could be revoked.[7] It seemed so unrealistic at that time that the threat barely made news.

By early May, Lam lost her only remaining argument for the amendments. Taiwan said it was against the extradition bill and objected to Hong Kong lumping its self-governing territory with the People's Republic of China. Even if the bill passed, the Taiwanese government said that it would not seek the extradition of Chan Tong-kai.

Still, she pushed on, and as she did, domestic opposition built. The issue energized the pro-democracy camp in a way that nothing had for years. Wu Chi-wai, the chairman of the Democratic Party who had clinked glasses with Lam a year earlier at the party's fund-raiser, stood up to speak against the chief executive at the legislature on May 9. Wu was generally a gentle person, a mild elder statesman in a raucous bunch. But that afternoon, in the wood-paneled chamber of the Legislative Council, he erupted in an eloquent tirade.

"Carrie Lam, I always thought you were human," he said, his body pitching forward with emotion. "You were born, raised, educated in Hong Kong, and you are a high-ranking official in Hong Kong, but you should know very well that the reason that one country, two systems existed in the first place, is that Hong Kong people are afraid of the Communist Party . . . you, smart ass, opened the firewall that separates China and Hong Kong, and our core value of one country, two systems in Hong Kong, you say it doesn't matter. . . ."

Wu continued: "Look at yourself, what do you see now? Apart from having the [Communist] party spirit and servility, you have neither blood nor humanity. . . . How many people need to take to the streets before you stop?"[8]

Lam pursed her lips and listened. When Wu was done, she called it slander and brushed him off. She continued to be unmoved when two days later, a procedural meeting on the bill descended into physical clashes between opposing lawmakers. One was carried out on a stretcher. She was doing the right thing, Lam told herself. Only one opinion mattered, anyway—Beijing's—and that one was trending in her favor. The highest levels of the Central Government were now publicly backing the proposals, convinced by Lam that she could deliver. In mid-May, the director of Beijing's Liaison Office, Wang Zhimin, met with some two hundred pro-Beijing loyalists in Hong Kong behind closed doors. He instructed them to fall in line and offer their full support to the chief executive and her extradition bill.

Meanwhile, global pressure intensified. In mid-May, Trump's secretary of state, Mike Pompeo, raised concerns that the bill would threaten Hong Kong's rule of law. On May 24 the European Union released an unprecedented formal diplomatic rebuke of the extradition bill. The démarche was agreed upon unanimously in Brussels by the bloc's twenty-eight member states despite their varied relations with China. Kurt Tong and his Canadian counterpart, Jeff Nankivell, met with Lam five days later, on May 29. "Our best advice to you is timeout," Tong told her. "Do a timeout on this thing, say we're going to do a review, put it on the shelf . . . and then go from there." Nankivell took the opportunity to raise the plight of the two Canadians detained in China, a reminder of why the world was terrified of Beijing-style justice.[9]

Their appeal to the years-long relationship with the chief executive did not work. Lam was combative and repeated her arguments to the pair, promising them there were enough safeguards. People didn't understand the amendments, she told the diplomats. It just needed to be explained to Hong Kong people. "They need to trust me," she said.

Lam summoned the city's diplomats in for a final briefing on June 6 before the bill's next reading six days later. Another diplomat who'd similarly worked with Lam for years approached her on the sidelines. "The degree of dissent here," he said, "is bigger than anything I've seen. Please reconsider."

Lam responded that the briefing was a courtesy. "We've got the numbers," she said. "We can do this."

That Sunday, June 9, 2019, corporate lawyers, students, housewives, religious leaders, artists, migrant workers, expatriates, the ultrawealthy, and the very poor took to the streets of Hong Kong. The Civil Human Rights Front had again called for a protest. The dress code was white, a color reserved for death in Chinese culture. The march looked like a giant funeral procession for the city. By the end of the day, more than a million people had turned up to protest peacefully against Carrie Lam and her extradition law.

Lam praised the protesters for their civility. Then she vowed to continue with the lawmaking process. "We were doing it, and we are still doing it, out of our clear conscience, and our commitment to Hong Kong," she said.[10]

———

TOMMY ARRIVED AT TAMAR PARK JUST AFTER 1 A.M. ON JUNE 12. HE CAME alone, unable to convince his friends to show up that early. Tommy made the decision to sleep on the street that night rather than catch the first train from Yuen Long at dawn. Before he left, he told his parents he was going to be staying over at a friend's house for the night. He didn't know much about this sort of protest but had seen videos of the tear gas from the Umbrella Movement. Tommy packed cotton gloves that he took from the art room at school, a pair of swimming goggles, a first-aid kit, and a foldable tripod. The tripod was a last-minute add. He figured it might come in handy against a police baton. Tommy took a picture of the gear, laying it on his bed on an orange sheet decorated in cartoon skulls, thinking he might want to have a record of his participation. Who knew when he might get to do it again?

Several companies from the Police Tactical Unit (PTU), Hong Kong's riot police, were deployed around Admiralty from the early hours of June 12, with orders to stop and search young people. Calls had been circulating online for people to "have a picnic" on the open green lawns of Tamar—a euphemistic call for protest. Police figured protesters would show up around 11 a.m., when the legislative session was due to start. Hong Kong's young people were not known to be early risers. But even before the police units could get into position, hundreds were arriving at Admiralty, slipping into the open expanse around the government buildings and staking out their positions for the night. At sunrise, they descended on Harcourt Road.

The first protesters started erecting barricades out of metal road dividers and redirecting traffic. Sympathetic motorists parked their vehicles across the road and walked away. By 8 a.m., Harcourt Road was occupied, an embarrassing development, given the security measures put in place ahead of the morning. Just as protesters had promised in 2014, they were back.

Pro-Beijing legislators rushed to take shelter at the police headquarters, fearing that they might be attacked.[11] Some forty thousand people thronged the government buildings. By mid-morning, entrances to the government buildings were closed. Civil servants were told to stay home. The Legislative Council president announced that the second reading of the extradition bill would be delayed until further notice.

It was the first victory of a movement that didn't quite know where to go from there. The participants knew that they would accept nothing less than the full withdrawal of the bill, but otherwise their demands were neither clear nor unified. Unlike in 2014, there were no obvious leaders or instructions. People did whatever seemed right to them in the moment. They quickly established points to distribute water, gloves, helmets, and surgical masks, fearing mobilization from the police. Others arrived with boxes of milk tea and brown bags of McDonald's fries and burgers. People bringing crates of supplies were met with cheers and applause.

Tommy milled around Harcourt Road, scrolling through Instagram. He saw a girl he'd known in primary school post on social media that she was there too. Tommy texted her, asking if they should meet up, and eventually found her in the crowd. As they weaved through the roads filled with people instead of red taxis and luxury sedans,

Tommy saw groups of protesters digging up bricks and zip-tying metal road barriers together to form a triangle-shaped weapon they called a "tank." He hung back and observed. When people called for supplies, he followed instructions and passed down whatever was needed. Tommy wondered how one became a leader in these streets, rather than a follower.

By afternoon, police were losing patience with protesters, some of whom were flinging empty water bottles, broken umbrellas, and helmets at officers stationed around government buildings. An order came down to PTU units from Rupert Dover, one of the six senior officers leading the response to the demonstrations that day.[12] Blue-eyed and fair-skinned, Dover was one of some sixty foreign-born, mostly British officers who remained on the Hong Kong Police Force, supposedly a testament to the unchanged nature of the city's institutions post-handover. Dover made a decision that would change the movement. His officers suited up, fastening their black gas masks around their faces and tightening the straps. They aimed their tear-gas guns at the sky and fired, the percussions of the explosions reverberating in the air before landing around the packed streets of Admiralty.

One canister landed at Tommy's feet. He was wearing his swimming goggles, so he had some protection, but his friend was panicking. He told her to close her eyes, and he took her hand and led her through the crowd. They were standing between the entrance of the Legislative Council and an office building called the CITIC Tower, a thirty-three-story building named after the Chinese state-owned company headquartered there. There were children around him, middle-aged parents, and teenagers, panicking, with nothing to cover their eyes or faces. Tommy, one of the few who still had any visibility, realized there were officers on both ends of the crowd and a line of metal barricades to their north. They were trapped. There was nowhere to go for cover but the lobby of the CITIC Tower. Both its main glass doors were locked, leaving just one revolving door to accommodate the hundreds of desperate people rushing to get in.

Police began firing again. Canisters rained down in the middle of the crowd, stuffed in a thin strip between the office building, barricades, and lines of riot police. Tommy did not have expertise in protests, but even he knew that the point of tear gas was to disperse people, not punitively trap them breathing in the fumes. It felt like the police were inciting a stampede. People around Tommy urged the crowd to stay calm to prevent anyone from getting crushed or killed. Groups who made it inside the CITIC Tower began smashing the locked doors, which eventually opened, allowing more through. Tommy saw volunteers washing out bloodshot eyes with water; others were in shock. Tear gas wafted in.

Violence escalated through the afternoon. Wu Chi-wai, the Democratic Party chairman, was out in the crowd along with other pro-democracy lawmakers, trying to act as a shield between the young people and the police. Wu approached the line of police standing between the Legislative Council, the building in which he worked and had been elected to, and the CITIC Tower. "I want to see your commander! I want to see your commander!" he bellowed as he walked toward the police front line, a blue surgical mask draped around his chin. He was alone, unarmed, nothing in his hands. A commander ordered an officer to fire tear gas at Wu. A canister clinked off the asphalt behind the lawmaker, who kept marching forward. A second canister bounced and then exploded next to him. Wu flinched but advanced. His rage seemed to overpower the effects of the gas. He reached the row of police, screaming at the officers behind their wall of riot shields before he was escorted away.

As the hours passed, officers fired more crowd-control weapons: bean-bag rounds, rubber bullets, and more than a hundred rounds of tear gas. Tommy heard the zips of rubber bullets and decided to leave. He was exhausted and afraid. His friend left with him. Tommy squeezed past people at the entrance of the Admiralty station, still appealing to the public for water, first-aid supplies, helmets, and umbrellas to shield against the bombardment of tear gas. He boarded a train and stepped into another world. People were commuting from work as though nothing had happened. Some had groceries and shopping with them; others were holding their briefcases as though it was a normal day in the office. Tommy's eyes had stayed dry through the tear gas. On the train, he started crying. It felt to him like he and thousands of others had suffered so much that day, "and all of you just feel nothing. It hurt me." Tommy told his friend he didn't think he could stay in Hong Kong. He couldn't bear to suffer this pain unless more were in it together. He wanted to give up.

———

TENS OF THOUSANDS HAD BEEN TEARGASSED THAT DAY. THE INDISCRIMI-nate weapon didn't differentiate between protesters or bystanders at work in one of the dozens of office towers around Admiralty. Officers in those few hours unleashed more force than they had throughout the seventy-nine days of the Umbrella Movement, and it wasn't just tear gas. A reporter was pepper-sprayed in the face; a teacher was shot in the eye with a police projectile and partially blinded. Police surrounded a man standing on a road alone and beat him repeatedly with batons. Officers hurled abuse at citizens. One told a priest at the demonstration to "ask your Jesus to come down and see us." An expert on crowd control called it an "essay on how not to police a protest movement."[3]

It was the first display of how police were willing to abandon their guidelines, morality, and humanity to stand as Beijing's soldiers. These were Hong Kong people—and some British expatriates—acting against their own city. They did it because they'd come to internalize that demonstrators were bad, disruptive, hated the government—hated the police. During the "Fishball Riots" in 2016 that saw Edward Leung and other localists jailed, officers were resentful that they'd been ordered to act with restraint. Commanders had told their juniors to just bear it when protesters threw projectiles and hit them, not to fire off tear gas. "Some of [the officers] were really happy for the chance at revenge," said a young riot police officer on the streets on June 12.

Tommy and many traumatized others returned home to see an interview with Lam playing on repeat on the government-aligned TVB. Lam opened by saying that her support for the bill remained steadfast. Then she pivoted to maternal disciplinarian, scolding young demonstrators. "I'm a mother too; I have two sons," Lam told two journalists who sat opposite her. "If I let him have his way every time my son acts this way, I believe we will have a good relationship in the short term. But if I indulge in his wayward behavior, he might regret it after he grows up." As she continued, Lam, as she had in the past, acted distressed. She stammered, on the brink of tears, as she described her love for Hong Kong in response to allegations that she had sold out the city. It was the opposite, Lam insisted. She had sold herself to the city. "My love for this place has prompted me to make many personal sacrifices," she said.[14]

Lam had pushed for this bill, watched thousands teargassed, others beaten on the streets—and then painted herself as the victim. It was a show of arrogance that galvanized the city in disgust. Off-camera, Lam was a little more conflicted. She had promised Beijing that she could deliver. The Communist Party wasn't exactly one to back down in the face of opposition on the streets, but this was evolving into a crisis even bigger than the one in 2014.

Lam sought the council of senior pro-Beijing heavyweights. One who had initially supported the bill told Lam it should be stopped.[15] If the government U-turned now, he said, at least the damage could be controlled. June 12 would be registered in Hong Kong's history as a violent, tragic day, but it would end there. Another urged her to say she would "withdraw" the bill so that it wouldn't seem like she might bring it back later in her term.

She didn't quite take the advice. Lam announced on June 15 that her government had decided to "suspend"—not withdraw—the legislative exercise, restart communication, and "do more explanation work."

It was a missed off-ramp that appeased no one. Pro-Beijing lawmakers felt that Lam put them in an impossible position by asking them to back the bill and then suspending it. They were going to be destroyed in upcoming elections. In a meeting that morning, a few hours before Lam's announcement, one pro-Beijing lawmaker erupted: "My colleagues have been fucked every day while explaining [the bill to the community]. Drop dead! Why don't you try facing the community and be fucked every day!"[16] Lam held a similar briefing with the opposition camp, who told her she was making a grave mistake. Wu, the Democratic Party chairman, pleaded with Lam.[17] He told her she still had a chance to pull the city back from the brink of disaster if she withdrew the bill and ordered a judge-led inquiry into the events. Lam sullenly told them she was sticking to "suspending" and walked out after half an hour.

Four days after police unleashed on protesters, on June 16, tens of thousands again gathered in Victoria Park. The Civil Human Rights Front had called for another protest. Some were holding up red posters of Lam with devil horns, the yellow sickle and hammer of the Chinese Communist Party blinding her eyes. Others cried as they held images of protesters covered in blood. Lam, like her law, was "evil." Five hours after the march was due to begin, people were still waiting at Victoria Park to exit. There were too many people ahead of them to move.

Organizers estimated the turnout at two million, almost a third of the city's population. It was the largest protest in Hong Kong history. Lam had opened a new chapter in Hong Kong and then entirely lost control of it.

CHAPTER 11

攬炒

LAAM CAAU

ICHMOND, AN UPPER-MIDDLE-CLASS NEIGHBORHOOD BY THE THAMES ON the outskirts of London, was an unlikely place to foment a revolution. On a balmy June day—a luxury even in Britain's notoriously fickle summer—visitors flocked to the bars and restaurants along the riverside, enjoying pints of beer and ice cream cones as airplanes flew overhead, en route to Heathrow Airport. Residents in light Barbour jackets walked their pedigreed dogs along the river path; others zoomed past in fixed-gear bikes or rented punts for a spin on the river. Mick Jagger, Angelina Jolie, and Brad Pitt had all called Richmond home at one point. It was here, in a cozy minimalist studio decorated in soft hues of gray and white, that Finn Lau—far from the rural New Territories where he'd grown up and from the perceived failures of his school years—was typing an epistle. It was one of several that would change the course of his life.

Sitting in his room, Finn opened the LIHKG app on his phone. Its yellow smiley-face icon was incongruous with the mood on the forum, a Hong Kong version of Reddit, but clunkier and harder to navigate. Finn had posted frequently since June 9, the first million-strong protest. Each post was shared and "upvoted," or endorsed, by hundreds if not thousands. It was now June 17. Everything had escalated so quickly since his first post, both in his own life and in his city. Yet some things remained painfully similar to Hong Kong's last failed movement. People on the forum were still fighting among themselves; the "wo, lei, fei" (peaceful, rational, and nonviolent protesters) against the 勇武 or "braves" (more radical front liners who wanted to channel their anger into violence against the police and government). Finn was frustrated. He moved his thumbs with furious speed:

> Please everyone listen to me, stop the internal discord, set a deadline, and fully escalate!
>
> I have never attempted only sleeping ten hours total all week, taking painkillers every day to withstand it! I'm doing this to help everyone win this battle!
>
> I've only got half a life remaining, I'm begging you to listen to me.
>
> The peaceful, rational, and nonviolent, and the brave fighters are like sword and shield, yin and yang, you can't do without one or the other!

(He marked the text in red and black and formatted it perfectly so the post would stand out—but also because he was still compulsively neat.)

> Braves, if you didn't have the peaceful, rational, and nonviolent ones [on June 12] as your backstop, how would you have made your name?
>
> Peaceful, rational, and nonviolent ones, if you don't have the braves holding out for you on the front lines, do you want to repeat the same mistakes of Umbrella? Umbrella won us halos worldwide, but then the world laughed at us for five years!
>
> Fucking rebuke each other after we're done fighting this battle, please!

He ended his post with a call to action, setting a deadline of 11 p.m. on June 20 for the government to drop rioting charges against those arrested thus far. "We must save them all," he wrote. In a post the previous day he had reminded those on the forum that Carrie Lam was a master at deception: "Every time she pretended to give in, and then hit back." Suspending the bill was not enough. "We can't fall for it again!"

If the government did not acquiesce, Finn proposed that both the "wo, lei, fei" and the "braves" fully escalate on June 21, besieging the government headquarters, police headquarters, and Government House: "I am kneeling and begging you, upvote posts with all your might, send this post to people you know, share it on Facebook, forward it to the pan-democrats. . . . Fight those motherfuckers!"

It was an impassioned, expletive-punctuated manifesto written by a shy twenty-five-year-old newlywed and rising star in a global surveying firm. Anyone who knew Finn would have described him the way his teachers did in primary school: polite, determined, respectful, reserved, quiet, "a nice boy." But here on LIHKG, he was not Finn Lau Cho-dik. He had stripped away the traits that masked a deep, sometimes explosive anger. On the forum, he was a different persona altogether. The words he typed would be distilled into a philosophy of mutual destruction best summarized by Katniss Everdeen in *The Hunger Games*: "If we burn, you burn with us."

———

FINN MOVED TO LONDON IN MARCH 2019, THE SECOND STOP IN HIS BUR-geoning career. The disappointment of his second-choice program at City University faded quickly after his first summer internship. The job of a quantitative surveyor, it turned out, wasn't traversing the city with a tripod over his shoulder. Finn was assessing bids from construction companies vying to build major infrastructure projects in Hong Kong and internationally. Some of his supervisors—generally the British expatriates, not the locals—jetted across the region to South Korea, Japan, and beyond, managing these projects. Finn had traveled overseas only once, to nearby Taiwan. The next summer, Finn clinched an internship at Mott MacDonald, the company responsible for the Channel Tunnel between France and the United Kingdom, the Aswan Dam in Egypt, and, more recently, express highways running through Silicon Valley. The firm assigned Finn to a team handling the expansion of Hong Kong's MTR network. Finn did so well that his higher-ups mistook him for a full-time employee, not a college student.

Finn spent the years after the 2014 Umbrella Movement frustrated by the direction in which Hong Kong was heading. He couldn't find any political ideology that aligned with his. Finn gravitated toward localism but was disgusted at its sometimes-ugly xenophobia against mainlanders, like calling Chinese tourists "locusts." Student leaders like Joshua Wong allowed little room for ideas other than their own. Finn decided he wanted to see more of the world. Mott MacDonald was one of the few firms that offered a pathway to a global career. He was offered a job after he graduated in 2015, and within three years he was posted overseas to Singapore, the Southeast Asian city-state so often compared with his own city.

Finn and Theresa married in the spring of 2018, in a pavilion designed to look like a chapel: triangular with floor-to-ceiling glass windows overlooking the ocean. They were different in so many ways, especially when it came to politics, but it didn't matter. They loved each other. Theresa told Finn she wanted an international life like his. Finn's salary did not meet the minimum threshold in Singapore to sponsor Theresa, so she could visit only as a tourist, flying back to Hong Kong every thirty days.

Finn was impressed with the vision of the Singapore government, which had worked to reduce its dependence on and outshine its much larger neighbors. Finn started to question the assumptions so often parroted to him in Hong Kong. If Singapore, smaller and with fewer people than Hong Kong, could be independent, why was it sold to Hong Kong as something ridiculous, impossible? Instead of great statesmen who could have pushed for a different fate, all Hong Kong had was rich and powerful developers, Finn thought. On New Year's Eve in 2018, he had watched fireworks race up into the sky behind the rooftop infinity pool of Marina Bay Sands and explode into a kaleidoscope of colors, feeling deep gratitude for the opportunity and yet aching for Hong Kong.

The Mott MacDonald office in Singapore was far more diverse than anywhere Finn had worked in Hong Kong. He discussed British politics, Australian football, and Southeast Asian history with his colleagues. One was a former officer in the Singapore Army, an experience Finn found fascinating and that had no parallels in Hong Kong, where military and diplomatic relations were controlled by China. Theresa was the only part of home with him in Singapore, but a sporadic one. He still wanted to be connected to Hong Kong. Sitting in a project-site office in the spring of 2019, Finn decided to download the LIHKG mobile app. He was mostly a lurker, reading celebrity gossip, reviews of computer hardware, and crude jokes that proliferated on the forum.

Finn moved to London in March 2019 after yet another promotion. This time, he made enough to sponsor Theresa. Finn was comfortable enough that he was sending money to his parents back in Hong Kong, allowing them to live an easier life. He had finally justified the overpriced English-language primary school in Kowloon Tong. Hoping to advance his education, Finn applied for a master's program at University College London (UCL). He easily got in.

Theresa was charmed with life in London. She insisted on Richmond, although they could afford only a small studio there. The young couple explored new areas every weekend: the kitschy shops and cozy bars of Seven Dials in Covent Garden, the seaside resort city of Brighton, the edgy northern borough of Camden. Theresa captured everything on her iPhone, building her Instagram profile with heavily edited photos enhanced with trendy filters. It was a blissful few months, until the upheaval back home.

———

EVEN FROM ITS EARLIEST DAYS, THE ANTI-EXTRADITION MOVEMENT WAS shaping up to be something different in Hong Kong's protest history. If the police response had changed, so had the tactics and methods of the demonstrators, influenced by past failures. Right before the start of the anti-extradition movement, the government convicted nine leaders of the 2014 Umbrella Movement with incitement to commit nuisance, sending Tai and Chan Kin-man to jail for sixteen months. Reverend Chu was spared prison, receiving a suspended sentence from the judge because of his age, health, and past public service. Joshua Wong was also jailed. Edward Leung, the localist leader, was serving an even longer sentence for rioting. It was a lesson in the vulnerability of the old model. If prominent pro-democracy activists took control at the start of 2019, it could open a new batch to arrest, making it easier to dismantle the whole movement.

The Civil Human Rights Front, which organized the first marches against the bill, pitched itself more as a coordinator than a leader. It would apply for protest permits, but it would not determine the course of the action. This new model of decentralization wasn't just built out of necessity. Many shared Finn's frustration with the pro-democracy movement's most prominent members, were sick of their infighting, and wanted to have a real say. "Leaderlessness," wrote a group of scholars studying the movement, "was treated not only as a fact but also an ideal."[1] Without any kind of central command, protesters turned to the website LIHKG—another legacy of the Umbrella Movement.

Many in 2014 rejected Hong Kong's established media organizations, which were slowly coming under control of pro-Beijing companies and proxies, continuing a trend from before the handover. Hong Kong journalists increasingly saw self-censorship as a problem, and the public no longer believed that the press was free.[2] In 2017 Hong Kong's securities regulator revealed that TVB, the free-to-air local broadcaster that transmitted scenes from Tiananmen Square, was owned by Li Ruigang, one of China's most powerful media tycoons.[3] Hong Kongers called it "CCTVB," a reference to the Chinese state-owned broadcaster. The *South China Morning Post* (SCMP), the city's most important international title, was also seen as compromised after it was purchased by Chinese e-commerce giant Alibaba in 2015. People started throwing financial support toward media organizations founded in the wake of the upheaval. The same year that Alibaba bought SCMP, a lanky, ginger-haired social activist and blogger named Tom Grundy founded *Hong Kong Free Press* through crowd-funding, billing his outlet as independent and devoid of pressure from pro-China tycoons. Gwyneth's employer, *Stand News*, along with *Citizen News* and *FactWire News Agency*, also emerged as a direct response to the censorship.

The Umbrella Movement didn't just change the nature of Hong Kong's journalism, but political discourse entirely. In 2014 online forum HKGolden—started as a nonpolitical site that featured consumer tech reviews and pricing guides—cemented its role as a hub for political dissent. But police began to crack down, and HKGolden acquiesced, giving authorities the IP address of a user who urged protesters to block subway tracks. He was arrested and released on bail.[4] HKGolden posted a notice asking users to refrain from inciting others and started limiting political content.

Users migrated to a new site that was easier to read on mobile devices: LIHKG. Publicity-shy techie Lineage Hui founded the site in 2016 and established measures to protect it against cyberattacks and censorship. He crafted the website's name by taking the first two letters of his first name and adding "HKG" in a nod to its predecessor. Users who wanted to sign up needed an email address from a Hong Kong–based internet service provider or a Hong Kong school or university. Once on, they could post under a pseudonym. A setting allowed users to turn the entire site into a fake Excel sheet to browse at work when their bosses were looking. And unlike Twitter and Facebook, users couldn't follow a specific person, only "upvote" or "downvote" posts they liked or rejected, meaning that no single person could dominate the conversation. Just like on the streets, the forum could not have leaders. Cantonese slang and codes that proliferated on the forum also made it difficult for outsiders to infiltrate.

LIHKG became a petri dish for ideas: neighborhood-specific protests, global advertisement campaigns, petitions, lobbying, and other efforts to "liberate" Hong Kong from Beijing's grip. The forum registered more than 36,000 new users between June and August 2019.[5]

FINN'S FIRST POST ON LIHKG WAS ON THE EVENING OF JUNE 9. HE HAD just returned from a march in central London in solidarity with the one back home. The frustration he felt in September 2014, when he was sitting on the streets, came back to him. Overseas Hong Kongers could do more than just chant. Finn remembered reading a post on LIHKG the day before, asking users to create a list of Hong Kong government officials whose immediate family held foreign passports. It was a requirement in Hong Kong to give up foreign citizenship to take up office, but family members were allowed to retain overseas passports. Carrie Lam's husband and sons both had British passports, as did the security minister's wife and children. The post on LIHKG was calling out this hypocrisy—of those who were ruining Hong Kong but had a get-out clause with right of abode elsewhere through their children. "Hong Kong can't be saved. So you fuckers have to stay here too, get cooked together," the person wrote.

Finn wanted to take it a step further. He changed his username to a new pseudonym, 我要攬炒 or "iwantlaamcaau." The phrase "laam caau," borrowed from Cantonese gambling slang, translated to "embrace fry." It encapsulated a philosophy that was gaining traction, a strategy of mutual destruction. Under the "laam caau" doctrine, protesters would strike at the heart of Hong Kong's safe, predictable business environment, calling for sanctions and the destruction of the international ties that underpinned the territory's survival. China still needed Hong Kong as a financial bridge to the rest of the world. China's own economy was also under strain, with US president Trump steadily escalating tariffs and trade barriers on Chinese exports. If Beijing and their proxies wanted to take Hong Kong's freedoms, Hong Kongers would destroy the city—and China itself.

Finn didn't think too much about the consequences before he typed, nor did he think to tell Theresa. Foreign lobbying was not illegal under Hong Kong law. Under the new handle, he wrote a post that was basically a recruitment drive. It was time to "turn up to turbo speed and get down to business," he wrote, and then called for anyone with a background in law, good English skills, and some free time to leave their Telegram handles in the comments section. "iwantlaamcau" would then invite them into a separate group. There, they'd divide up labor as they began investigating the foreign family ties of each Hong Kong pro-establishment official and drafting letters to respective governments. "iwantlaamcau" suggested creating teams to cover specific countries, including the UK, the US, Australia, and Canada. The goal would be to dox senior officials, releasing personal details and those of their foreign spouses and children, while also urging foreign governments to revoke the privileges. "Labor is limited," he wrote; "we are racing against time, and urgently need help."

The response was overwhelming. Every hour, the list of comments grew longer, with Telegram usernames such as "honeymilk," "unbelievable," and "RIP." Finn asked only for basic information, like where the person was based and their job. Within hours, Finn was overseeing half a dozen Telegram groups. They were anonymous to one another, built only on trust and their singular purpose. Finn organized them by location: the US team, the UK team, the Japan team, and so on. He named his group the "laamcau team" and later gave it an English name, Hong Kong Liberty. Soon he was spending more time talking to these online strangers than to Theresa. She, too, was distracted. Theresa fell deeper into the manicured world of Instagram as Finn went further into Telegram and LIHKG.

Within weeks, there were dozens more groups like Finn's. Some were focused on raising awareness of Hong Kong's plight by translating informational materials into different languages. Others, formed by graphic designers and artists, created posters and flyers. In Hong Kong, some facilitated protester safety within the city, alerting users to police movements at demonstrations. One group was for foreign journalists who wanted to find specific types of people to interview. We joined that one and many others, although they quickly drained our phone batteries with constant pop-up notifications. Their security protocols were impressive, requiring us to take a selfie with our business card and a code they'd send over beforehand to verify our identities as reporters.

It wasn't just the young who were organizing and mobilizing. Hong Kongers in their mid-thirties and forties, without the mettle to go to the front lines but with financial resources, set up groups to distribute food coupons, provide temporary housing to younger protesters at risk, and help in other ways with their money. They were volunteers known as "parents," playing the role of the elders among the "kids." These were entirely grassroots initiatives, independent of the pro-democracy groups that had anchored Hong Kong's civil society for the past three decades. Telegram, like LIHKG, was becoming so central to the mobilization that it quickly rose to being one of the most downloaded apps in Hong Kong, adding almost a hundred thousand new users in a month.[6] A new kind of movement—networked yet decentralized, held together by a singular focus and an almost blind trust—was forming.

———

Chu Yiu-ming weds Dorothy Leung, 1972.
(*Courtesy of Dorothy Leung*)

New Mass Transit Railway tubes wait to be fitted underwater in Chai Wan, 1978.
(*South China Morning Post via Getty Images*)

Martin Lee, in the middle and front row, and Chu Yiu-ming, behind him, protest in Hong Kong in support of students at Tiananmen Square, 1989.
(*LightRocket via Getty Images*)

Finn Lau with his grandmother, 1996.
(*Courtesy of Finn Lau*)

The royal yacht *Britannia* arrives at Victoria Harbor ahead of the July 1, 1997, handover of Hong Kong from Britain to China.
(*AFP via Getty Images*)

Protesters on Harcourt Road leave messages promising to return as police clear the Umbrella Movement campsite, December 11, 2014.
(*Tom Grundy*)

Chinese President Xi Jinping swears in Carrie Lam as the chief executive of Hong Kong and her cabinet, July 1, 2017.
(*Getty Images*)

Chan Kin-man, left, Chu Yiu-ming, and Benny Tai, right, as they enter court to be sentenced for their role in the 2014 Umbrella Movement protests, April 10, 2019.
(*AFP via Getty Images*)

Over a million people protest against the extradition bill on June 9, 2019, kicking off months of large-scale sustained demonstrations.
(*Deacon Lui*)

Protesters who broke into the Legislative Council graffiti the emblem of Hong Kong and hang the British colonial-era flag over it, July 1, 2019.
(*Associated Press*)

Protesters in hard hats use umbrellas and other shields to protect themselves from a police water cannon on Harcourt Road, September 15, 2019.
(*Deacon Lui*)

Stand With Hong Kong used crowdfunding to buy advertisements in newspapers globally promoting the pro-democracy cause. Eighteen ads were published in thirteen countries in August 2019.
(*Courtesy of Finn Lau*)

Gwyneth Ho and Sarah Van Meel dress up for one last night together in Amsterdam before the pandemic closed borders across the world, March 13, 2020.
(*Courtesy of Sarah Van Meel*)

Activists from the "resistance camp," including Gwyneth Ho (*second row, right*) and Joshua Wong (*first row, left*), hold a press conference after winning the most votes in the pro-democracy primary election, July 16, 2020. All are now in jail or exile.
(*Associated Press*)

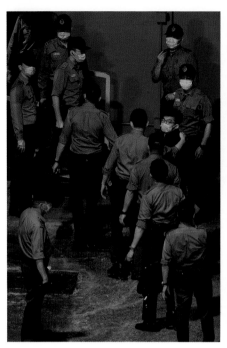

Joshua Wong escorted by officers into the Lai Chi Kok correctional facility, March 2, 2021.

A Zodiac boat carrying Tommy and four others sails across the South China Sea towards Taiwan, July 17, 2020.
(*Kenny*)

Finn Lau and Catherine Li at Finn's graduation from his master's program at University College London (UCL), June 30, 2022.
(*Alan Lau*)

An illustration of Gwyneth by her friend Sarah, inspired by the MIKA song "Staring at the Sun."
(*Sarah Van Meel*)

ALONG WITH FINN'S POST, UNIVERSITY STUDENT UNIONS WERE ADDING TO
calls for a protest on June 21. The online and offline directives served to
reinforce each other.

Protesters also wanted to commemorate a painful event that had
unfolded a week earlier. After the clashes of June 12, a thirty-five-
year-old man wearing a yellow raincoat stood at the top of a lattice of
scaffolding erected outside a luxury mall in Admiralty. He unfurled a
white banner, affixing it to the metal with black tape. Scrawled on the
banner in Cantonese and English were pleas: "No extradition to China,
total withdrawal of the extradition bill, we are not rioters, release the
students and injured, Carrie Lam step down, help Hong Kong." Hours
later, despite efforts by firefighters, police, and bystanders, the man fell
to his death in an apparent suicide. Years later, an inquest found belongings in his backpack including a black T-shirt with the words "I am
lost in Hong Kong" and a notebook that carried his final words: "I felt
dejected about this Hong Kong. . . . I pondered these past few months
but could not find an answer to the future. [The decision] today is my
wish. The government is the cause of it all."[7]

After his fall, Marco Leung became "raincoat man," an iconic symbol of the perceived indifference and cruelty of the government. In an
already emotional city, Leung was seen by many as a martyr, the first
to lose his life ostensibly because of the government and its despised
bill. There was little discussion about the complexities of suicide and
mental health. For days after, the walkway where he fell to his death
was obscured by mounds of white chrysanthemums, memorials, and
tribute artwork, stretching beyond the perimeter of the mall. Grieving
protesters never knew Leung. They didn't have to. Their collective pain
reinforced itself; some felt almost guilty, responsible for his death by not
having done enough to stop Hong Kong from getting to this point. It
was a sentiment repeated among those who were middle-aged and older:
*If only we did more, if only we had guaranteed Hong Kong's democracy ear-
lier, our young wouldn't be here, fighting, dying on the streets.*

Before Tommy joined the unauthorized protest on June 21, he made
a stop at his local supermarket and bought two cartons of brown eggs.
Still a novice to civil disobedience, he took measures to ensure that his
fragile ammunition would be intact when he needed it. He opened the

carton, draped layers of bubble wrap over the eggs, closed the package, and cocooned it with more bubble wrap. Tommy then wrapped the carton in a plastic bag, gently placed it in his backpack, and traveled across Hong Kong with the cargo.

Around 11 a.m., Tommy joined the crowd in briefly blocking access to the government headquarters, as they had on June 12. This time, there were no police—but the protesters weren't going to wait until they arrived. They swarmed around the city, rushing inside other government buildings, blocking exits, and forcing civil servants to end work early. Each time they achieved their goal, they dispersed and moved on to a new location.

The black-clad protesters were guerrilla fighters engaged in urban combat. It was a strategy borrowed from one of Hong Kong's most famous residents. Bruce Lee discovered kung fu in the city and was memorialized along the harbor in his classic "ready to strike" pose, molded as a bronze statue. In 2019 the pro-democracy movement resurrected his memory in a different way. They used his words to guide their resistance: "Be formless, shapeless, like water. Now, you put water in a cup, it becomes the cup. Put it into a teapot, it becomes the teapot. . . . Be like water, my friend."

The crowd of protesters settled on their last target for the day, the headquarters of the Hong Kong Police Force. Once outside the gates of the imposing building, Tommy recognized a group of friends from college. He saw more familiar faces as he looked around. He didn't anticipate how comforting their presence would be. It was the best he'd felt in weeks.

By nightfall, the roads around the police headquarters were blocked, rendered impassable by traffic. Police presence around the building was almost nonexistent. Protesters could reach right to the front of the building. Officers stayed inside, peeking out of windows at the crowd. At one point, a spokeswoman for the police said the force respected the peaceful rally and wouldn't launch a clearance operation. Joshua Wong, who had just been released from jail after serving his last sentence related to the Umbrella Movement, was rallying the crowd.

Tommy unwrapped his parcel. His friends laughed at him. "Of course Tommy brought eggs," they joked. He took aim and threw. The slop of white, yolk, and cracked shell fell to the pavement below, well off its intended mark of a police officer standing by an open window. Tommy's limp tosses kept missing his target; he was never very good at sports. He got through just half his haul before he packed up the eggs up and stuffed them back into his bag, slightly embarrassed and his ego a bit bruised.

Before he left, Tommy looked back at the cement wall marking the entrance of the police headquarters, stained yellow with yolk. "Fuck the popo" was graffitied in blood-red spray paint. They had made their point. It was now time to "be water": flow back home and prepare for the next fight.

———

AHEAD OF JULY 1, THE HONG KONG GOVERNMENT ANNOUNCED IT WAS moving dignitaries celebrating the twenty-second anniversary of the handover indoors. Their press release cited "bad weather"—but it wasn't raining. Meteorologists called off a thunderstorm warning at 6 a.m., and the month was shaping up to be the hottest July on record.[8] Just hours after dawn, the sun beat down on the city. Temperatures would rise to 90 degrees Fahrenheit by afternoon.

A truthful statement, on this especially significant day for Beijing, would have been too embarrassing for Lam and her government. Ahead of the annual ceremony, calls had circulated for protesters to disrupt the event. Authorities ascertained, correctly, that it was easier to block off access to a convention center than to an open square. They would keep officials inside the hall, away from potential protests, even if that meant they had to watch a live feed of the flag raising on a small screen. It was better than the alternative.

Tommy was still groggy when he arrived at the area around Golden Bauhinia Square at 6 a.m. He'd had some trouble sleeping the night before, a little anxious. The eggs, he decided, were stupid. Today, July 1, would be his first real fight. He had even packed a full respirator that he'd swiped from the art room at the university and a yellow hard hat.

Tommy felt like he was ready, spurred on by the large-scale marches of the previous weeks. He and hundreds of others pushed forward to the frontline officers around Bauhinia Square only to be met with pepper spray and batons. Outnumbered, they fell back. The ceremony inside went ahead.

About twenty minutes after those clashes, Carrie Lam entered the convention center. It was her first public appearance in weeks. Lam Siu-por, her husband, stood beside her in an ill-fitting suit that hung off his small frame. The pair sang the national anthem as the Chinese and Hong Kong flags rose in the square outside. Lam then took to the podium and gave a short speech. She was somewhat conciliatory. After the "incident" of the past months, Lam said, she would "learn the lesson and ensure that the government's future work will be closer and more responsive to the aspirations, sentiments and opinions of the community."[9] The work of a more open government, she said, would start with her. Lam clinked champagne flutes with her predecessors and smiled for the cameras, as if someone had pulled a string on a doll and bared its teeth. The ceremony concluded within half an hour—but it had happened. Given the political environment, that was victory itself for the government.

Tommy and the others had failed their first task, but they were just getting started. Police had granted the Civil Human Rights Front a permit for their annual July 1 march, which would kick off around 3 p.m. Interest was significantly higher than in any other time since 2014. Soon, tens of thousands of "wo, lei, fei"—the peaceful, rational, nonviolent protesters—would march down the parallel street along the sanctioned route. They had numbers that the "braves" never would.

The "braves" decided they would rest for a while at a corner of Harcourt Road, away from the police, and vote on their next course of action. Tommy had actively sought out this crowd but, sitting among them with their hard hats and gas masks, was a little wary. Until that morning, they were just random usernames to him, grouped together on the streets only as a result of the Telegram group. If he wanted to do more at the protests, trusting these strangers was the only way. He couldn't find willing partners elsewhere. On the weekends, Tommy and his friends—mostly girls a few years younger—experimented with film cameras or rummaged through Mee & Gee, a crammed thrift store filled with garish apparel, where salespeople recognized him for his outlandish purchases. These friends knew he was impulsive and had a propensity for doing "crazy" things. They loved to remind him of when he snuck into an abandoned hospital and the security almost called the police. Tommy felt they sometimes looked at him like he was a different breed. He knew their limits. In this emerging battle, he was looking for more than friends. Tommy wanted comrades.

Tommy paired up with two others from the Telegram group. He didn't know much about them, but at least he could see their faces. One of his new teammates was just nineteen. A speaker addressed the group. The "braves," he said, would try to break into the Legislative Council building that day. They would take back power on July 1, 2019, the anniversary of the day they were returned to China without so much as a referendum. They hoped the peaceful marches would provide them with cover, if not support, for this escalation.

Over the next hours, some prepared. They collected metal poles, trolleys stuffed with cardboard, metal road dividers, bricks, and whatever else they could scavenge from the street and nearby construction sites. Then just before 3 p.m., groups stationed at different ends of the Legislative Council began hammering on the thick panes of glass surrounding the building. Moderate pro-democracy lawmakers tried to stop them; one, Claudia Mo, told them to consider their futures. "Ten years in jail, is it worth it?" she urged. The lawmakers were ignored. The next phase had begun.

Tommy walked around the perimeter for a while, watching. Then someone passed him an iron bar. He took it and swung at the glass with all he had. It bounced off without making a dent. He tried again. It felt like he wasn't doing anything impressive, just embarrassing himself. "I was just too weak," he said. Tommy watched others trying to do the same. It seemed entirely futile. There were more layers of security inside, including locked metal shutters that would have to be pried open somehow if the plan was to succeed.

The fortification was by design. After the 2014 Umbrella Movement, the Legislative Council commissioned a security report. It found that the building, with its open design, was susceptible to attacks, more likely from protesters than terrorists. Independent security consultants advised that the Hong Kong government reinforce the glass walls that were a hallmark of the complex with anti-blast film. On their recommendation, authorities also installed the roller shutters and metal barricades around and inside the building.[10] The upgrades, they thought, made the building impenetrable.

Realizing he was no match for the glass, Tommy set his sights elsewhere. His team was trying to obtain the blueprints for the Legislative Council building, hoping they could map out all its entranceways, passages, and tunnels. Maybe they could find another way in or anticipate police action if protesters did eventually get in. Others, stronger than him, kept smashing. Peaceful marchers were beginning to flow through the parallel street. Some took a fork in the road to alert the crowd of the brewing action around the Legislative Council, appealing to them for help and support. They jumped and flailed, "Help the Braves! Stop marching along this route! Come to Harcourt Road!" Middle-aged residents, parents with kids in tow, the elderly: thousands broke off from the main, authorized protest march to surround and protect the younger radical protesters.

By nightfall, the metal fences around the legislative building were missing some of their poles, ripped off by protesters and turned into spears. People were breaking whatever they could, spray-painting graffiti, and digging bricks up from the road. Standing beneath the entrance of the building, the lights still on, was a sea of yellow hard hats. After six hours of trying, they were still determined to make their way in. The glass had finally been ripped away in spider-webbed sheets. There was a metal shutter in their way now and, behind them, hundreds of riot police who had curiously not made efforts to disperse the crowd.

Around 9 p.m., officers who had been standing guard behind the metal shutters simply left. In two straight lines they marched away, got into their vans, and drove off. The three Police Tactical Unit companies stationed in the building—some 360 officers—had received a command to withdraw. The Legislative Council's own security team, a division separate from the police, was baffled. Minutes later, the young men and women in yellow hard hats marched up the escalators of the Legislative Council. They had made it in.

Hundreds began filling the chamber. Stepping over shards of broken glass and mangled metal, protesters roamed the halls and began tagging them with slogans. "HK is not China," someone sprayed in black on one of the pillars. Others destroyed portraits of the Legislative Council president and his predecessors. A man in a white helmet with a white mask strapped across his face began climbing the brown leather chair reserved for the Legislative Council president. He reached up with a can of black spray paint and, under a shield of umbrellas protecting his identity, began spray-painting the red-and-white emblem of the Hong Kong Special Administrative Region. He blacked out "The People's Republic of China," leaving only "Hong Kong Special Administrative Region." That was their sole allegiance. Beneath it, across the raised desk of the council president, several others hung the colonial flag of Hong Kong with a blue British ensign and the city's coat of arms.

It wasn't just a rejection of the extradition bill, but of everything that had transpired since Margaret Thatcher met with Deng Xiaoping at the Great Hall of the People. One graffitied message in the chamber that night, however, appeared directed more at Carrie Lam than Beijing: "It was you who taught me that peaceful protests are futile."

Tommy didn't have a can of spray paint. Instead, he plastered the chamber with stickers his friend had designed, mocking the police. He was still focused on finding possible routes the police could use to surround the protesters. Those inside the chamber were on edge, buzzing with excitement and paranoia. That they had reached this inner sanctum felt like a trap, a way to encircle the core of the movement and take them down en masse. Reporters were live streaming and documenting, which could also subject recorded protesters to arrest. Aware the world was watching, the young demonstrators kept their vandalism targeted. They destroyed no books, only portraits. They left money behind for drinks they took out of the vending machine. They didn't damage the media room where journalists worked.

Tommy blocked some elevator shafts and doors to empty rooms with chairs and debris in a haphazard effort to cut off what he randomly guessed might be secret entrances to or exits from the building. The full day of action had made him hungry. He pushed through the crowd toward the exit and left for dinner. As he was eating, the protesters inside deliberated their next course of action. One young man inside the chamber stood on a lawmaker's desk, pulled down his blue surgical mask, and in front of cameras—face visible to all—began to speak. "The more people here, the safer we are!" he shouted. "Let's stay and occupy the chamber; we can't lose anymore!"[11]

Many wanted to leave instead. They wanted to end the siege and to maintain the "be water" tactic. Some brought up the 2014 Sunflower Movement, where the Taiwanese legislature was occupied by students worried about a trade pact that could expose the self-governing island to political pressure from Beijing. Protesters wanted to replicate their standoff and spur a similar movement for autonomy through occupation. But if Hong Kong was not China, it was also not Taiwan. None of those involved in the Sunflower Movement were found guilty; courts decided their actions were justified civil disobedience. Protesters in Hong Kong could face up to ten years in jail for rioting. As they debated, Hong Kong police televised a message saying they'd give the protesters only until midnight to leave. Then they would storm the building and arrest anyone left inside.

A consensus emerged. The protesters would exit the chamber but, before they did, would use the moment to clarify their movement. The unmasked protester, a graduate student named Brian Leung, read out a declaration, drawn up by both those inside the chamber and those online. It crystallized into five demands: fully withdraw the extradition bill, release all arrested protesters unconditionally, withdraw the classification of their movement as a "riot," open an investigation into the police behavior, and—underpinning it all—implement universal suffrage in Hong Kong. They wouldn't stop until these five demands were met, "not one less."

Most began streaming out. Four demonstrators wanted to stay. They said they would rather die than exit on their own. The majority reached another consensus: there would be no more martyrs, no more deaths like Marco Leung's. They would remove the remaining protesters against their will. Dozens rushed back into the building to remove the four, minutes before the midnight deadline.

————

GWYNETH HO WAS A FEW WEEKS INTO HER SUMMER BREAK. SHE WAS BACK in Hong Kong, just as she had planned, reporting for *Stand News* while waiting for the second year of her master's program to begin. How that month had unfolded was beyond her expectations.

Almost immediately after touching down from Denmark, Gwyneth found herself on the streets, part of *Stand News'* small but agile team. She still didn't know much about live streaming, the online outlet's preferred mode of news gathering. *Stand News'* live coverage sometimes reached more than a million viewers, and reporters were meant to deliver an unfiltered look at the protesters to this growing audience. It required constant attention to her phone, which frustratingly had just overheated and shut down. She never knew the right balance between adding her own commentary and letting the scene speak for itself. Gwyneth turned her phone back on and restarted her Facebook live stream. Just then, she saw a group of protesters reentering the chamber and ran to follow them. "Why are you rushing in here?" Gwyneth asked the girl next to her. She thrust her microphone close to capture her answer.

"Because we were notified through Telegram and learned that four protesters had decided to stay," the girl answered. "So we all decided to come up here to carry them with us, and get them out of here." The young protester started sobbing: "If they don't leave, we won't either." A boy was holding her hand, leading her into the chamber.

Gwyneth's own voice over the live stream cracked: "Aren't you scared that you won't be able to get out if you enter here now?"

Now crying heavily, the girl answered, "We are all scared, but we are much more terrified that we will not see the four of them tomorrow. That's why we will enter here together, and leave together. . . . This was a decision we all agreed upon."[12]

The protesters physically carried out the remaining four and dispersed. By the time the police fired tear gas just after midnight, the streets were mostly quiet. Protesters left in their wake millions of dollars in damages, but no lost lives and few injuries.

———

CARRIE LAM REEMERGED SOME TWENTY HOURS AFTER THE HANDOVER ceremony at a 4 a.m. press conference. She contrasted the two groups: the peaceful marchers participating in the regular July 1 event and the "extreme use of violence" of those who stormed into the legislature. "I hope the community at large will agree with us that with these violent acts that we have seen, it is right for us to condemn it," she said.[13]

She was banking on conventional wisdom that such acts would divide the movement. More moderate Hong Kongers, the narrative went, would turn on the more radical faction. The movement would lose popular support. Participants would descend into infighting. There was precedent for this prediction. Hong Kong prided itself on a post-handover protest culture that was overwhelmingly peaceful and civil. In 2014 moderate protesters condemned even those who shattered windows. How could popular support be maintained for people who had broken into the seat of Hong Kong's government?

Instead, a cross section of society kept demonstrating. Mothers held a rally reiterating that their children were not rioters. Protests spread out of Admiralty to populous residential centers of the New Territories. Lennon Walls with colorful sticky notes proliferated, covering campus walls, underpass crossings, overhead bridges, subway stops. Protesting became interwoven with daily life. Reverend Chu, conscious that he could attend only low-risk authorized rallies because of his suspended sentence, joined thousands of other "silver-haired" marchers to show it wasn't just young people fighting for Hong Kong. They could not run to the front lines or withstand clouds of tear gas, but the elderly "could express the idea that we are unanimous in the movement," Chu said. In his heart, Chu still wanted peace and negotiation—but believed that by the time the first rounds of tear gas were fired in September 2014, and then again on June 12, 2019, the government had closed the door on anything but the emergence of radicals. "We are not qualified to criticize them," he said of those taking more extreme measures. Those who stormed the Legislative Council, those who helped supply gear to them, journalists like Gwyneth Ho who captured and broadcast the scenes, front liners like Tommy, overseas activists like Finn, and the aging Chu—they were 兄弟爬山, 各自努力 "brothers climbing mountains together, but with their own efforts."

A new mantra began to emerge after July 1: "Do not split." It inspired a solidarity in Hong Kong that would endure. Week after week, strangers sacrificed their time, sleep, and money, risked their careers, their safety, and their liberty for people they did not know, bound together by a love for Hong Kong and united in the impossible hope that their actions could somehow save it.

Tommy, watching the news of the Legislative Council break-in at home later that night with his mother, recognized himself in the footage playing across every channel. "Look at how crazy things are!" his mother said. Tommy stayed silent. Officials were threatening a litany of charges against those who entered the chamber.

Perhaps it really was a trap, Tommy thought. He was frequently messaging the nineteen-year-old he'd met on the streets some forty-eight hours earlier. The teenager had seen himself on the news, too. He suggested that Tommy leave Hong Kong with him, just for a while, in case police showed up at their homes or started charging those inside with rioting. Tommy couldn't explain why he trusted him, but he did. He was Tommy's 手足 or sau zuk, a Cantonese phrase that translates to "hands and feet." They were bound together against a common enemy. Tommy still didn't know what his friend had studied, what his family was like, or where he lived, but he boarded a flight with him the next day to Taipei. He told his parents he was going on a quick holiday with friends.

Before July 2019, Tommy's trips to Taiwan involved bubble tea, fried chicken, and other street snacks. This time, Tommy found himself with some "real fighters," associates of his nineteen-year-old comrade. They seemed to be in Taipei evading arrest in Hong Kong, but Tommy didn't want to ask questions. They showed him how to mix Molotov cocktails, adding bits of Styrofoam to make the flaming liquid viscous and tacky.

They told him how to neutralize tear-gas canisters by dropping them into airtight containers to snuff out the burning or covering them with traffic cones to contain the smoke, then dousing them with water. They taught Tommy how to throw better to avoid a repeat of his egg-tossing failure. It wasn't so much that Tommy wanted to take this path. He felt that without a discernible future or much to lose, he had to.

Police did not show up at Tommy's parents' apartment, nor were they charging anyone involved in the break-in with rioting. Maybe he had not been identified by authorities after all. Figuring that he was at low risk of arrest, Tommy returned home. It was time for him to be brave.

CHAPTER 12

7.21

ALMOST EVERYONE LIVING IN YUEN LONG HAD HEARD THE WARNINGS. In the days before July 21, 2019, rumors circulated in forwarded messages, then by word of mouth. The substance was cryptic but carried the same theme, alerting residents to possible violence in the neighborhood directed at those supporting the protest movement. "Please try to stay out of Yuen Long after noon on Sunday," one such message read. "If you do go there, wear white, don't wear a mask. The bosses in Yuen Long had a meeting and decided to wear white shirts, they don't want to hit the wrong people." Others came from the aggressors themselves and were far more graphic: "If you wear a mask in Yuen Long, both your arms and legs will be amputated."

Yuen Long, in the northern New Territories, was an insular, rural community. On the edge of Hong Kong, close to the border with Shenzhen, it was a stronghold for triad gangs such as Wo Shing Wo—the second-largest triad in Hong Kong—Wo Hop To, and 14K. In Yuen Long these elements of Hong Kong's underworld intermingled with local officials and rural power brokers, creating a form of informal self-rule that felt closer to the territory's hardscrabble past than its modern present. The demographics had started to shift in recent years. There were new arrivals from the mainland and a sizable ethnic-minority population. Young, recently married Hong Kong couples, some with babies in tow, settled into newly opened housing developments, drawn by the relatively affordable property prices. Tommy's parents had moved his family there when they unexpectedly had another child ten years after Tommy was born. Gwyneth Ho grew up there. The neighborhood was a distinctive juxtaposition of modern condos and malls butting up against aging multistory village houses, their exteriors covered in glossy tiles.

After July 21, Yuen Long came to represent more than the multitude of contradictions contained in Hong Kong. The neighborhood's name and the date—7.21—would become shorthand for the chilling lengths to which Beijing-backed forces would go to terrify the city into submission. That day, the Hong Kong police and government effectively allowed pro-Beijing thugs to brutalize their people—and did little to stop them.

Calvin So, twenty-three, was a lifelong Yuen Long resident. From his childhood, his parents schooled him in the unwritten code of the neighborhood, telling him which villages to avoid and where not to wander. He too had heard the rumors in the days before July 21, but paid them little mind. It was a Sunday, and he had a long shift cooking at the Le Grand Pokka Café, a family restaurant inside a large shopping mall.

When So checked his phone before helping close up the restaurant at 9 p.m., he saw a post about a group of men gathered in a nearby park that he passed daily on his walk home. It was odd, he thought, but not cause for alarm. Anyway, the protests that day were taking place on Hong Kong Island, far from Yuen Long. He saw no reason to stray from his normal route back to his apartment. When he neared the park, So saw that the loitering group of men had swelled in size. There were dozens now, maybe more than a hundred milling about. All wore white shirts. More troubling than the coordinated outfits was the fact that many held thin wooden rods. A few were adorned with the Hong Kong or Chinese flag. As he passed, So remarked to no one in particular, "Wow, really so many white shirt people."

The banal comment was enough to attract one man's ire. "What did you say?" he yelled. So kept walking, but the man and others started to keep pace alongside him. They heckled as they walked. The small crowd attracted others. So walked more briskly, hoping that they would fall back. When the first blow thudded across his back, So tried to ignore it. The men, he thought, were just trying to scare and rough him up a bit. Another hit followed; within a moment the street was the scene of a violent frenzy. The men lashed So across the back. Some pounded his head and neck with their fists. "Hit him! Hit him!" a man screamed over and over. So pleaded with them to stop, to no effect. When he finally freed himself, So ducked into a 7-Eleven for safety. The attack lasted just minutes, but the men had transformed his back into a grotesque mess of deep purple welts.

––––––––

GWYNETH WAS AT HER PARENTS' HOME, ALSO IN YUEN LONG, WHEN SHE noticed a clip of So's assault spreading online. As was often the case, she was behind on her deadline. After her July 1 reporting in the protester-occupied Legislative Council, she had experienced a burst of viral fame. Her new fans called her "Sister Stand." It was a moniker of affection, but it made Gwyneth uncomfortable. She was more comfortable laboring over long, analytical pieces behind a screen. Gwyneth thought a journalist should be a fly on the wall. That wasn't possible when people saw her as part of the movement itself.

Struggling with too many thoughts, including on her own role on July 1, Gwyneth did what she knew best: she wrote a lengthy post and published it on Facebook. She was trying to adapt but lamented that "having a phone in your hand for a very long time makes it not only difficult to get contacts of interviewees, but also difficult to synchronize with the changing atmosphere of the scene." It made her, she said, "unable to feel what the protesters feel, which seriously hinders your ability to empathize with them." Still, the virality of her coverage emphasized to her the power of media in this movement. The response from her interview with the young woman running back into the Legislative Council chamber had been "really big," she wrote, "enough to the extent that it scared me." It pushed even moderate pro-democracy sympathizers to endorse the break-in at the Legislative Council and humanized the protesters. Gwyneth recognized that the impact was many times that of the long-form pieces, which appealed largely to insiders. Her views on journalism began to shift in those weeks. "I can only say, I hope that I can slowly find the balance," Gwyneth wrote.

Gwyneth's challenges with virality were fairly unique, but on July 21 she faced a problem shared by any journalist covering the 2019 protests.

The diffuse nature of the movement meant that several newsworthy events often happened at the same time across a huge swath of Hong Kong. A reporter could be immersed in covering one demonstration, only to realize that another had kicked off elsewhere. Covering everything was impossible. The video circulating of So's attack was a horrifying scene but not yet the biggest news of the day. That afternoon, around 430,000 people had joined a peaceful march called by the Civil Human Rights Front. It was the seventh Sunday since the movement began on June 9. There were sporadic protests on weekdays, but the largest crowds usually turned out on Sunday. Knowing by now that marchers would likely deviate from the authorized route, police prepared for a curveball. They took extra precautions and erected towering plastic barricades filled with water near the Legislative Council to prevent it from being stormed again. Officers glued down sidewalk bricks to keep protesters from ripping them up to use as projectiles.

The police were, again, a step behind. Rather than focusing on what were now their regular targets—the symbols and institutions of Hong Kong's government—a large group of demonstrators continued west across Hong Kong Island. Their target was Beijing's Liaison Office, the most prominent symbol of the Chinese Communist Party in Hong Kong.

Protesters formed human chains and ferried supplies down the street to those laying siege to the building. They spray-painted the walls with graffiti and pelted the gaudy gold and red emblem of China affixed to the building with paint-filled balloons. Protesters splattered the emblem with more and more black splotches until it was all but unrecognizable. Thousands roared in approval. As they cheered, members of the crowd broke into a call and response: "光復香港," some cheered. "時代革命," others shouted back. Romanized as Gwong Fuk Heung Gong, Si Doi Gaak Ming, it translated to "Liberate Hong Kong, Revolution of our times," and was Edward Leung's campaign slogan from 2016, when Tommy began following the young candidate. Once reserved for a political fringe that the government had tried to silence through imprisonment, the slogan was now a rallying cry, shouted in front of Beijing's representative office.

The incident was the first direct attack targeted at Beijing. It was unclear how security forces, in Hong Kong and on the mainland, would respond to the new provocation. Gwyneth urgently needed to get there to relieve her colleague, who had been covering the day's protests for hours.

Gwyneth headed to Yuen Long station to catch the train. While waiting, she hoped to snap some pictures of demonstrators returning home as they changed out of their black outfits and into clothes left behind by sympathetic strangers. This was a relatively new tactic, meant to help them blend into the crowd after they left the streets.

Assistance went beyond the donated T-shirts. Other residents volunteered as medics operating underground clinics, drivers to ferry protesters back home, or spots to monitor and report on police activity. Some left spare change at ticket machines so protesters could buy single-use subway cards, erasing evidence that they had traveled to a demonstration. Those unsuited for the front lines wanted to support those taking disproportionate risk for their collective futures.

Subway stations were considered safe spaces, largely off-limits to police. Officers generally allowed demonstrators to enter subway stations, hop on trains, and disperse without conflict. Gwyneth assumed she would be safe inside the station if there was further violence beyond the beating that So had endured. If there were more conflicts, she reasoned they'd be on the streets of Yuen Long.

As Gwyneth entered the station, it became immediately apparent that something was wrong, as were her assumptions about safety. Marauding groups of men in white shirts, like the one she saw in the video beating Calvin So, rushed past her. They freely roamed the halls of the vast station, hitting people with bamboo sticks seemingly at random. A cacophony of profanities and terrified cries echoed throughout the station.

Gwyneth looked around and didn't see any police officers, not the regular patrol cops dressed in blue or the riot police in their green fatigues who in the past weeks had been filmed hitting protesters with batons and teargassing Hong Kong neighborhoods. Gwyneth dipped into a bathroom. Inside, she saw a middle-aged woman with blood pouring from her head. She told Gwyneth she had been attacked, hit two or three times by men with wooden canes before they sprinted off.

Gwyneth slipped on her fluorescent yellow vest with PRESS stamped across the back. She was the only reporter there; most others were congregated at the demonstration on Hong Kong Island. Gwyneth then went back out and began recording.

She positioned herself in the relative safety of the station's paid area, separated from the main publicly accessible hall by turnstiles and a waist-high metal and glass barrier. Standing with the journalist was a crowd of demonstrators returning home along with everyday commuters pinned in by the mob. On the other side were dozens of the men in white shirts. Some in white kept pitching forward, waving their sticks in the air. Gwyneth could see smug, sinister expressions on their faces. Unlike the protesters, they didn't bother to obscure themselves with surgical masks.

A few of those stuck behind the subway gantry with Gwyneth attempted to defend themselves. They hurled bottles of water at the crowd when they approached the barrier. Some opened their umbrellas for protection, but they were outnumbered.

Gwyneth began live streaming from her phone to the *Stand News* Facebook page at 10:40 p.m., roughly an hour after So was attacked.

"Hi everyone, this is. . . ." Gwyneth hesitated for a beat before restarting her introduction. "*Stand News* viewers, this is Yuen Long station," she said. Gwyneth relayed to viewers what the woman in the bathroom told her and commented on what was unfolding. She sounded like a dispatcher radioing for help. "I will repeat again," she said a few moments later, as if to convince viewers, and maybe herself, that what they were seeing was indeed real, "this is live from Yuen Long station."

———

ABOUT SEVEN MINUTES LATER, MOST OF THE MOB STARTED MOVING TO another part of the station. Gwyneth tapped her subway pass, exited the paid area, and followed, filming as she walked. She was fixated on the smartphone, the world around her reduced to a tiny screen. It made her a little slow to react. A man in a peach-colored shirt, the buttons undone as if heading off on a beach holiday, appeared behind her. She swiveled to her left to capture him reaching over the turnstiles and smacking one of the trapped people with his stick. The man noticed Gwyneth filming him. He rushed toward her in a manic sprint, lifted his rod in the air, and struck her multiple times. Gwyneth let out two screams as she fell to the tile floor. From the ground, she continued to film while trying to protect herself as the man flailed violently above her.

Back on her feet a few moments later, Gwyneth struggled to hold her phone steady as she recorded more of the unfolding attacks. One man grabbed the top of a metal trash can and swung it like a hammer, just missing the head of his intended target, a man in a gray rock-climbing helmet who was trying to rush to Gwyneth's side. A group of men surrounded another in a black T-shirt and brown pants, standing directly in front of Gwyneth. One of his attackers, dressed in a white shirt and a black Louis Vuitton belt, looked straight into her camera, waving a bamboo stick in his left hand like a deranged practitioner of martial arts. Someone slammed her to the ground a few seconds later. Her camera captured a swirl of fluorescent lights and tiles. She screamed again.

Elsewhere in the station, the savagery continued unabated. Passengers hiding in the train above the main hall were easy targets. The men entered through the open car doors and bloodied them. One desperate victim fell to his knees and begged them to stop. Where Gwyneth had initially been filming, a heavily pregnant woman lay on the floor in distress. Two uniformed police officers who were dispatched to the station just before 11 p.m. glanced around at the scene and casually strolled away down a pedestrian bridge, never making an effort to intervene, not even turning back to see what was unfolding behind them.

———

SINCE THE POLICE'S HEAVY-HANDED CONFRONTATION WITH PROTESTERS on June 12, the clashes were turning more violent. A week before July 21, protesters and police had faced off in a suburban mall. One man bit off part of a policeman's finger after the officer tried to gouge his eye. The Hong Kong Police Force was seen more like occupiers doing mercenary work for Beijing rather than as a legitimate policing unit.

At Yuen Long on July 21, police had the opportunity to prove their professional, unbiased role. Unlike the prior weeks, the public was begging them for help. Some 24,000 panicked calls were placed to emergency services over a period of three hours, alerting them to the scenes unfolding in Yuen Long and asking for assistance. It was not the first the police had heard of the brewing attacks. A week prior, members of five separate triad groups joined a WhatsApp group to discuss plans to "defend their homeland," Yuen Long. As the triad groups coordinated their plans for July 21, a detective sergeant from the anti-triad bureau that oversaw the area was reading along. He had managed to gain access to the WhatsApp groupchat, giving him unfettered insight into the plans, even before rumors reached the residents of the neighborhood.

It was unusual for so many triad groups to come together with a singular purpose. They often clashed over turf and their share of illicit businesses. The Chinese flags they were carrying—and historical precedent—suggested their allegiance in this coordinated attack. Even in 1989, when the triads assisted Reverend Chu in getting Chinese dissidents into Hong Kong, he was under no illusion that the gangs were allies. It was a working relationship, in response to a singular event that created sympathizers even in the Chinese state media. In normal times, the mafia-like organizations had been willing to do the dirty work of brute intimidation when Beijing officially couldn't. In 1984, in planning for the handover, Deng remarked that the triad groups wielded disproportionate influence and said there were "many good people" among them.[1] In 1992 China's public security minister publicly said that Hong Kong triads were "patriotic." Triad members were allegedly involved in clearing the Mongkok campsite during the Umbrella Movement in 2014.

It took thirty-nine minutes from the start of the attack on July 21 for police to arrive. When around forty officers equipped with body armor and riot-control gear gathered outside Yuen Long station, they were noticeably more restrained when dealing with the mob of men than they were on the streets with protesters. There were no rubber bullets or bean-bag rounds, not even a foot chase. Instead, officers allowed the men to exit without issue. The delay in responding to calls for help coupled with the hands-off approach to dealing with the thugs enraged the station crowd, which began calling the police corrupt. Confronted, the police left just before midnight. Staff at the subway station rolled down safety shutters at the exit closest to three rural villages.

The mob was not finished. Some thirty white-shirted men returned at 12:28 a.m., standing behind the metal bars of the shutter.[2] Believing he was safe, one man poked his umbrella through the rollers. The sense of security proved false. The men pulled and kicked the metal gates, and began prying them up from the floor. Once there was enough space to slip under, they charged back in, and the attacks started anew.

At least forty-five people were injured that night. None of the men in white were arrested.

Videos exploded online. One was of a visibly agitated officer offering a flippant response when reporters pressed him on the force's sluggish response: "Sorry, I did not look at the watch." Another was a clip of a fervently pro-Beijing lawmaker gleefully shaking hands with members of the mob like a mayoral candidate on the campaign trail. The incident would eventually come to be defined by a photo: a riot officer with his hand amicably placed on one of the white-clad men's shoulders. It was an awfully gentle way to treat someone suspected of assault.

————

THE FAILURES TO INTERVENE EXTENDED FROM THE POLICE TO THOSE WHO ostensibly controlled them. Inside the secure confines of Government House, Hong Kong's leadership was blithely unaware of the crisis in Yuen Long. It would have remained so had Betty Fung not needed to use the bathroom.

Fung, one of Carrie Lam's few trusted aides, was huddled with Lam and a handful of advisers that night, monitoring the protests on television. For security purposes, the officials left their phones outside the room. The reliance on mainstream TV reports, as well as their disconnection from the internet in a movement that organized itself on social media, would prove to be an embarrassing mistake. When she checked her phone on her way to the bathroom, Fung saw that a group of young staffers were posting about an attack in Yuen Long station. She responded with surprise, and then incredulity. You "can't just rely on

YouTube clips," she wrote, warning that there was a lot of "fake news circulating around." Her younger colleagues were stunned that after nearly two months of protests, top officials in government were just watching TV, seemingly unaware of live streams, LIHKG, and Telegram channels.

Lam's administration should not have needed Fung to alert them, nor should it have been so difficult to connect the dots. The government already knew who some of the men were. On July 20, some twenty-four hours before the attacks began, the political assistant to the Secretary for Constitutional and Mainland Affairs attended a banquet in a rural village in Yuen Long. The Constitutional and Mainland Affairs Bureau is responsible for liaising with authorities on the mainland, and the secretary himself was a close adviser to Lam. It was part of a slew of festivities held in the preceding weeks that involved members of Beijing's Liaison Office and pro-Beijing lawmakers. At a separate community event about a week prior, the local head of the Liaison Office told Yuen Long residents to have the "persistence and courage to maintain social peace and protect our home" if confronted by protesters, according to a recording obtained by Reuters.[3]

At the banquet, guests celebrated the inauguration of newly elected village leaders. They were treated to food, a traditional dragon dance, and fireworks—banned since leftist riots in 1967 but displayed in the village with impunity, in front of all the high-ranking officials. There was some overlap between the membership of these rural political bodies and of the triad societies. Triads provided muscle to the rural committees, intimidating and strong-arming opponents.

At one point in the July 20 celebrations, Yuen Long village leaders posed for a group photo. Standing among a line of men arranged in a neat row behind three suckling pigs, laid out on a table draped with a red tablecloth, was a man identified by the *Times of London* as Stephen Ng.[4] Gwyneth captured Stephen on her live stream from Yuen Long station the next night, wooden stick in hand, shouting at and then beating an unarmed, defenseless man. Stephen was wearing the same Louis Vuitton belt, its "LV" hardware as clear in her footage as it was on the night of the feast.

The government officials attending these celebrations ahead of the attacks offered hints that they knew what was about to unfold. The political assistant to the secretary for mainland affairs had invited some others to join him at the banquet on July 20. He gave them a very specific dress code: wear only white.

———

WHAT TOOK PLACE ON JULY 21, 2019, UNLEASHED A FLOOD OF EMOTION: denial, disbelief, shock, grief, and anger. When 999 emergency calls were ignored, when clips of the light-touch approach to the men in white went viral, trust in the police cratered. On the streets, people began to call the police 黑警 or haak geng, combining the characters used to describe triad societies and the police, implying they were as "dirty" as the gangsters themselves. Protesters spoke of collusion between the police and the triads in planning the attacks. Active coordination between the triads and the police force was never proven. But the police knew, and they did nothing. A speaker at a pro-police rally the day before the attacks told supporters to "take the cane out . . . and discipline the kids." Many police officers outright sympathized with the men in white. On WhatsApp groups, frontline officers in unrelated units praised the men in white for "teaching the kids a lesson," saying that they had used the "perfect weapons" for the job. They believed the injured civilians were just crisis actors, that all the victims were protesters and legitimate targets. The men in white had helped police punish people who were disrespectful of their government and of China. It was permissible because it was done in the name of the country.

Researchers at the Chinese University of Hong Kong found that 43 percent of the Hong Kong public had zero trust in the police in the months following the Yuen Long attacks. That percentage would grow. Thousands of others joined Tommy in believing vigilantism and radical violence were the only way out. Accountants and other white-collar professionals learned how to make Molotov cocktails. Others took defense classes. Overseas, activists with video and design skills frantically documented and advertised the incident, attaching the evidence of the attacks to letters to human-rights groups, the United Nations, and foreign governments. After 7.21, police were more widely seen as targets who should be doxed, sanctioned, and even violently attacked.

The 7.21 events spurred even the passive into action. For the first time that next weekend, Tommy's mother tagged along in a protest condemning the Yuen Long attacks. He was shocked when she agreed to go. She had thrown away his protest gear on several previous occasions to try to dissuade him. But Yuen Long was their home, where they lived. She wanted to understand what was happening. (However, she remained convinced that the protesters' efforts were futile.)

Calls for an independent inquiry into the police force's actions grew to encompass a huge and diverse cross section of the city. A former chief justice championed a judge-led inquiry, saying that it would help to uncover the truth and have a "therapeutic effect on society." Former government secretaries, academics, and university leaders as well as religious groups urged Carrie Lam to set up a body to independently investigate what went wrong. Two pro-Beijing lawmakers broke with their colleagues to support it.

Lam, once again, missed the off-ramp. She brushed these calls aside and, in private, staunchly defended the police. Speaking in a meeting after the attacks, she rejected any allegations of collusion, saying that she had full trust in her police force—the embattled leaders of the police unions had even cried in front of her, Lam said. She reminded those in attendance that Hong Kong had no military of its own to fall back on. Without the police, she warned, it would be the People's Liberation Army handling the protests.

Even through her staunch defense, Lam knew how she now looked. In a meeting with just a few people after 7.21, she brought up her husband, the quiet Lam Siu-por. Even he, Lam said, believed that she had erred. He had chided her using a Chinese idiom, translating to "sinner through history." As she recounted his words, Lam's voice cracked.

CHAPTER 13

INTERNATIONAL FRONT

B EIJING WAS INITIALLY CAUGHT FLAT-FOOTED BY THE HONG KONG PRO-
tests. Unlike Article 23 and the interpretation of universal suffrage,
the extradition law was a local initiative, pushed by Carrie Lam. In their
first foreign interviews, Chinese officials distanced themselves from
Lam's mess, telling the BBC that Beijing had given "no instruction, no
order" on the extradition amendments.[1] Privately, they were livid, perhaps even more with the chief executive than the protesters. Lam had
told them opposition to the bill would be negligible. When millions were
on the streets of Hong Kong, "they started thinking, what the hell is
going on?" one pro-Beijing lawmaker said. "They are most furious at the
government's misjudgment."[2]

But they gave consent. They said to Lam, "Yes, go ahead."[3] When the
demonstrations escalated—when protesters took their fight directly
to the Liaison Office, using slogans of the independence movement—
and were celebrated as a brave democratic uprising in the West, China
believed it had to act. The stakes were getting higher. On October 1 the
People's Republic of China would celebrate the seventieth anniversary
of its founding. The Chinese Communist Party was obsessed with this
marker, given that its closest comparison—the USSR—survived almost
sixty-nine years before its collapse. By August, Beijing's response was
coalescing.

Beijing broke its silence on the protests in a press conference on
July 31, publicly backing Lam and her government. No matter their feelings, abandoning her then would have looked like a concession to the

protest movement. Days later, Chinese state media posted a video from the Shenzhen police showing a simulated response to a riot. It looked like a low-budget film re-creation of central Hong Kong. In the drill, the Shenzhen police quickly won, overwhelming the "rioters" in yellow hard hats with tear gas and police dogs. A spokesman for China's Hong Kong and Macau Affairs Office made a blunter threat in a news conference, the same day the video was released: "I want to warn all the criminals to not wrongly judge the situation and take restraint for weakness. Those who play with fire will perish by it."[4]

Beijing soon used the term *color revolution* to describe Hong Kong, characterizing the protests as the "most serious situation" since the 1997 handover. This descriptor held with it an ominous undertone. A "color revolution" denoted something deeply sinister to Beijing and its allies in Moscow. They looked at the "color revolutions"—the Yellow Revolution in the Philippines against Ferdinand Marcos, the Velvet Revolution that led to the collapse of Communism in Czechoslovakia, the Orange Revolution in Ukraine—not as inspirational mass uprisings against dictatorial rule, dovetailing with the end of the Cold War in the 1980s. To authoritarian hardliners, a "color revolution" was a deliberate, coordinated effort by the United States to foment extremist ideology, promote economic instability, and extend its hegemony. The end goal was American control and global dominance. As China's nationalistic *Global Times* newspaper asked, "How many evils have been committed in the name of democracy?"[5]

The Hong Kong government and Beijing's other allies in the city had to nod along, feigning outward agreement with China's leadership. But they knew what was unfolding in their city and why. Even Carrie Lam initially dismissed claims that the protests were the work of foreigners when asked directly by an official in her administration during a private meeting. Quietly, work had started within the Hong Kong government and among the more progressive pro-Beijing lawmakers to push for an obvious solution. They wanted Beijing's blessing to meet the protesters' two key demands: the full withdrawal of the extradition bill, accompanied by an independent investigation into police actions and the origins of the crisis.[6] These were the two most logical and most deliverable of the five demands, a way to pull Hong Kong back from the edge.

The reply from Beijing was an unequivocal no. In a meeting in Shenzhen on August 7, pro-Beijing Hong Kong lawmakers were told that there was "no room for compromise," that this was "not a good time to respond to any of the five demands from the protesters."[7] It was a decision straight from the Central Government, which, having lost faith in Lam, was now calling the shots. There was no room to maneuver. The establishment would have to get in line or suffer the consequences.

If Chinese officials had looked back at Hong Kong over the past three decades, they might have noticed some consistency. The response to the Tiananmen massacre, the anxiety that manifested in a mad dash to grasp second passports before the handover, the fears of Article 23, the pushback against the national education proposals, the seventy-nine-day street occupation that followed the denial of universal suffrage—all of it stemmed from a deep distrust of Beijing that intensified with every broken promise. This was not the way that the Communist Party operated. Unable or unwilling to acknowledge these legitimate grievances, Beijing pushed its own narrative. Paid protesters, "color revolution," Hong Kongers as pawns of foreign powers—first the United Kingdom and now the United States. These lines echoed the logic that Deng Xiaoping used after authorizing the killings on June 4, 1989. But Beijing, under the leadership of Xi Jinping, was prepared to take this false narrative one step further.

THERE WAS NO FOREIGN INTERFERENCE BEHIND THE PROTESTS. THEY were locally driven, planned, and organized. We covered the protests every weekend and never saw American men in sunglasses hand over wads of cash to demonstrators, contrary to the caricature put out by Beijing. It must have been hard for Beijing to understand the spontaneous love for a place that would push people to fight for it, having tried and failed to systematically manufacture Chinese patriotism within Hong Kong. The Chinese Communist Party routinely paid people to show up at pro-China rallies, and it might have assumed that a similar type of coercion was happening on the other side.[8] But the movement was entirely a manifestation of Hong Kong's will, sparked by Lam and her mishandling of the extradition bill, and then fueled by the police's unconstrained use of force.

This did not mean that the Hong Kong protests were happening in isolation. Hong Kong was one of the most international cities in the world. Its people were some of the most well-traveled, scattered in foreign universities and multinational corporations. Its airport received more than sixty million passengers yearly. Harnessing the power of international support was a key tactic of the movement. By late July, hundreds were staging sit-ins inside Hong Kong's International Airport to broadcast their demands, raising awareness of the city's plight with every arriving passenger. These demonstrations were organized by aircrew including from Cathay Pacific, the prestigious flag carrier of Hong Kong that symbolized its status as a global city. One Cathay Pacific pilot, landing home from Japan, used his pre-landing announcement as a form of advocacy: "Don't be scared by all these people wearing black shirts sitting at the arrival hall. . . . Feel free to talk to them, and try to know more about Hong Kong if you want to." Before telling the cabin crew they had half an hour to landing, he added in Cantonese, "香港人加油," or "Heung gong yan, gaa yau." This statement, which directly translates to "Hong Kongers, add oil," was believed to have originated from a cheer used to motivate drivers during the Macau Grand Prix in the 1960s, but since the Umbrella Movement had become a ubiquitous cheer encouraging persistence at pro-democracy protests.

These ground efforts were bolstered by seasoned activists who, dating back to the 1980s, knew they had allies in Washington, Paris, Ottawa, London, and other democratic capitals. Hong Kong's status as a freewheeling financial hub rested on the support of international governments, which treated the city differently from mainland China under the "one country, two systems" arrangement. Throughout the post-handover history, when one system seemed to be exerting itself over the other, activists would turn to the most powerful democracy in the world—the United States—to serve as a bulwark against Beijing's encroachment. Martin Lee, as founder of the Hong Kong

Democratic Party, met with President Bill Clinton in 2000 and then with Vice President Joe Biden in 2014 after Lee retired as a lawmaker.[9] Reverend Chu was old friends with Nancy Pelosi. When she was a young congresswoman in 1991, he gave her a banner honoring deceased protesters that she unfurled in Tiananmen Square. The activists formed ties that allowed them to act as emissaries for the democracy movement. They were consistent in their messaging, dating back to the 1980s: *We are the city that stands between authoritarian rule and the democratic world. Use your leverage to keep us autonomous, and to help promote our democracy.*

In 2019 Lee, now in his eighties but still fighting for democracy, made the rounds in Washington opposing the extradition bill. Other Hong Kong activists easily got an audience with higher-ups in the Trump administration, especially *Apple Daily* founder Jimmy Lai. Lai was beloved by the Republican Party and was an old friend of conservative *Wall Street Journal* editorial-board writers who rose to positions of influence under Secretary of State Mike Pompeo. They had the kind of access and star power within Washington that the Hong Kong government, much to its frustration, struggled to get. But it was Joshua Wong, the face of the 2014 movement, who stirred the most excitement in DC. No one else in the movement commanded the same level of foreign attention. Although he was in jail when the 2019 protests started, his reputation as a diviner of democracy was undiminished. The day of his release, he was mobbed by reporters and did hours of interviews with the largest TV networks in the world.

The feelings among those in his own city were more complex. Joshua was not universally loved, still seen as too much of a one-man show. Demonstrators bristled when he was erroneously referred to as a leader of the movement; theirs was now a decentralized and leaderless one. Amid these new dynamics, Joshua realized that his best contributions to the protests could be made in the international arena, not on the city's streets. His name recognition gave him a bullhorn that dwarfed anything he could shout at a rally. Together with Jeffrey Ngo, a loquacious doctoral student in history at Georgetown University, and Nathan Law, the disqualified lawmaker who was one of his closest allies during the

Umbrella Movement, Joshua worked on building Hong Kong's international front.

With Hong Kong squarely on Washington's radar, American foreign-policy advisers wanted a firsthand look at the situation. A delegation from the Senate Foreign Relations Committee landed in early August and, like other all visitors, wanted face time with Joshua. Because the US consulate was oddly designed, with little space for meetings and strict security protocols, bringing in visitors was a hassle. The consulate instead arranged for Joshua, Nathan, and two other young activists to meet with the staffers at the nearby J.W. Marriott Hotel.

Consulate staff had the unenviable role of directing the visitors and serving as their local fixers. That day, the task fell to Julie Eadeh, the head political officer who had served in Hong Kong since 2017. Eadeh went up to the group and told them the staffers were ready. Unbeknownst to Eadeh or any of the activists, someone in the lobby was waiting for this moment. They surreptitiously snapped a picture of the five. Shot from a low angle, the photo showed Eadeh, in a white-and-black dress with red heels and an Issey Miyake tote over her shoulder, clutching a thick stack of papers in her arm. The four young men stood awkwardly, readying themselves for the meeting by tucking in their shirts. It was a wholly unremarkable scene.

The first article about the meeting was published alongside the photo by *Ta Kung Pao* newspaper on August 8, just before 4:30 a.m. Along with the banal snapshot of Eadeh and the young activists, the paper published what it described as a groundbreaking scoop. The "story" dug into Eadeh's "so-called" diplomatic career, with information on her postings dating back more than a decade. It cast her as a master of subterfuge who was skilled in subversion and had a personal hand in destabilizing the Middle East. Now, the article implied, she was directing the Hong Kong protests, sought out by Joshua, Nathan, and the others to stir trouble. This was Beijing's smoking gun—"solid evidence" that the US was behind the protests. It wasn't enough to target Eadeh. The article published the name and a photo of her husband, who was also a US diplomat, the names of their two young children, and the years they were born.

Ta Kung Pao claimed to be much like any other Hong Kong media outlet, but the Liaison Office controlled the newspaper and used it as a tool to bully and intimidate its adversaries. The article acted as the starting gun for an unprecedented disinformation campaign. Over the next days, the number of articles about Eadeh multiplied. The *People's Daily*, the official newspaper of the Communist Party's central committee, published a story on her. *China Daily* produced a video montage of Eadeh from her public webpages. More details were published, including Eadeh's parents' names and her hometown in the Midwest. Chinese diplomats and state-linked accounts amplified the story on social media. Messages flooded Eadeh's social media accounts. One user threatened to kill her children. A photo of her mock funeral went viral.

The harassment was not confined to cyberspace. Eadeh noticed that a white minivan started to trail her and her family whenever they left their apartment in the Mid-Levels neighborhood, including when she dropped off her children at school. Sometimes, the people tailing them hoisted cameras with large lenses, conspicuously snapping photographs as they went about their daily errands. The insistent harrying distressed and infuriated Eadeh. Her mother called from the US in tears, confused about why her daughter was being so viciously targeted.

Some months later, a video game promoted by Chinese state media allowed players to beat pro-democracy figures with a baseball bat. It was called *Everyone Hit the Traitors*. Eadeh was one of the targets. The *Global Times* claimed to have interviewed someone fond of the game. "The practices of these modern traitors have long been irritating," the supposed player said. "While they are free in real life, at least in the game they should pay for what they have done."[10]

A report to the Hong Kong police yielded no action. Nor did efforts to raise the issue with China's Ministry of Foreign Affairs in Hong Kong. It was deeply shocking not just to the US consulate but also to the broader diplomatic community in the city. Washington was quick and public in its condemnation. "I don't think that leaking an American diplomat's private information, pictures, names of their children, I don't think that is a formal protest, that is what a thuggish regime would do," a spokeswoman for the State Department told reporters in Washington. Beijing didn't stop. Higher-ups debated pulling her out of Hong Kong, but Eadeh chose to stay until the end of her rotation in July 2020.[11]

Washington was far from a monolithic, coordinated force. Reaction to the Hong Kong protests had thus far been divided. Those on the Right who had long viewed China as a threat pushed sanctions. US law enforcement agencies saw the Hong Kong police as kindred, and defended the force used against protesters. Perhaps the most important group on Hong Kong policy, the State Department, was filled with bureaucrats who were convinced they knew how to navigate Hong Kong's government and dismissed Deputy National Security Advisor Matt Pottinger and Trump's other China hands as too hawkish. The doxing of Eadeh and her family awakened the Washington bureaucracy to the kind of regime they were facing in China and to the Hong Kong government's inability to control Beijing. Ivan Kanapathy, then the National Security Council's director overseeing Hong Kong, describes it as a moment "when everybody was like, 'Okay, it's just done. We can't work with these people. It's us against them.'"[12]

Settling in with their morning papers over a cup of coffee, readers from New York to Barcelona, Tokyo to Paris, found similar advertisements on August 19. The images varied depending on where they were printed: a bloodied pair of goggles, young men and women holding wooden shields shrouded behind clouds of tear gas, police unleashing pepper spray on civilians. Above the images, translated into nine languages, were variations of the same appeal: "Bear witness to Hongkongers' fight for freedom. Tell our story—especially if we can no longer do it ourselves. Fight for Freedom. Stand with Hong Kong."[13]

Those trying to look for the group behind the campaign wouldn't have found much. A QR code printed on the ads linked back to a website called freedomhkg.net, created by a "group of Hongkongers from all walks of life, living in Hong Kong and across the world." On the website, they offered only the explanation that they had raised over $1.5 million from 20,000 donors to fund the ad campaign.

Finn Lau opened his Telegram app to see the first real-life photos of the ads, printed in actual newspapers, coming through on his phone. Dawn was breaking over Tokyo and Seoul, but Richmond was enveloped in darkness, still and quiet at this time of night. He was careful not to wake Theresa as he messaged other members of his team with congratulations.

———

When Finn pressed "publish" on his first LIHKG post in June, he had no network, resources, history of political organizing, or social circle beyond his academic and professional one. He was gifted at his job but otherwise a regular Hong Konger without the celebrity of Martin Lee, Jimmy Lai, and Joshua Wong, whose personal histories were intertwined with the evolution of the pro-democracy movement. With every recruit, his team grew in influence, successful in part because they lacked the prominence of those who came before them. Their anonymity allowed them to push boundaries and largely dismiss concerns about their personal safety and legal risk, shrouded behind the cover of pseudonyms that existed only online.

Finn, along with core members of his team, slept little, working across three time zones to coordinate and execute their projects. They took their corporate training and turned it toward lobbying and activism. By mid-July, they had racked up a list of achievements: targeting officials eligible for foreign passports like Secretary for Justice Teresa Cheng, documenting police abuses and collating them into memos for the United Nations and Amnesty International, and publishing a letter to the editor in the *Financial Times* (which the paper took down when it realized that the letter was submitted under a pseudonym). They were working together without even knowing one another's full names or faces, but each victory built trust.

With every action, Finn tried to distill the meaning of "laam caau," the ideology that had fundamentally changed the nature of the movement. He and other activists hoped that Hong Kong would unravel if the foundation that underpinned its special treatment—the Sino-British Joint Declaration—was declared breached. Because they were in

London, he wanted to focus on lobbying British politicians. It was a bit optimistic, but he hoped that Britain would hold China responsible as the other signatory to the declaration. "Laam caau"—"Embrace fry" or "Burn with us"—was more than an ideology. It was a blueprint, with the decimation of Hong Kong as a financial center as its end goal.

This campaign, bigger than anything Finn's team had executed before, would need a focused effort. Finn decided to split off the UK chapter of his original "laam caau" team into a new organization: "Stand with Hong Kong." The simple English name, he thought, would make it easier to pitch to Western politicians. Then Finn returned to the LIHKG forum to articulate why the Sino-British declaration should be a focus. It went viral again. The thousands of "upvotes" gave him the confidence to launch the crowd-funding campaign. Within nine hours, their new group raised more than $380,000. Money kept pouring in.

Finn shared the success of the crowd-funding effort with Theresa, proud of himself. All he received back was apathy. Theresa wasn't following the protests like he was. She didn't think about politics much and was unmoved by what was happening back home. "Why are you doing this?" she asked Finn. It seemed to her like a waste of time.

He pushed aside her skepticism, deciding instead to take his activism a step further. Armed with capital, Finn and Stand with Hong Kong began to emerge from the online world of LIHKG and thrust themselves into the world of lobbying—but still with their identities protected. They engaged a London-based PR firm to represent them. The firm, 89Up, could not reveal too much about its clients when it reached out to journalists and politicians, representing them vaguely as a group of pro-democracy activists. Interest in the Hong Kong protests was so high that people were willing to put aside their doubts and work with the group despite the condition of anonymity. Stand with Hong Kong grew into a legitimate voice representing the nature of the movement: faceless, identified only by the ideology that it stood for. While battles were ongoing on city streets, these activists were waging their own on the international front, fighting for Hong Kong in Washington, London, and the United Nations—all arenas that Beijing believed it should dominate.

Everything in Finn's life was secondary to the movement. He had asked his managers at work for time off. He ignored the tension in his marriage, now devoid of adventures to the chilly British seaside or casual dinners in London's Covent Garden, and Theresa's cold stares as he worked silently in their living room. Although he had started his master's program at University College London, he could barely focus in class. He was being pulled in different directions, but Hong Kong always took precedence. His teammates had no idea who he was or that he had other commitments beyond the movement. From the way he operated, they thought he was a robot functioning in overdrive.

Eventually, more through necessity, members of Stand with Hong Kong started seeing each other's faces. Finn was working with one of his teammates on the newspaper ads when something urgent came up. The teammate thought to just call him. Finn was surprised when the man turned on his camera, but without much thought he did the same. On the other end, back in Hong Kong, was twenty-nine-year-old Andy Li Yu-hin.

It was a little uncomfortable at first. Until then, Finn had known him only by a rotation of cryptic Telegram usernames and by the fact that he owned an IT company. Hearing Andy speak at a halting, clipped pace, thin, greasy hair framing his squarish face, Finn thought he was exactly the archetypal computer geek he'd expected. Still, he trusted him instinctively. He didn't care how he looked, only how he worked. Only Andy rivaled Finn's own ethic, similarly able to work for days without sleep.

There was one instance when Finn decided unilaterally to make himself known to a teammate in person. At the end of July, Hong Kong activists in London rented out one of the city's beloved red double-decker buses, campaigning for the newly elected prime minister Boris Johnson to put Hong Kong on the top of his agenda. Sitting on the top deck of the bus, Finn noticed a young woman some rows in front of him, her light-brown dyed hair bright against her all-black outfit. Finn had an intuition that this was the person he'd been talking to for hours since she'd organized "Sing for Hong Kong," a demonstration where she and others traveled around London singing protest anthems.

Catherine Li was distracted and about to get off the bus when Finn tapped on her shoulder. She turned around, slightly annoyed. He spoke so softly that she strained to hear him. "Are you 'Jasmine'?" he asked. "I'm 'HK'"—using his Telegram username—"I'm the one you've been talking to on Telegram. . . ." He trailed off.

The exchange lasted just minutes before Catherine rushed off to Trafalgar Square, where hundreds were gathered for the protest she had helped organize. As she walked, she smiled a little to herself. Catherine had expected "HK" to be a short, overweight, pimply nerd. Because he seemed to spend so much time formatting and changing the colors of his LIHKG posts, Catherine thought he was probably the kind of guy who had been repeatedly rejected by women and spent his life online. She'd chosen "Jasmine" because she loved the character in Disney's *Aladdin*, specifically the feminist version from the live-action remake that came out that year. It seemed to encapsulate her personality well, but it turned out that Finn's pseudonym masked his true self. Finn— "HK," "iwantlaamcau"—was nothing like she had expected. He was tall, well-dressed, and had angular cheekbones, a slightly clefted chin, and a wide smile that brought out his dimples. Catherine thought he was kind of handsome.

———

Weeks after her assault at Yuen Long, Gwyneth Ho was still suffering from the aftereffects. She was diagnosed on the night of July 21 with a mild concussion and discharged from the hospital the next day, but the nausea she felt when she looked at her phone screen lingered. Gwyneth was constantly drowsy and found it hard to focus. Kathryn had been texting her all through that summer: sometimes she heard back; sometimes she didn't. She was relieved when Gwyneth replied almost immediately on the morning of July 22, promising that she would get some rest. Gwyneth fought through the discomfort to reply to everyone who asked. *Don't worry about me*, she kept repeating. *I'm fine.*

By the time she recovered, Gwyneth found she had morphed within public perception into something other than a journalist. The attention she received before was nothing compared with that after the July 21 attack. It seemed like everyone recognized her. Strangers stopped her on the streets, telling her how brave she was, how courageous she was facing the mob. Online, she was elevated to a symbol of the movement.

Gwyneth was uneasy with the attention. She didn't like being seen as a martyr or as a singularly special person. Gwyneth thought she was just doing her job, reacting to the environment around her. She was especially annoyed when people said they felt bad for her because she was a woman. The man who had shielded her from more attacks, also a journalist, did not receive the same kind of sympathy. She thought it reeked of misogyny. Her family took it even less well. They told Gwyneth she was being reckless and was asking for more beatings when she kept filming from the ground, even after the gangsters had already assaulted her. Gwyneth as a journalist had spent months asking protesters to explain their decisions. They almost always replied similarly: in the moment, you don't think too much; you just follow your instincts and do what feels right. Gwyneth understood what they meant. She was no different from the tens of thousands who had stood against the brutality of the state in one way or another.

"The reason that a reporter became famous in this movement is because all the protesters were faceless," she wrote. The morality of those fighting back the thugs at Yuen Long went to the person recording the scene, "with a name, a surname, and a face." But she was "only dust," insignificant compared with the heroism of her fellow citizens. There were dozens who were beaten more seriously, who were more nervous yet fought back. Hong Kongers were brave beyond imagination, she thought. Gwyneth was simply proud that everyone could use the footage she captured as a professional journalist, giving it more credibility than videos from activists or citizens.

Temperatures were finally beginning to cool after the humid summer when Gwyneth was preparing to leave Hong Kong to start the second year of her master's program. On August 31, friends in Hong Kong threw her a farewell party. It started with hot pot and ended with karaoke, two quintessential Hong Kong pastimes. The mood was as light as could be, given the atmosphere in the city. Gwyneth's friends presented her with going-away gifts. One was a candid photo of her looking like a hamster with puffed-up cheeks. They sang late into the night, playing songs from Cantopop singer Anthony Wong and his duo, Tat Ming Pair. It was Wong who'd first introduced her to a place called Amsterdam in one of his songs; she'd romanticized the idea of living there. But looking around at her friends that night, Gwyneth really didn't want to leave. She had started her master's program thinking it would better equip her as a reporter or provide a new career path. It now seemed irrelevant. Over the summer, experiences had tied her fate together with that of Hong Kong's. She feared that the movement was now escalating to the point where people would start dying. She wanted to stay to bear witness.

Still, out of obligation rather than desire, Gwyneth stuffed her suitcase full of souvenirs for her friends back in Europe: delicate butterfly earrings, pu'erh tea—and some mooncakes, a treat she was saving for the first day of the Mid-Autumn Festival. Without excitement and with her mind only on Hong Kong, Gwyneth flew to the Dutch capital and started her second year at the University of Amsterdam.

This phase of the program was more demanding, and the cohort smaller. Kathryn had dropped out. Gwyneth was now staying on her own in a spartan single room in a dormitory complex that looked nothing like the canal-lined image of Amsterdam she was expecting. It was dark when she woke up and dark when she biked home after classes. Gone were the carefree days of cooking elaborate meals and having late-night parties. Students were anxious about their internships, grades, and careers. Gwyneth had none of these professional concerns. She couldn't even keep herself interested in the program, which mostly discussed political communication in democratic societies. "I have never voted in a real democracy," she thought when her professors asked questions. "How am I supposed to discuss this with you?"

Unaccustomed to hearing from her, the head of the program was surprised to receive an email from Gwyneth in early September with a request. The program was very strict about attendance, and Gwyneth was asking for permission to miss a single class to travel to the United States. A group of activists, she said, had invited her to Washington, DC, to talk about covering Hong Kong and to journalistically document their lobbying efforts. She didn't tell the professor why they'd invited her specifically—that would mean explaining the Yuen Long attacks, her role in them, and the symbol she had become.

The professor knew only that Gwyneth was from Hong Kong and was passionate about what was happening. It came up sometimes, given that Hong Kong was a major news story. But the program had students from all over the world, including Myanmar, Belarus, Ukraine, and Lebanon, whose homes were similarly teetering on crisis. Gwyneth, unlike some of the other students, did not describe herself as an activist, and she kept a low profile. He felt that Gwyneth was almost apologetic about her request. Of course she could miss class, he replied. She should be proud that she was asked to attend.

Kathryn, back in Seattle, received a WhatsApp message. It had again been weeks since she had heard from Gwyneth. "You won't believe this: I am coming to the US next week," Gwyneth wrote, with the caveat that she'd be traveling only to the East Coast.

"Not to me :(," Kathryn replied. "Why though?"

It was "lobbying stuff," Gwyneth said, for a bill that was making its way through the US Congress that would support the Hong Kong movement. She told Kathryn she would be speaking at one event—"shit, so nervous," she added—and would otherwise cover the work of the delegation.

"Thing is," Gwyneth wrote to her friend, "I became a famous victim because of being beaten up . . . so I guess it's my responsibility now to help raise awareness. . . ."

It was Joshua Wong who reached out to Gwyneth, inviting her to join his delegation on a weeklong trip to New York and Washington. He and other activists wanted to make a splashy, final push for a goal they had been working on for months—one that would rewrite the relationship between the US and Hong Kong, and China itself. Like Finn in London, activists focused on Washington wanted the US government to answer a fundamental question: could Hong Kong still be seen as separate from China? Relations between Washington and the territory were defined by the 1992 Hong Kong Policy Act, legislation that spelled out Hong Kong as a separate jurisdiction for customs, trade, tax, and other purposes. It was built off the Sino-British declaration and rested on the principle that life would go on "unchanged" there. With such seismic changes underway, activists believed that Washington needed a new Hong Kong policy.

Joshua and others wanted Congress to take up a piece of legislation known as the Hong Kong Human Rights and Democracy Act. The act was first floated by longtime supporters of their movement, Republican senator Marco Rubio and Republican representative Chris Smith, in 2014. It received tepid support then amid a lack of focus on Hong Kong or even China. Five years on, the legislation could be easily dusted off, refreshed, and updated, hastening bureaucratic processes.

The US legislation required Congress to certify yearly whether Hong Kong was still autonomous enough to deserve special treatment apart from the mainland. If the determination was that it wasn't, the 1992 policy act would be reworked. Hong Kong could lose trade privileges. It also opened a pathway to economic sanctions against those who curtailed the city's freedoms. The act carried with it implications that a place was slipping further away from international norms. American sanctions were slapped on countries like North Korea and Venezuela, not financial darlings like Hong Kong. Hong Kong's democracy activists were desperate to see it passed.

Joshua, in planning the trip, knew it was disingenuous of him to claim to represent the movement as it was now. He wanted co-speakers who were participants in some of the most pivotal actions the city had seen since June. He picked a team: Brian Leung, the young man who took off his mask in the Legislative Council chamber on July 1; pop star and LGBTQ+ activist Denise Ho; and Gwyneth.

Denise Ho was the first mainstream Cantopop singer to come out as a lesbian, and for her pro-democracy advocacy she was banned from performing or distributing her music in China. She could speak to the economic punishment that China inflicted against those who stood against it. Brian Leung, twenty-six, had become a personification of the "braves" when he stood up on a wooden desk in the chamber of the

Legislative Council on July 1, took off his mask, and read the demands of the movement. He was also a doctoral student at the University of Washington, studying comparative politics. Joshua believed that Gwyneth represented something different from the group—she exemplified the brutality of the system, testament to the breadth of its cruelty. Joshua, Brian, Denise: they had all chosen to stand against the system. Gwyneth hadn't.

Gwyneth was thrilled to be part of the team. She was curious about the inner workings of international lobbying and knew that Joshua would have never invited a "regular" journalist to embed with him. They permitted her to write her usual intellectual-driven essays on the power of lobbying for the movement, but otherwise she had to treat any closed-door meetings with US politicians as off the record.[14]

It was just Gwyneth, Brian, and Joshua in New York. The rest of the group was preparing for a congressional hearing in Washington, the highlight of the two-city tour. As Brian and Joshua strategized and planned for the days ahead, Gwyneth didn't interject much. She saw her role as observational. She did take it upon herself to be somewhat of a caretaker, particularly because these younger men seemed incapable of looking after themselves. Joshua wore suits only on this sort of occasion and didn't know how to iron his shirts properly, so Gwyneth did it for him. (On a previous lobbying trip in Germany, another female activist also helped Joshua with his shirts and arranged his taxis.)[15] Gwyneth alerted Brian that the tags on his new suit were still visible and cut them off. She thought they looked like teenagers going to prom rather than well-known activists.

Their meetings started at 8 a.m. the next morning. New York City being the media capital of the world, the trip included the headquarters of global media outlets—Reuters, NBC, Time, CNN—all eager to hear from Joshua amid the roiling protests back in his home. With each interview, they fielded difficult questions on the movement's increased use of violence and whether it was detracting from their goals. The trio's last stop was the *New York Times* headquarters in midtown Manhattan, an impressive building that expanded across half a city block with a double facade of glass and crisscrossing ceramic rods. For many young journalists, it is a mecca. Gwyneth wasn't impressed. She was too focused on perfecting the group's talking points with the American reporters. When they were done, Joshua and Brian took a selfie at the front of the building, under steel letters that read "The New York Times" in the paper's signature Adobe Garamond font. Gwyneth was nowhere in the photo.

It was almost time for dinner. Joshua hunched over his phone, scrolling to see what restaurants were nearby. Gwyneth wasn't familiar with the city and wanted to get her bearings, so she also opened Google Maps on her phone. Zooming out so that Manhattan's neat grid layout filled her phone screen, Gwyneth realized they were close to the south end of Central Park. It was one of the few places she wanted to see while in the city. She thought this might be a good moment to offer up the mooncakes—calorie-laden pastries filled with white lotus paste that she had been carrying in her bag all day.

It was the first day of the Mid-Autumn Festival, which symbolized reunions between family and loved ones. It was a happy coincidence that the trip to New York fell on the right day. When Gwyneth packed the mooncakes from Hong Kong, she envisioned eating them alone in her dorm room in Amsterdam. Now she could share them, the way they were meant to be eaten.

"Should we go to Central Park and have some mooncakes?" Gwyneth suggested. Brian and Joshua looked up from their phones, confused. They appeared to have forgotten what day it was amid their hectic schedules, but were happy to indulge her. It was a small piece of Hong Kong so far from home.

The New York Times building and Central Park were more than a dozen blocks apart. Joshua thought they should call an Uber, but Gwyneth stopped him. She wanted to walk. She had a romantic image of the city at dusk, where "the setting sun penetrates the thick air and falls on the glass curtain wall." Traversing Manhattan on foot made her feel like a protagonist in a film. But as they made their way north, Gwyneth felt they were a little out of place. She looked at the two men with her. Joshua by now was a frequent target of Chinese state media, lumped as a traitor along with Julie Eadeh at the US consulate and other American officials. Brian had also been pinpointed—not yet by the courts, but by former Hong Kong chief executive Leung Chun-ying, who said he would offer a bounty of $64,000 for information that could lead to Brian's prosecution. Gwyneth had spent much of her career covering dissidents on the mainland. She knew there could be no neat, movie-script ending for her friends. She didn't consider where her own journey would take her.

The sun had set by the time they arrived at the park. Gwyneth pulled out the plastic-wrapped mooncake, stuffed in her bag among a jumble of reporter's notebooks, pens, and name cards. She realized she hadn't brought a knife to cut it. There was only a wine shop nearby, and with no knives for sale they settled for a corkscrew. Trying her best with the curly metal, Gwyneth worked to cut the hard pastry into quarters. It wasn't at all the right tool for the job, the crust of the mooncake too thick for the thin piece of wire. Joshua watched her with an expression of befuddlement and impatience. The pieces of mooncake were flattened and unappetizing by the time Gwyneth was done. They ate them anyway, sitting under a canopy of trees that blocked the yellow glow of the full moon overhead. Gwyneth turned on Spotify and played Cantopop songs. The three sipped beers and spoke for hours about relationships, crushes, food, their families, life itself. For just one night, they forgot the adult roles they had thrust themselves into. They let the pressure fade away, remembering the young people they were.

―――――――

ON SEPTEMBER 18, JOSHUA WONG AND DENISE HO TOOK THEIR SEATS ON A panel of five testifying before the Congressional-Executive Commission on China (CECC). This was the second hearing on Hong Kong that year, but in the six months since the first, interest had surged. CECC staffers borrowed a room from the Senate Foreign Relations Committee.[16] It was still too small. All its roughly 150 seats were taken. Staffers removed designated media seats and crammed journalists at the back, but there was still overflow out into the corridors of the Capitol.

Denise Ho spoke to the brutality that Hong Kong police had been inflicting on the population while hiding their ID numbers and warrant cards. Hers was not a plea for "foreign interference," she said, but "for universal human rights," "for the freedom to choose." Joshua spoke of how his sacrifices were "minimal" in the present leaderless movement and appealed for Congress to stand with Hong Kong.

Immediately after the hearing concluded, Joshua, Denise, Nathan Law, and other activists gathered with Senator Todd Young of Indiana to launch a new DC-based nongovernmental organization. It was a watershed moment. Very few overseas democracy movements have representatives with access to the highest levels of Washington. Even fewer have a permanent lobbying presence in the United States. Hong Kong now had both.

The organization introduced its founder and managing director, Samuel Chu Muk-man. He wasn't as well-known as Wong or Ho. But his surname was etched into the very history of the modern pro-democracy movement, of everything that had led them up to this point, a testament to Hong Kong's enduring, generational struggle. Samuel was the second-born son of Reverend Chu Yiu-ming.

———

CHU HAD SENT SAMUEL TO CALIFORNIA IN THE EARLY 1990S, NOT KNOWING what his son's path would be. It turned out strikingly similar to his own, but with a more progressive twist. Samuel entered the seminary but decided to pursue a pastorship at a Presbyterian church rather than a Baptist one like his father's. He became a community organizer focused on liberal causes in America: LGBTQ+ rights, marriage equality, expanding social services, including health care and free school lunches. Samuel got involved in the progressive Jewish community, training rabbis on how to update their activism from the days of Martin Luther King Jr. so they could be more relevant to the American Left in the twenty-first century.

Working on food insecurity, Samuel met a range of Democratic lawmakers, including Jim McGovern, the longtime Democratic representative from the Massachusetts second congressional district. In the spring of 2019, McGovern took on a new role as the chair of the CECC. Samuel had just returned from Hong Kong, where he watched his father stand trial because of his role in the 2014 Umbrella

Movement. In a meeting, McGovern joked that they rarely spoke about Hong Kong, where Samuel was from. "What should I be doing or paying attention to?" the congressman asked. Samuel had actually come prepared with an English translation of Reverend Chu's mitigation speech, an emotional recounting of his childhood, faith, and lifelong struggle for democracy delivered in the style of a sermon. Samuel pointed McGovern to the extradition bill—helping, along with Joshua's efforts, to lay the groundwork for the Hong Kong work that the committee would undertake for the rest of the year. In May the CECC held its first hearing on the extradition bill.

For the past three decades, Samuel's life had been riddled with doubts. He was plagued by the question of whether he was a Hong Konger or an American, shrouded under his father's huge shadow and still coming to terms with the upheavals that he'd experienced. In the summer of 2019 it felt like all those circumstances had led to his calling. Crucially, after living in the US for almost three decades, he was now a citizen. In those months, a Hong Kong–born American citizen whose family was part of the earliest iteration of the city's pro-democracy movement was exactly who was needed—particularly one who understood what it took to set up a nongovernmental organization and navigate the world of 501(c)(3) incorporation. Joshua's compatriots, Jeffrey Ngo and Nathan Law, joined the new organization as board members.

Basking in the attention of Washington, it felt to those activists that everything they were working toward had come to fruition. Together, they had ensured that the issue of Hong Kong was front and center and that the Hong Kong Human Rights and Democracy Act was on the top of Congress's agenda. A month after Joshua Wong's appeal to Congress, the US House of Representatives unanimously passed the bill by a voice vote.

On her flight back from Manhattan to Amsterdam, Gwyneth scribbled furiously, trying to piece together everything she had experienced over the past week. Before this trip, she saw international lobbying as something complex, requiring a special type of skill. But in the gilded halls of Congress and in penthouses in New York, it seemed that attendees from academics to human-rights practitioners wanted to hear her story even more than Joshua's sound bites. She kept asking Joshua and Brian how they made sure that their work was representative of the broader movement. Did they raise anything on LIHKG? Was there any democratic process or negotiation? The answer was no; it was just a few guys strategizing in hotel rooms on the East Coast. Gwyneth, more confident than she had felt in years, believed that she could do it herself.

CHAPTER 14

ARRESTED PERSON

TOMMY FASTENED A POCKET-SIZED GOPRO ON THE LEFT SHOULDER strap of his hiking backpack before heading out to the streets on September 29, 2019. Blended into the dark canvas of the strap, the camera was a relatively new addition to his growing kit. Tommy first started using it like a thrill seeker would, drawn in by the novelty of the protests. Friends warned him that his behavior was reckless, but Tommy characteristically ignored them. It was his way of proving, perhaps to himself, that he was really there. With the movement entering a darker place, Tommy believed that his camera could also provide some accountability.

A month earlier, on August 31, officers from a police tactical unit stormed subway cars at Prince Edward MTR station in the Kowloon district. The force had received calls about clashes between protesters and counterdemonstrators, and had sent an elite squad known as "raptors" to respond. Once again, a subway station became a theater for a brutal attack, this time with the police as perpetrators. They whacked passengers and protesters with their batons, soaked horrified commuters holding their hands up in surrender with geysers of pepper spray, and body-slammed teenagers to the floor. An emergency warning played on repeat, the blaring dinging competing for volume with the screams of passengers and the crash of riot shields on tile. Authorities closed the station off, including to medics and journalists, while officers were inside. A video of a first-aid worker pleading with police to be let in raced across social media and Telegram channels. Those inside only captured part of the scene; authorities refused to release the full CCTV footage of the violence.

Amid deep distrust of the police, some in the movement—even elected lawmakers—were convinced that murder and a subsequent cover-up had taken place inside the MTR station. Independent journalists found no evidence to substantiate the theory. The only missing person who "disappeared" after the Prince Edward attacks later reappeared as an exile in London. But over the past four months, so much that was once unthinkable had happened. Police had fired hundreds of rounds of tear gas within residential neighborhoods, imbuing family meals with noxious fumes. Officers had allowed gangsters to assault a journalist, a pregnant woman, and other random commuters at a subway station. Children as young as twelve had been arrested. Everything unfolding was unbelievable, so the idea that the police could have taken lives and covered it up seemed believable. Even before the Prince Edward attacks, there was a growing paranoia, with groups of people convinced that demonstrators had been "suicided" by police, their bodies dumped into the harbor or hidden after being arrested and killed. Online sleuths filled Reddit threads and the LIHKG forum with theories on the suspicious death of a fifteen-year-old student. They held memorials and prayed for her soul as another victim taken by the state.

Protesters like Tommy saw themselves as vigilantes keeping tabs on the brutality. He kept the GoPro running throughout the day at every protest. He hoped the footage could help identify protesters if there were "disappearances" or capture police doing something out of line like firing tear gas into a packed crowd, firing rubber bullets at close range, and other violations (there were dozens of these incidents at each protest). After the demonstrations ended, Tommy uploaded the footage to his university computer hard drive, creating a repository that also chronicled his own journey from a bystander on the fringes to a balaclava-clad protester in full black bloc.

———

THE HONG KONG GOVERNMENT HAD TRIED ITS BEST TO STAVE OFF DEMON-strations ahead of that last September weekend. Carrie Lam, having withdrawn the extradition bill, finally decided to hold a public dialogue.

She wanted to appear to be listening as she had promised, to put on a show of a government engaged with its people. After weeks of planning, on a Thursday evening in late September, Lam faced 150 Hong Kongers who were chosen among thousands to directly address the leader. "You are useless at governing," one woman barked at her, shaking with anger. Another repeated the slogan of the protests to her face: "Five demands, not one less!" Lam was emotionless and took copious notes as if she were hearing these grievances for the first time. When it was over, Lam was trapped inside the stadium for four more hours, blocked by protesters who gathered outside. It was the first and last of such sessions. She never faced the public again.

The timing of the dialogue made it seem like a last-ditch attempt to pacify Hong Kongers ahead of October 1, the seventieth anniversary of the founding of the People's Republic of China. Mainland authorities had gone to extreme lengths to ensure a trouble-free event, banning balloons and even captive racing pigeons from taking to the skies, citing the birds as possible aviation-security risks.[1] Online censors worked frantically to purge Chinese cyberspace of any modicum of dissent. Chinese police were on high alert. The day was meant to be celebrated with a parade of astounding scale to showcase China's emergence as a global military power and Xi's unrelenting consolidation of authority. More than 150 bombers and armed forces planes would streak above Beijing. Below, 15,000 military personnel would march in tight formations. During rehearsals, they had worn diapers to avoid wasting time with bathroom breaks.[2] Top commanders coyly hinted that the parade would showcase new weapons. The only thing that could spoil Xi's festivities was Hong Kong.

Protesters in the territory had planned their own slate of events leading up to China's national day. They would mark the last Sunday before the holiday, a day traditionally reserved for protest, with an "anti-totalitarianism" march. The date coincided with the eightieth anniversary of the day when Germany and the Soviet Union divided up occupied Poland. For the first time, the rally shifted beyond Hong Kong and toward China's actions in other regions. Sister rallies were held in Taiwan, Sydney, Toronto, and elsewhere.

Among the hundreds of thousands of demonstrators in Hong Kong flew the sky-blue Kökbayraq flag, representing Xinjiang region, where Uyghur Muslims and other ethnic minorities were subject to gross human-rights abuses. There were T-shirts and banners bearing the snow lion emblem of Tibet, the mountainous region and stronghold of Buddhism that was seized by Communist Chinese forces in 1951. Demonstrators decried "ChiNazis" as they held signs of the red Chinese flag, its yellow stars rearranged as a swastika. They pasted stickers of this altered flag on bus stops and storefronts throughout Central. Posters scattered on the street depicted Xi with the toothbrush mustache and comb-over of Adolf Hitler. This protest was organized largely online, not by the Civil Human Rights Front. Police banned the march, but protesters continued anyway. They carried a global warning: "Yesterday, it was Xinjiang and Tibet. Today, it is Hong Kong and Taiwan. Tomorrow, it will be the free world."

―――――

OUR OFFICE WAS LOCATED ON THE SIXTH FLOOR OF ADMIRALTY CENTER, which provided an unobstructed view of Harcourt Road and the main government buildings. We watched months of protests from this perch. When there was a lull, we would race up to our desks to file stories and update editors while keeping watch. When demonstrators began to move or the police launched a particularly aggressive clearance operation, we raced down to the ground floor to document. The demonstrations in this area had taken on a familiar routine. A handful of protesters braved the speeding cars to walk into Harcourt Road, taking with them traffic cones and metal road barriers. A trickle of others followed suit once traffic began to slow. Then, when the road was largely clear of vehicles, a deluge of bodies began to fill the lanes. A few taxis or buses would try to weave their way through as the crowds grew thicker, but eventually traffic halted completely. Protesters would hold the road for hours, chanting slogans, chatting with their friends, and obsessively checking Telegram for where to go and what to do next. Some trudged up the overpass near the PLA garrison and taunted the Chinese soldiers below. The elevated roadway provided a panoramic view of the Kowloon skyline that could otherwise be glimpsed only from a speeding car. In quieter moments, we spotted young couples holding hands as they looked across the empty highway out to Victoria Harbor, watching the sun set.

This movement had taken over our lives, too, everything we spoke about, dreamed about, and wrote about. It was overwhelming to recognize we were part of all this. Sometimes it felt like we didn't have enough words or the right ones. It was impossible to convey everything—the volunteers delivering bags of food, the medics rushing to help strangers, the shopkeepers who opened their doors to let groups of fleeing protesters in so that they would be safe from the police. In the face of such wanton state cruelty, we often felt we were witnessing the best of humanity.

On September 29, police had a surprise for the protesters, who had become somewhat complacent. As thousands of people milled about on Harcourt, some tossing rocks at government buildings, dozens of officers sprang from hidden doors in the exterior of the Legislative Council building. The sudden stampede of people caught our attention six stories up. We watched as demonstrators tried to scatter, tripping and falling over one another and struggling to scale the concrete road dividers to escape. Officers tackled those who were too slow and slammed their batons down. Blood pooled on the black asphalt. Police officers were trained to avoid the head, legs, and chest of protesters. That afternoon, they were targeting exactly those fragile skeletal parts. We rushed down to the street in time to capture Rupert Dover commanding the elite "raptors" tactical unit as they charged down a side street toward another major thoroughfare filled with hundreds of protesters. "Go, go, go!" he yelled as he sprinted.

The masked protesters scattered into the roads and cut-throughs. We didn't know him then, just one of the almost identical figures we watched racing through the streets, but Tommy was among them. Before the raptors burst out of the Legislative Council doors, he was using a slingshot to launch stones at officers, who were returning fire with dozens of cans of tear gas. Tommy was not strong, but over the past months, he had become quick. Speed mattered most when it came to escaping arrest.

Tommy was running when an officer stepped forward and shouted at him to stop. Juiced with adrenaline and fear, Tommy paid no attention. He kept going, but the officer clipped Tommy with his riot shield as he ran past. Tommy's pink iPhone sailed from his hand. He froze, spun, and reached back to retrieve it. The officer was faster. He already had the phone in his hand. Tommy's hesitation gave the officer enough time to lunge. He grabbed Tommy, who was slowed by his large backpack, and wrestled him to the street.

After months of close calls and escapes aided by blind luck, of watching friends and fellow demonstrators picked off by police, Tommy's turn had come. It was his first arrest. He found himself oddly calm. "Oh," he thought, like it was matter of fact, "this is it." Seconds later, the panic set in: "Shit. Fuck." Hoping to be spared a lengthy and uncomfortable booking procedure, Tommy began to scream, "I need to go to the hospital." Officers ignored him.

Around him, captured demonstrators yelled out their names and ID numbers to social workers, a practice that had become common since the Prince Edward attacks. Arrested people wanted to be recorded, fearing they would be "disappeared." Officers bellowed commands and pounded their plastic shields on the ground, creating a rolling clangor meant to intimidate. We weaved between the piles of officers and shot close-ups of faces pressed into the ground by police. Strewn across the street were supplies hastily jettisoned by those who'd fled: cotton gloves, broken respirators, and mangled umbrellas. Some of the arrested briefly fell unconscious. One had to be carried by police because he could no longer walk.

It was among the most aggressive police responses in seventeen weeks of protests. Elsewhere in the city, an officer blinded an Indonesian journalist in one eye when he fired a rubber bullet at close range. She was live streaming for a publication whose readers were mostly domestic helpers.

The officer's narrative of Tommy's arrest, dictated later in an official report, described his actions as a model of cordial professionalism. In his version of events, he restrained Tommy with the assistance of another officer, using zip ties to bind his hands. He clearly informed

Tommy that he was under arrest for taking part in an unlawful assembly. With tear gas still wafting through the streets, the officer put Tommy's respirator back on his face to allow him to breathe more easily. When Tommy asked for water, the officer kindly obliged, lifting Tommy's mask to allow him a sip. In the report, Tommy was reduced to just an abbreviation, AP, for "arrested person."

It was a sanitized version of events. As Tommy was flailing, hoping to escape, the officer repeatedly punched him and continued hitting him when he was held on the ground. Once Tommy was sufficiently subdued, the officer yanked down his mask, leaving him to choke on the tear gas and gasp for breath. Tommy begged for it to be put back on. The officer refused to help him. His face burned from the chemicals. Eventually, officers hoisted Tommy from the road and dragged him over to the sidewalk. They set him down near a light post, lining him up with others who were too slow to outrun the blitz.

———

PRUDENCE WAS ONE OF TOMMY'S CLOSEST FRIENDS. THEY WERE IN ART class together, ran for student council together, shopped together, and hiked together. But on the streets at protests, she largely stayed away from him. Knowing his penchant for adventures and impulsiveness, Prudence turned down his invitations to follow him to demonstrations. She was one of the many who thought he should stop carrying his GoPro. Prudence had seen Tommy slipping further into the crew he had met on the streets at protests. This was a part of his life she could not fully access. Prudence still spent every weekend staring at her phone, waiting to see if her WhatsApp messages to Tommy had two blue ticks, indicating he had read them. She worried about him.

That Sunday evening, Prudence was with another mutual friend of Tommy's from school, waiting to board a flight back home from Seoul after a weekend of barbecue and shopping. Messages started arriving on their phones. "Has anyone heard from Tommy?" "Have you seen the news?" She shot off a message to Tommy, then stared at her phone again, waiting. It stayed unread as the boarding calls for her flight began. Perhaps he had fallen asleep back home, she hoped, without much faith.

When another friend forwarded a photo of a young man in black athletic leggings and a black shirt being led by two officers, her heart dropped. The man's face wasn't visible. He looked down at the road, and his hair hid his features. But one of his shoes was captured perfectly in the frame. It was black and looked a bit like a wet-suit bootie. Tommy owned such a pair. How many others arrested that day could have the same ones? She checked her messages again. Still no blue ticks, still no response from Tommy. The confirmation Prudence didn't want came in a video clip as her flight was about to depart. A TV cameraman panned over the dozens of arrested protesters and zoomed in on what was undoubtedly Tommy, with his thickish lips and broad nose, sitting on the ground. His face was framed by a black balaclava. His bulging eyes darted back and forth. Tommy's backpack was still strapped to his shoulders, the GoPro intact. Prudence felt like she couldn't breathe. She started crying, oblivious to the looks around her. For the first time, everything felt real.

Tommy was taken east along Victoria Harbor to the North Point police station. The scale of the day's arrests became apparent to him as he stepped off the transport van just before 8 p.m. The parking lot adjacent to the station was transformed into a processing center to handle the volume. Police that day arrested nearly 150 people across the city. Dozens of them sat in neat rows—some fidgeting, others dozing off—waiting for their names to be called, fingerprints and statements to be taken. Industrial fans whirred in the parking lot, providing some comfort in the 80 degree heat.

Police inventoried Tommy's backpack. The contents were testament to his journey from a young man once unsure about tossing eggs to one who was facing a ten-year rioting sentence. There were zip ties for tying metal railings together once they were pried off their hinges and fashioned into a blockade. Tommy had a multitool pocketknife with a hammer for "renovating" a target. He carried a spare subway card to disguise his movements through the city. There was a sole memento of a simpler time in his life: a plaid shirt thrifted from Mee & Gee, where he and Prudence spent their weekends fooling around with sequined tops and outlandish pants. It was Tommy's favorite shirt.

Police kept Tommy's GoPro. The footage he captured would later be used during trial to identify others arrested alongside him and confirm their actions on the streets.

Volunteer lawyers arrived at North Point that evening, knowing that the sheer number of detainees would need representation. The young lawyer assigned to Tommy told him he'd be released only if he paid a bail of roughly $1,270. Tommy knew his family couldn't afford it. They had barely enough for his youngest brother's school tuition. Still, he told the lawyer to call his parents, not sure who else to ask. Tommy tried to be cavalier, joking with the police officers taking down his details and making friends with the other detainees. But it hurt to know he was adding to the burden already carried by his family. His parents were hardly speaking to each other, the financial struggles fraying their already-strained marriage. Tommy played a big role in raising his ten-year-old brother and wondered if he'd now be judged by him. He thought about how he'd explain the arrest to his grandmother. Tommy whispered with the other arrestees. Although their backgrounds and ages were different, they were coming to the same conclusion. Everyone was "wondering about whether or not they'd be able to go back to school, or get a decent job."

While he was waiting for his forty-eight-hour detention period to lapse, held incommunicado, Prudence was working through a solution. They were so close that she had his passport details and ID number. She found his lawyer, solicited donations from his friends, and paid Tommy's bail.

———

TOMMY WAS STILL IN JAIL WHEN DAWN BROKE ON OCTOBER 1, 2019. THE arrest of dozens like him did nothing to keep thousands of others off the streets. Demonstrators were already converging across the city. Hong Kong government officials were again forced inside to watch a flag-raising ceremony (Lam was spared the embarrassment, having left Hong Kong for Beijing to attend the gaudy celebrations there). Authorities canceled the planned fireworks display. The mood quickly turned explosive. Protesters were pugnacious, many girding for a fight. With no centralized location serving as a natural rallying point, people spread out across Hong Kong Island, Kowloon, and the New Territories.

Running skirmishes quickly turned into ferocious brawls in numerous neighborhoods. The day spiraled into violence. The police, stretched thin, turned again to tear gas, firing 1,400 rounds and deploying water cannons filled with water laced with stinging blue dye to hunt down and mark protesters. Then came a major escalation.

In the New Territories, an eighteen-year-old student and his teammates were battling with police officers. He had come prepared for this fight with a black helmet, a shield fashioned out of a blue pool float which he kept slung across his left arm, and a pole in his right hand. When one officer became separated from his colleagues, the young man and around ten other demonstrators set on the lone officer, knocking him to the ground and beating him. He then turned his sights on an officer who had come to aid his fallen comrade, using the pole to hit him. The officer, in a full-face respirator, turned back as the teen swung the pole at his arm. He aimed his aging revolver at the young man and fired once. The protester tried to swing the pole again but fell backward, screaming in pain. It was the first time that police had shot a protester with live ammunition.

Tommy was still awaiting his release as ambulances rushed the young protester to hospital. When the volunteer lawyers briefed him and others about their release, no one asked about their own cases. They wanted to know what had happened on National Day. How big were the crowds? How intense were the clashes? The lawyers told them about the shooting. The mood in the room sank. *They really used a gun.* Tommy could hardly process it.

What was meant to be a celebration of the superiority and longevity of the Chinese Communist system turned into a humiliating split screen contrasting this propaganda with a city in revolt. Rather than uninterrupted coverage of the grand ceremonies, global news coverage flipped between the perfectly synchronized ceremonies in Beijing and the chaos in Hong Kong. Standing in Tiananmen Square, Xi praised the "one country, two systems" framework and said that it would "maintain lasting prosperity and stability" in Hong Kong. Thousands of military personnel goose-stepped through Beijing in rigid formation. A fleet of helicopters spelled out "70" across the sky. When the sun set, an orchestra performed under the glow of an enormous fireworks display. Lam beamed as she took in the pageantry, but the stability that Xi spoke of was elusive. News cameras showed live footage of her city. Fires smoldered on the streets. The air was again thick with tear gas. A young man lay in the hospital with a gunshot wound, along with some seventy others. Across a destroyed subway station, someone had mockingly spray-painted "Happy Birthday."

————

HONG KONG WAS ONE OF THE BIGGEST STORIES IN THE WORLD, LEADING newspaper front pages after the dramatic escalation on October 1. The dynamics would soon reach a broader cross section of the US public when one of the most American—and yet internationally exposed—of institutions became caught in China's crosshairs. On October 4, Daryl Morey, the general manager of the Houston Rockets, tweeted a photo. It had the logo of Finn's organization and the slogan "Fight for Freedom Stand with Hong Kong." Morey quickly deleted it but could not stave off the ensuing fallout. Within the hour, Morey's team was rushing to distance themselves from him, and NBA players were proudly declaring their love for China. The nakedly capitalist basketball league itself was groveling, hoping to preserve its $1.5 billion streaming deal with Chinese internet portal Tencent and its agreement with state broadcaster CCTV to air games in the country.[3] The Rockets, which in 2002 drafted Chinese superstar Yao Ming, was one of most beloved American sports teams in China. Beijing wanted nothing less than Morey to be fired. Because he kept his job, China punished the league by pulling broadcasts for most of its next three seasons. The Rockets specifically were kept off Chinese screens for fifteen months. It cost the NBA nearly $400 million.[4]

The NBA debacle added to the clamor around Hong Kong in the Beltway. Support was bipartisan, but it was Republicans who approached the cause with the most vigor. Whereas Pelosi, McGovern, and a host of Democrats with a longtime commitment to human rights in China were fully behind the movement, others within the party saw the issue as peripheral. Representative Alexandria Ocasio-Cortez, the progressive star from Queens, did not reply to a request from Joshua Wong and his contingent to meet on their Washington tour. Most Democrats were focused domestically, trying to protect their own democracy from the efforts of President Trump, who was hurtling toward his first impeachment.

Two Trump allies were the loudest and most performative champions of Hong Kong. Ted Cruz, the Texas Republican, traveled to Hong Kong in mid-October, the highest-ranking member of the US government to visit. Cruz made a point of wearing all black, a sign of solidarity, he said, with the protesters, whom he found to be "inspiring." Not to be outdone, a few days later Josh Hawley went to the streets of Mongkok, the heart of radical protests since the 2014 Umbrella Movement.[5] Hawley, with his suit and slicked hair, stood out among the teens running in athletic gear and yellow helmets. He tweeted updates of a nighttime standoff between protesters and police. Both men invoked Berlin, casting Hong Kong as the new center of a global struggle between democracy and Communism. Both pledged to support the Hong Kong Human Rights and Democracy Act, which was fast making its way through both the House and the Senate. Their trip coincided with yet another rally in Hong Kong in support of the US legislation. Joshua Wong, back in the city, was at the front of the throng, leading the group in bellowing chants of "Pass the act!"

After the humiliation on National Day and as more senators started turning up, greeted by Hong Kong demonstrators waving the American flag, Beijing was now certain that this was the work of a foreign power—the US—seeking the fall of the CCP. They were "convinced," said Michael Tien, one pro-Beijing lawmaker. "You are talking about Communist China. The one thing they hate is their own people going to a foreign government asking for help, and particularly this foreign government, who is trying to nail China."[6] Hong Kong was demonstrating that they did not want to be Chinese, that their identity was their own. This was the reddest line of all. Xi Jinping, speaking the same weekend that Hawley was cruising around Mongkok, delivered an unvarnished warning: "Anyone attempting to split China in any part of the country will end in crushed bodies and shattered bones."

The growing radicalization of the protest movement also shaped Beijing's views that this was mob violence, funded by people who wanted to turn Hong Kong Chinese against mainland Chinese. Anti-China sentiment had moved beyond emblems of the state—the Liaison Office, the Chinese flag—to people from the mainland. Protesters in mid-August took their hatred for China to a shocking new level when they attacked and tied up a reporter from the *Global Times*, the Chinese state media outlet, and another man whom they believed to be an undercover Chinese agent. By October, the victims became regular mainland Chinese. A Mandarin-speaking banker in the central business district was heckled and told to go back to China. When he replied, "We are all Chinese," the crowd was further incensed, and shouted back, "We are all Hong Kongers!" Then someone in all black emerged, punching the man repeatedly outside his office building. The humanity we had seen on the streets for months appeared at the time to be fading, replaced by a moral ambiguity and ugliness. Tommy's comrades encouraged him to take more radical action, to attack police officers. He tried to "train" his mind. Sometimes in his dreams he could punch someone, kick them, even shoot them. "But I didn't do it," he said, "because I don't think I am ready to hurt people."

The trajectory of the violence kept ticking upward. Protesters were engaging in more targeted vandalism that made the Legislative Council break-in appear tame. They sought out businesses with connections to mainland China or pro-Beijing businesspeople. Starbucks stores were smashed because of the pro-Beijing position of the local franchisee. Chinese state banks began to erect protective walls around their outlets to keep them from being ransacked. Still, protesters made a point of never stealing from the places they wrecked. What appeared to be a homemade bomb was set off near a police car, and a police station was hit by more than a dozen petrol bombs. There were some who appeared to simply want to hurt anyone who disagreed with them. When a man tried to stop protesters from vandalizing a subway station, they doused him in flammable liquid and set him on fire. The man lived but was badly injured. During a fight between protesters and pro-China residents, a seventy-year-old cleaner was hit in the head with a brick and died.

The same "do not split" ethos that led to acts of self-sacrificial bravery early in the protests made it difficult for anyone to criticize these actions without being seen as standing against the whole movement. Pro-Beijing commentators and state media seized on the largely isolated incidents. They conveniently ignored the millions of peaceful marches and creative displays of dissatisfaction over the months—which they censored on state media—and broadcast this violence, painting the entire movement as a vicious, xenophobic mob, paid and encouraged by Americans to topple the Communist Party.

Tommy tried to lie low after his arrest, not wanting to cause more strain on his family. But even as he largely stayed off the streets, the police found him. In November, officers showed up at his home and told him he was under arrest for the second time, again for rioting. They had matched his fingerprints to those on a bunch of stickers inside the Legislative Council chamber on July 1. He was now facing a prison sentence totaling thirty years.

———

IN EARLY NOVEMBER, HONG KONG MARKED THE FIRST CASUALTY WHOSE death was directly connected to confrontations between police and protesters. Chow Tsz-lok, a twenty-two-year-old computer science student at a Hong Kong university, fell from a parking garage while police officers were dispersing protesters nearby. He went into a coma and died a few days later from a severe brain injury. A Rubicon had been crossed. The city was seething. A new protest slogan took hold on city streets: "Hong Kongers, take revenge."[7]

Protesters responded to the death with "Operation Dawn," the first coordinated effort to disrupt Hong Kong on a Monday, the start of the workweek, with a general strike. The goal was to cause widespread traffic disruption across the territory, stalling Hong Kong. It worked. Most of the city's subway stops were forced to shutter, stopping thousands from making their way to work, a much greater inconvenience than the normal weekend protests. That morning, a traffic cop shot another protester at close range. He survived, but the rage kept snowballing, plunging the city into a state of anarchy. The video of the protester falling to the ground spread through Telegram channels and Facebook groups. University students joined the strike, turning their campuses into staging grounds from which they threw projectiles onto the nearby train tracks to disrupt commutes. Police, for the first time, fired tear gas and other crowd-control weapons directly into university campuses, starting first with the Chinese University of Hong Kong.

Black-clad demonstrators moved from one campus to another, facing off with police who described them as a "cancer" spreading across universities. Universities evacuated their dormitories and suspended classes. Eventually, hundreds retreated to Hong Kong Polytechnic University, known more widely in its shortened form, "Poly U." A cluster of rectangular brick buildings and cylindrical towers, Poly U's campus sat like an island encircled by a ring of major roadways crisscrossed by pedestrian bridges and flyovers linking the university to the dense residential neighborhoods nearby. Protesters decided that this would be their fortress, and they loaded it with supplies. Behind its red-brick walls, they created a production line to make petrol bombs, cooked meals in the cafeteria, and repurposed classroom furniture to fortify their position. These guerrilla soldiers, now more experienced in the art of warfare, created giant slingshots from which they fired off impressive firebombs at the police officers just outside the campus walls. An arrow fired from commandeered archery equipment impaled an officer's leg.

In occupying Poly U, protesters abandoned the "be water" approach that had for months allowed them to avoid being cornered. Coming off the high after securing the campus, some began to realize they had made a grave tactical mistake. The geography of the campus easily allowed police to cut off access in and out. Unlike some of Hong Kong's other universities, surrounded by vast hiking trails through dense country parks, Poly U's campus was entirely urban. The protesters had trapped themselves.

Officers settled in for a siege and reveled in their advantage. They taunted the protesters stuck inside, blasting Cantonese love songs over a loudspeaker. The titles of their chosen tracks: "Ambush from All Sides" and "Surrounded." As the days wore on, the mood among those inside shifted from one of bold defiance to panicked desperation. Tommy was at his own campus deliberately staying clear of Poly U, Gwyneth was halfway across the world in Amsterdam, Finn was in London, but all were glued to the live streams, horrified.

Some tried to make a run for it from Poly U and were quickly apprehended. One group made it out by abseiling from a pedestrian bridge onto a nearby road and hopping on the backs of waiting motorbikes, which sped them to safety as police scrambled to react. Some of the escapees fractured legs or broke arms in the process. A group crawled to freedom belowground, using maps supplied by an employee of the city's Drainage Services Department.[8] They walked for hours through the sewer system, a vast network of subterranean pipes and tunnels teeming with skittering cockroaches. The most dedicated ones stayed to fight, taking turns bombarding the police with Molotov cocktails and withstanding rounds of tear gas and water-cannon blasts, then rushing back to shower themselves, screaming and writhing in pain. Gwyneth canceled a trip to Northern Ireland. *What is the point?* she thought. *My home is a war zone.*

It was the closest Hong Kong got to its Tiananmen moment. The whole city seemed to be at a standstill, watching to see if police would rush in and open fire on the demonstrators. They ended up waiting them out, letting the hard-core front line of the movement battle it out internally with terrified students and demonstrators inside who just wanted to leave. The nauseating smells of rotting garbage, unwashed bodies, maggot-infested food, and unused petrol bombs that piled up after a week were testament to a movement that had begun to lose itself. Exhausted and defeated, most surrendered after seven days. The siege ended without more loss of life. By the time the campus was cleared after twelve days, police had arrested 1,377 people, 318 of them under the age of eighteen. During their battles with protesters, officers had fired 1,458 tear-gas rounds, 1,391 rubber bullets, 325 bean-bag rounds, and 265 sponge rounds. Nearly 4,000 petrol bombs and 573 weapons were seized from inside the campus.

It was the last battle for the "braves." Police had effectively neutralized the radical core of the movement. A few people remained on campus long after thousands were gone, sleeping amid swarms of flies, disappearing into darkened classrooms when they heard footsteps, descending deeper into mental breakdown.

It seemed, after almost six months of solidarity and endurance, that the movement had lost its way. The explosion of fiery violence should have ended it. But as officials began to assess the damage from the weeks of extreme tumult, Hong Kong headed to the polls—and delivered a resounding victory for the pro-democracy movement.

———

THE DISTRICT COUNCIL ELECTIONS, HELD ON NOVEMBER 24, 2019, WERE the closest thing the city had to a representative vote. Since their roles were created by the British in 1982, district councilors did not have glamorous jobs. Like city councilmen, their daily schedule usually involved helping elderly residents struggling to use digital formats to pay their bills, dealing with pest-control issues, and overseeing upgrades to their neighborhoods. They were members of the lowest rung of government but the only ones elected entirely by the Hong Kong people after appointed seats were abolished in 2013 ahead of the last District Council election. The local vote was held every four years.

Pro-Beijing lawmakers, who had seen their offices thrashed over the past months, had a bad feeling about the elections. A rout at the polls was exactly what they feared when they cursed Carrie Lam for asking them to support the extradition law, then pulling it back. But no one wanted to disappoint the bosses. The Liaison Office in Hong Kong and their other allies sent briefs back to Beijing that a "silent majority" would come out and vote for pro-establishment politicians, in a repudiation of the chaos that had gripped the city for the past six months. After Poly U, they believed their own narrative more than ever. Some state media outlets had gone as far as to prewrite their coverage of a sweeping victory.

Voting lines snaked through the city starting well before 7:30 a.m., when the polls opened. There had never been so much interest in a local election. Because there was no overseas voting, some Hong Kong residents overseas paid to fly home. Nearly three million people, representing over 71 percent of eligible voters, cast ballots, more than double that of the last local election. By contrast, less than 60 percent of American voters cast ballots in the 2016 presidential election that saw Donald Trump win.

Voters nearly unanimously wiped out their pro-Beijing rivals. Candidates from traditional pro-democracy parties and novices who took campaign portraits wearing full-face respirators and hard hats won more than 85 percent of the contested seats, taking control of seventeen out of the eighteen district councils. Almost all of the new entrants to politics were in some way affiliated with the protest movement. A journalist who filmed the Prince Edward station attacks won a seat, as did a police department veteran who had quit her position over the handling of the protests. Joshua Wong had been disqualified from standing for advocating for Hong Kong's "self-determination," but a hastily arranged replacement candidate trounced the pro-Beijing incumbent. Pro-democrats had experienced their biggest electoral victory in Hong Kong history.

It was a referendum with an unambiguous answer. The elections were fought around just one issue: whether the candidate stood with the movement or with the pro-Beijing establishment. Even after six months of demonstrations crippled the city, left hundreds injured, shrouded weekends under a haze of tear gas, and turned academic institutions into battlefields, the majority was still behind the protesters. Blame for the chaos fell squarely on the government and Beijing for pushing Hong Kong to this point. There was not a single act of violence on Election Day and in its aftermath. This, after all, was exactly what Hong Kong had been fighting for since its earliest days as a special administrative region under China: the right to vote for their leaders.

The Human Rights and Democracy Act was sitting on Trump's desk in Washington as the results from the District Council elections became clear. The Senate unanimously passed the bill on November 15, sending it back to the House, where it passed 417 to 1. It was a rare display of American bipartisanship at its best, amid bitter and deeply divisive impeachment proceedings. Nancy Pelosi celebrated the bill's passage as "a day of mutual respect for democratic freedoms, the courage of the young people there to speak out, and also [a] day of great bipartisanship in the House of Representatives and the United States Senate. . . . It hardly gets any better than that."[9]

There was just one hurdle left. The president, for all his tough-on-China bluster, was reluctant to sign the bill. To Trump, the entire US-China relationship was predicated on his trade deal with Xi Jinping. He was obsessed with the idea that China had been ripping off the United States for years. His problem with Beijing had nothing to do with its human-rights record. Anything that could scuttle the deal would have to wait. Speaking on *Fox & Friends*, Trump suggested the impossible: "We have to stand with Hong Kong, but I'm also standing with President Xi. He's a friend of mine. He's an incredible guy. . . . But I'd like to see them work it out. Okay? We have to see and work it out. . . . I stand with all of the things that we want to do, but we also are in the process of making the largest trade deal in history. And if we could do that, that would be great."[10]

Eventually, as markets closed for the Thanksgiving holiday, a distracted Trump, pushed by his allies and members of the Republican Party, signed into law the Hong Kong Human Rights and Democracy Act, opening a pathway to sanctions against those responsible for crushing the city's freedoms. Trump got his trade deal, signed in January 2020—but China didn't follow through on the promises in the agreement. It was a failure.

Taken together, the District Council elections and the passage of the act provided an impetus to keep fighting. It opened the possibility of a wholesale restructuring of Hong Kong's domestic politics and international relations. But more than pro-democracy control of the district councils or a pathway toward sanctions, what 2019 created was a Hong Kong nation. They believed themselves to be their own people, with the Bauhinia flag and their own identity, entirely separate from the oppressor ruling over them. The nation even had its own anthem, written and sung in Cantonese rather than English borrowed from the British or Mandarin from the mainland. It was created—in true 2019 fashion—by an anonymous online composer who drew his inspiration from other national anthems and revolutionary songs, including "Battle Hymn of the Republic," written by abolitionist Julia Ward Howe during the US Civil War. He posted the lyrics on LIHKG and tweaked the song with crowd-sourced feedback. Lyrics included the slogan "Revolution of Our Times." Anonymous volunteers came forward to record a music video. He uploaded it to YouTube with scenes of the demonstrations, where it was viewed 1.5 million times in a week. The anthem, "Glory to Hong Kong," became an emotional rallying cry for a hurting city, sung by weeping crowds in suburban malls, in underground subway stations, and in the bustling heart of the business district.

Beijing had never been more disgusted with Hong Kong. Since Deng and Thatcher first met in 1982, China's policy toward the city could be best described like a pendulum, "swinging that way and swinging back the other way," one official within Carrie Lam's administration said. "It has always been that way, for the past decades." After the District Council elections, after Hong Kong became a tool for the US to bash China, "even the doves became hawks." Beijing was working through the perfect solution that would reconfigure the city from top to bottom, from the unreliable intermediaries at the Liaison Office to the incompetent caretakers of the local government to the radical black-clad protesters who dared reject what it meant to be Chinese. By January 2020, Xi had sent trusted lieutenants to a Beijing hotel room to work on a draft of a new law he wanted in place within the next six months. Its implementation would be aided by a crisis of a different kind.

———————

MEDICAL PROFESSORS FROM THE SCHOOL OF PUBLIC HEALTH AT THE UNIversity of Hong Kong were enjoying their Christmas holiday when they were interrupted by urgent messages from contacts at the World Health Organization and fellow doctors working on the mainland.[11] A mysterious illness, they were told, was spreading fast in the Chinese city of Wuhan.

Having suffered through the worst of the 2003 SARS epidemic, Hong Kong was home to esteemed doctors like Keiji Fukuda and Yuen Kwok-yung, who had spent their careers studying this family of viruses that causes respiratory illness in humans. They had been tapped before by the WHO to investigate the origins of the 2003 crisis, exacerbated by the Chinese government's opacity in response to the first cases. The WHO asked them again to be on standby.

Alarm spread among the group. China's looming spring festival, the largest human migration on the planet, would begin in a week. Wuhan was a major transportation hub and was just four hours by high-speed rail from Hong Kong. Thousands traveled between the two cities every day. All cases of this new virus in Wuhan seemed to trace back to a single seafood market, and its symptoms—fever, shortness of breath—sounded much like the SARS virus.

The Hong Kong government was also perturbed by the news coming from its counterparts on the mainland. On New Year's Eve, as Hong Kong protesters were preparing for their first large-scale demonstration of 2020 and as Tommy was camping with his friends on the shores of Ham Tin, planning to flee, Lam rushed to convene an urgent, late-night meeting. The only item on the agenda was this as-yet-unknown virus. Officials decided to put hospitals on alert and place frontline doctors and nurses on notice.[12] The health minister, speaking to reporters after the conclusion of the meeting, couldn't offer much else by way of details.

"The situation in Wuhan," she said, "is unusual."

PART THREE

ONE COUNTRY

CHAPTER 15

A HANGING SWORD

B Y JANUARY 1, 2020, HONG KONGERS KNEW EXACTLY WHAT TO DO AT protests. The cadence of ambling down the streets from Victoria Park to central Hong Kong during an authorized march, banners in hand and throats sore from belting out slogans, was familiar. The unpredictability of the police was also part of the calculus. Few were really surprised when the police halted the march halfway on New Year's Day, and to avoid arrest they simply slipped away into the labyrinth of walkways connecting Central and Admiralty. Not Finn Lau Cho-dik, who was among the crowd. He wasn't in a hurry to go. It was his first time at a street protest in Hong Kong since the movement began in June 2019.

Finn had flown halfway across the world to be there. He wanted to feel what it meant to be teargassed, to help wash the stinging eyes of elderly men and women unprepared for the fumes, to build barricades around police lines to protect fellow demonstrators. Those months in London, shrouded in anonymity behind a username and a screen, were a compromise. Finn couldn't be a "wo, lei, fei" or a "brave" because he wasn't in Hong Kong. He had settled for "iwantlaamcau," the anonymous provocateur organizing actions from afar. All he wanted was to be back home, even when the cost became clear.

When Finn first floated the idea of a trip to Hong Kong, Theresa wordlessly removed her wedding ring and placed it on a table. The unsubtle threat marked a low point in their deteriorating relationship. Finn, for the last few months, had been relegated to the couch in their small studio. Theresa was growing resentful. She had never cared for politics. Watching Finn on hours-long calls with his teammates and glued to Telegram angered her. She needed more attention than he was giving her—and rather than providing it, he went further by suggesting that he return to Hong Kong. They both knew this came with the possibility of arrest, something Theresa was not prepared to deal with. She did not sign up for life as an activist's wife. She believed that Finn should consider her circumstances. Still waiting for her nursing license, Theresa depended financially on Finn. All the privileges that came with life in London rested on Finn's immigration status. Theresa was not prepared to give it up, certainly not for this vague idea of democracy in Hong Kong.

The gesture set Finn aback. He urged Theresa to reconsider. Finn sometimes harbored ill feelings toward Theresa too, but he always wore his wedding ring, a thin band of gold and silver twisted like a vine. They had designed the rings together. Theresa's was almost identical, except studded with small diamonds. Their lives were meant to be forever intertwined. Finn believed somehow that both his love for Hong Kong and for Theresa could coexist. He spent the next hours promising Theresa that he was still committed to her and would reconsider the trip.

She put the ring back on. He dropped the subject of returning to Hong Kong. As the weeks passed, Finn slipped deeper into a kind of grief that he found hard to fully comprehend. He lost his appetite, couldn't sleep, felt constantly distracted and burnt out. Finn searched the internet to make sense of his symptoms and believed he was experiencing a form of depression. At the core was his distance from Hong Kong. Finn felt like he wouldn't be able to go on fighting from afar if he didn't experience what it meant to be on the streets. He confronted Theresa with the subject again the next month, in November. Again, she removed her wedding ring. The silent treatment this time lasted for days. When she eventually deigned to speak to him again, Theresa told him she would allow him to go, but only if she took her own solo trip somewhere in Europe. Finn had never stopped her from traveling and told her he was fine with her plans. He noticed that the ring was still absent from her slim finger.

Finn left for Hong Kong in late December. He knew he needed to be careful. He had been involved in so much over the past few months—calling for sanctions, working with British politicians to punish Hong Kong, popularizing the "laam caau" philosophy. Just one of these would have made him a target. Finn opted to stay in a hotel in Wan Chai instead of with his parents, hoping to minimize his contact with them. He also wiped his devices before taking to the streets on January 1, 2020. The collection of apps on his phone—LIHKG, Telegram, WhatsApp—held the identities of Stand with Hong Kong's core members, information that would be valuable to authorities. Finn left only LINE, the South Korean messaging app he used primarily to communicate with Theresa.

His precautions couldn't have staved off his arrest that night. Police on January 1 came prepared with a new tactic, one meant to put an end to the protests after seven long months. Their focus was no longer just violent front liners. Anyone demonstrating or even just hanging around the area was a target. Finn was walking back to his hotel when police pushed him into a "kettle," corralling him behind orange plastic tape. The hundreds detained alongside Finn included human-rights monitors in identifying vests who were neutral observers. Finn glanced at the strangers around him, locking eyes with some. Words weren't needed to convey their shared feelings: frustration, fear, confusion—but most of all, solidarity.

The crowd of detainees was so large that Finn managed to briefly evade the attention of officers and record a voice note. "I'm being arrested," he told a close friend, assuming correctly that the message would reach a wider group, including his parents and Theresa. Finn stuffed the phone in the front pocket of his jeans and raised his hands high up as officers shook canisters of pepper spray at them.

Police bused the mass to two nearby police stations after holding them for several hours on the streets. Finn was brought to North Point Police Station, plastic zip-tie cuffs fastened around his wrists. Tommy didn't know Finn and had left before the march was declared illegal, but was watching the scenes on a live stream on his phone. He was reminded of his own forty-eight-hour detention at the same location.

Finn again found moments away from officers' attention amid the chaos in the police station. His hands fastened behind his back, he managed to extract the phone from his jeans pocket. Finn opened LINE and typed a message to Theresa. "Love you," he wrote in English. It was all he could manage with limited mobility. Her response came immediately, as short as his: "Fuck you." Police confiscated his phone minutes later.

————

FINN WAS HELD FOR TWO DAYS. HE HAD A CRIPPLING HEADACHE BUT NO access to medication. He asked to use the bathroom but was made to wait for four hours. The hundreds detained with him had to share a single phone to call their lawyer or family members. Many waited more than twelve hours to get legal representation. A prison cell, Finn thought, would have been a luxury, an upgrade from the uncomfortable plastic chair without shelter in the Hong Kong winter night. The conditions were compounded by Theresa's message, playing repeatedly in his head, taunting him: "Fuck you," "Fuck you," "Fuck you." It was torture.

Officers kept Finn's phone even when they released him on bail. It joined the repository of devices police had amassed since June, thousands of iPhones in all hues alongside Android models and laptops. Authorities were intent on cracking these devices, hoping that information within would reveal the leadership of the movement. They refused to believe that the protests were decentralized. Finn wondered what officers would think when they read Theresa's last message.

Finn knew it was foolish to stay while the police had his device, which could reveal who he was beyond just his legal name, Lau Cho-dik, and see him arrested for crimes committed under the pseudonym "iwantlaamcau." He scrambled to get a flight out of Hong Kong. To avoid being tracked, Finn booked a one-way ticket from Hong Kong to Singapore, then another on to London.

In Singapore, Finn had a layover of about ten hours. It felt comforting to be back in the city-state where he and Theresa had started their married life together. He wandered around their old neighborhood and ate at their favorite twenty-four-hour South Indian restaurant, dousing bits of flaky flatbread in a thick chicken curry. He spent a few hours at

Changi Airport, where he watched a giant new indoor waterfall cascade from the ceiling, surrounded by terraced jungle foliage. He knew that Theresa would have loved it. She would have taken lots of photos for her Instagram account. Nothing about her upset him in that moment; Finn just wanted her beside him. Finn and Theresa had a tradition where they wrote cards to each on special occasions—birthdays, anniversaries. Because he was in Hong Kong, his Christmas card was late. He picked up a few and spent the flight home filling them with his fastidiously neat handwriting. There was so much he wanted to say that he needed two full cards.

Finn walked through the door to their Richmond studio and took a deep breath. He wasn't sure what to expect. He could see Theresa inside, unpacking her suitcase from her trip. The apartment was small enough that she would have heard him enter, but she acted like she hadn't. Apprehensive, Finn asked for a hug. She eventually turned around and embraced her husband, a limp exchange devoid of warmth. Finn asked if they could sleep in the same bed, as they had when they were first married. She briefly considered before replying: "Just for tonight." Her response left him more uneasy than comforted. Finn decided he was better off on the couch. He left the Christmas cards on the counter and told Theresa to read them.

The next night, Theresa suggested they have dinner together at one of Finn's favorite restaurants, Nandos, on the Richmond riverside. Theresa was sweet, thoughtful, and attentive, for once looking directly at Finn and not her cell phone. She told him to order whatever he wanted. They talked for hours. Finn felt like the woman he married was finally sitting in front of him again. It was the happiest he had been in months. He believed they had somehow managed to salvage the relationship.

Back at their apartment a few hours later, Finn found Theresa at the dining table, holding the cards he had written. He took a seat next to her and realized she was crying. Theresa passed Finn her phone. "Please," she said, "read what I've written." He felt a wave of nausea come over him and the headache return.

The note started with platitudes like "You deserve better," and "I'm so sorry it has come to this." Finn skimmed quickly, looking for a particular word. He found it staring back at him: "divorce." For only the third time in his life, he began to sob.

———

FINN HADN'T EVEN STARTED PROCESSING THERESA'S WORDS WHEN HE heard a few days later through an intermediary that Jimmy Lai, the brash *Apple Daily* founder, wanted to meet with him—face-to-face, in Taiwan. Lai would be there amid a fiery electoral campaign that would determine Taiwan's new leader. Lai was not part of Stand with Hong Kong but knew one of Finn's colleagues. The millionaire pro-democracy supporter had also helped front payments for the newspaper advertisements while Stand with Hong Kong waited for the crowd-funding deposits to clear. Lai now wanted to ask Finn something in person. To ease the inconvenience, he offered a business-class ticket.

Finn agreed to go. Sinking into the plush leather seat, he tried to ascertain which development over the past two weeks was most surreal: his arrest, his impending divorce, or that he was about to meet Jimmy Lai, an outsized figure of the pro-democracy movement.

His arrival in Taipei coincided with some of the final rallies of the reelection campaign of the incumbent Taiwanese president, Tsai Ing-wen. Tsai was heading off contender Han Kuo-yu, whose Kuomintang Party advocated for closer ties between Taiwan and China. Finn was surprised to hear how central the lesson of his city was to Tsai's campaign message—that Beijing couldn't be trusted and that Taiwan could never accept Hong Kong's arrangement as a pathway to reunification. "Young people in Hong Kong have used their lives and shed their blood and tears to show us that 'one country, two systems' is not feasible," Tsai said at a rally the night before the elections. "Tomorrow, it is the young people of Taiwan's turn to show Hong Kong that the values of democracy and freedom overcome all difficulties."[1]

Finn and Lai met on January 11, the same day Taiwan went to the polls. Lai, perhaps not coincidentally, had picked this day to ask about another upcoming election—that of the Hong Kong Legislative Council, planned for that September. "Would you want to run?" Lai asked. He explained that this was a different kind of vote—one that would build off everything, including the "laam caau" and "do not split" philosophies, to deliver a resounding victory for the pro-democracy camp. It would start with an unofficial primary election to ensure that the strongest candidates were put forward.

Finn didn't have to think hard before declining the offer. Even though Theresa's reaction was no longer a consideration, he wasn't ready to be an activist with a public profile. Finn still saw himself as a chartered surveyor. He had never harbored ambitions in politics and wasn't prepared for his identity to be known outside his inner circle. However, he could get behind the idea of the primary and told Lai as much.

The meeting ended within a few hours. Once Finn declined Lai's offer to run, there wasn't much else to discuss. He headed out to Tsai's party headquarters in Taipei right after she declared a landslide win against her pro-Beijing challenger. The young Taiwanese around him were jubilant, but it felt to Finn like a shared victory. Hong Kong's sacrifices helped deliver Tsai's victory. Beijing, by strangling Hong Kong, had lost Taiwan for generations to come. The now hollow nature of "one country, two systems" had shifted the geopolitical landscape. Finn believed then that his pain—the headaches, the depression, the divorce—was worth it. This was what it meant to burn together.

―――――

THE ELECTION STRATEGY LAI DESCRIBED TO FINN IN TAIWAN WAS THE LATest idea from an old rabblerouser: Benny Tai, the law professor who'd helped launch the Umbrella Movement with Reverend Chu Yiu-ming and Chan Kin-man in 2014. Tai was barely out of jail for his role in those protests when he floated a plan more radical than anything he'd previously suggested. This time, it wasn't occupation that would be the "most lethal weapon." Hong Kong's very constitution, Tai suggested, could be manipulated to bring about genuine "laam caau," moving the philosophy from the streets to governance. To do this, the pro-democracy camp needed a simple majority within the Legislative Council, a goal so far unachievable under a system rigged in Beijing's favor. The historic win at the District Council elections that past November suggested that it might now be within reach. Tai often gave his election strategies outlandish names that sounded like military call signs—Operation ThunderGo, Project Storm. This time, he opted for simplicity: "35 Plus," denoting the number of elected seats needed for the plan to become reality.

Tai distilled the ideas in an article published in April 2020 in Lai's *Apple Daily*, titled "Ten Steps to Real Mutual Destruction—The Inevitable Fate of Hong Kong." A legislative majority, he argued, could be achieved only if a primary vote was held first. It was the only way to achieve cohesion in the fractious pro-democracy camp and overcome ballot splitting, directing supporters to vote more strategically. Once the camp had a majority of the members in the Legislative Council, they would use their roles to monkey-wrench the system: reject funding proposals, vote down the budget. This could prompt a constitutional crisis that would force the resignation of the chief executive. Tai wanted to weaponize Beijing's system against itself.

Holding a public primary election was a novel idea in Hong Kong politics. Tai would have to build the vote from scratch—polling stations, volunteers, a voting system, and election security. Crucially, candidates would need to pledge that they would abide by the results. This meant that current lawmakers running for reelection risked being ousted even before the election but also that a new slate of candidates without affiliations to major parties could now theoretically be elected.

It was a thrilling suggestion that came just as the movement was working out the next step in its fight. Joshua Wong, unbowed by his disqualification after the local elections, wanted to run but knew that an all-male slate of candidates would look bad for his political party. There was one woman who'd impressed him since their trip to the East Coast. He saw her brand, "Sister Stand News," as something he could use, something that would appeal to even the most modest pro-democracy supporter as an encapsulation of what had transpired in the city over the past months. "Lam," he told her, using her nickname, "you'll have the full support of our party, of our resources."

Gwyneth had spent her career analyzing and processing, plagued by what it meant to be something between an observer and a participant. "Thousands of words after another, I dug into the most subtle details, trying to eliminate misunderstandings between different spectrums and camps, and promote the purest exchange of ideas, but the records have never been able to keep up with the evolution of politics," she wrote. "I can only watch. The gap widens day by day." On July 1, 2019, when she captured the girl rushing back into the chamber to save the four protesters, when she saw Brian Leung take off his mask and address the crowd, her beliefs started to crystallize: "Only action can heal the scars of the movement and lead it to a better direction."

Her decision felt surprisingly simple. Gwyneth had been thrust into some of the most decisive moments of the protests. It was her responsibility to feed that into the movement, to use her status to do something more than stand on the sidelines with her phone. Anything else would be a waste. Before then, she hadn't even shouted "Liberate Hong Kong, Revolution of Our Times" once, but now she could declare it proudly, unencumbered by the pretense of objectivity, her voice more powerful because of who the movement had made her.

She was still in Amsterdam, finishing her studies, but told Joshua she was ready. Gwyneth would return to Hong Kong not as a journalist for *Stand News* but as a political candidate. It wasn't just activism or lobbying that appealed to her. Gwyneth wanted to participate in the crescendo that was moving away from the streets into the establishment itself. For too long, pro-democracy lawmakers had been resigned to the part of the "loyal opposition," playing along in the facade without any real power. The "35 Plus" plan was an "impossible agenda," but it was a chance, she said, to "initiate a political crisis."

———

THE PUBLIC WAS ALREADY ON EDGE WHEN THE FIRST CASES OF THE NOVEL coronavirus arrived in Hong Kong in mid-January, where painful memories of the SARS outbreak and the 299 lives it took still lingered nearly twenty years on. The suddenness and randomness of the deaths had terrified residents then, and they still remembered the frontline medical workers who fought the outbreak as heroes. The first public hospital doctor to die during the crisis was buried in Gallant Garden, a cemetery for civil servants and uniformed officers who perished in the line of duty. She was awarded Hong Kong's Gold Medal for Bravery. Many still believed the SARS deaths would have been contained had it not been for China's attempts to hide the outbreak from the rest of the world.

Even as their own government continued to look for cues from Beijing on how to proceed, Hong Kongers in early 2020 responded to the news of this new virus by following their own intuition. Without an official mandate, surgical masks began to appear on more faces outside of protests. The number of commuters on subway trains and buses dropped as people voluntarily stayed home. Residents leaned on each other, not the government, to keep Hong Kong safe.

The protests and the still-developing public-health emergency collided almost immediately, the latter helping to further agitate and compound grievances from the actions. Just after cases were first discovered in Wuhan, people across the political aisle were calling for Carrie Lam to close the border to the mainland. It was an awkward decision. Lam's government had declared the outbreak an "emergency," its highest level of preparedness. Closing the border to the mainland, though, would be snubbing Beijing, admitting that the mainland wasn't able to stop the spread of cases. It was also unclear if Lam had the authority to do so. After the mess she had created in Hong Kong, Lam had little leverage on the mainland. The outbreak underscored Lam's untenable position between her obligations to—and instructions from—Beijing and what her own people saw as necessary for their safety. She stopped short of closing the border fully, shutting some of the checkpoints but leaving others alone, including the airport and the Hong Kong-Zhuhai-Macau bridge she had helped open with Xi Jinping.

As the end of January neared, researchers at the University of Hong Kong presented alarming evidence showing that the number of cases in Wuhan had been severely undercounted. The number reported from Chinese officials was about 2,800 people infected. Based on their modeling, researchers estimated the true figure was closer to 44,000. The virus was spreading much faster than people realized, they said at a quickly arranged press briefing on the university's medical campus, with sustained human-to-human transmission already occurring in major mainland cities. The virus would not be contained to Asia. Those outside of

China who believed they would be untouched by this new virus, like SARS, were wrong. As Gabriel Leung, one of the researchers and a government adviser on the coronavirus, warned, "We have to be prepared that this particular epidemic may be about to become a global epidemic."[2]

Four days later, the World Health Organization said just that, declaring the coronavirus a Public Health Emergency of International Concern. Countries including Singapore began to ban all travelers from the mainland. Lam continued to keep Hong Kong ports open. Even the resistance to this decision was shaped by 2019, led by a new union that emerged during the movement along with dozens of others hoping to change workers rights' advocacy. The Hospital Authority Employees Alliance convinced some eight thousand medical workers to strike. They embarrassed Lam and her government, who soon looked like they were losing control. Household staples like toilet paper and rice disappeared from shelves of grocery stores. Prices of surgical masks skyrocketed. Latex gloves were nowhere to be found.

Lam had made her name as a civil servant with political savvy at the height of the SARS crisis. After precipitating months of political unrest, her reputation was tanking further and trust in her government cratered as this new global pandemic swept through her city. As one Bloomberg columnist put it, the semiautonomous financial hub, once known as a bastion of global trade and capitalism, was showing signs of a failed state.[3]

———

BY FEBRUARY 2020, GWYNETH NO LONGER LIVED ALONE IN AMSTERDAM. The scarcity of student lodging had forced her Belgian friend Sarah Van Meel to move in the previous November. They were in the same friend group with Kathryn back in Denmark, and had continued to the University of Amsterdam together. The room was about 170 square feet, maybe a little smaller. Gwyneth laughed Sarah off when she worried about the intrusion into Gwyneth's privacy. Buy a mattress, wear slippers, and stay, Gwyneth told her.

Gwyneth slept on a single bed and Sarah on an air mattress on the floor (they swapped when Sarah was unwell). There was only one desk, which looked out on a tree, its branches sad and bare in the winter. In those tight confines, Sarah heard all of Gwyneth's sighs, curses, and exclamations. "Oh, fuck," Gwyneth said suddenly one day, looking at her computer screen. She was reading about the coronavirus back in Hong Kong. Sarah, liked most Europeans, figured it was just another virus spreading through Asia. Gwyneth had lived through SARS and knew the gravity of what was unfolding. This was not something that could be isolated.

Winter in Amsterdam tended to put life in slow motion, everyone a little more content to stay in the confines of their homes, struggling with the gray dampness and the early sunsets. But the pandemic—now named COVID-19—put everything in superspeed. Italy became its first major epicenter outside China, the virus ripping through elder-care facilities and overwhelming hospitals. Correspondents turned from their usual fare of Vatican goings-on, migration, and politics to writing about death, disease, and social disruption.[4] The Netherlands recorded its first case on February 27, carried by a man who had traveled to Lombardy, in northern Italy. Cases climbed. By mid-March, cafés, restaurants, coffee shops, and Amsterdam's famed sex clubs were all closed. Universities moved to online only. Gwyneth and Sarah were running out of time, their days together numbered as forces beyond their control shifted their everyday routines and movements.

The two friends were chatting one evening that March in their dorm room. Gwyneth's desk chair was turned to face Sarah, a bottle of beer cradled in her hand. Sarah was on her mattress on the floor, her curly, freshly showered hair wrapped in a towel. The Christmas lights from December were still up, illuminating the mess around them with a multicolored glow. The chaos of their environment mirrored their own minds, but they were content to be with each other. Sarah knew that when Gwyneth drank, she got a little freer with her emotions. She tried to be quiet and to focus on her friend's words. She intuited that Gwyneth had something important to say.

Gwyneth told Sarah of her decision to run in the upcoming election. "You should cherish the human rights you have in your own country," Gwyneth told her, "while we try to fight for them ourselves." She didn't fully convey the gravity of what she had signed on to do—Gwyneth knew, even then, she would likely be jailed. Her mental preparation started from the moment she decided to run. Gwyneth hoped Sarah would know she was trying to say good-bye.

Soon, Gwyneth began hearing rumors that Hong Kong would be closing its borders. University of Amsterdam students from across the Asia-Pacific and other parts of the world were receiving similar messages from their home countries. Everyone was in a mad dash to get home. Sarah helped Gwyneth pack her belongings into two suitcases, grabbing shirts and dresses at random and leaving behind anything superfluous. They received a message from another friend in their crew who wanted to say good-bye before she left for Denmark. They decided to see each other off with one last night biking through Amsterdam—but in style, fully dolled up.

Gwyneth and Sarah picked dresses in their favorite color, blue. Gwyneth's was silk with white flowers, a belt wrapped around its waist. She put on a pair of heeled silver boots. It looked like she was going to a Christmas party. They stopped by the supermarket—restaurants were closed—and bought a quiche. They pedaled through the city, Gwyneth in front of Sarah, her long black hair carried by the wind. Their buoyant laughter and chatter were among the few sounds in the streets that night, emptied by the force of this virus no one fully understood. Gwyneth was so filled with joy, with adrenaline, with purpose. As she pedaled, Gwyneth let herself be free. She knew she wouldn't have many more nights like these.

Gwyneth flew back to Hong Kong. The city closed its borders to all outside travelers—including those from the mainland—a day later, on March 25. Hong Kong would remain largely closed for the next two years with harsh quarantine restrictions, cut off from the world as Beijing began to inflict its revenge on the city that dared stand up to it.

———

THE WORLD HEALTH ORGANIZATION REPORTED IN EARLY APRIL THAT over a million cases of COVID-19 had been confirmed worldwide, marking a more than tenfold increase in less than a month. Protests had effectively ended in Hong Kong. The health risk was too acute and harder to avoid than even arrest.

With the city quietened, governments distracted, and the world in chaos, Beijing pushed ahead in complete secrecy on a completely different type of threat to Hong Kong. The American and British intelligence community had picked up only some rumors with scant details. Beijing's loyalists in Hong Kong were mostly in the dark. The public knew nothing at all. It was only by the first week of May that the broad contours of this plan started to trickle out beyond a small circle in Beijing. The law, by then, was all but inked.

The Chinese government, diplomats and pro-Beijing stalwarts in Hong Kong heard, had prepared a new security law tailored for the city. Rather than revive Article 23, a local legislative process, Beijing had taken a drastically different approach. It had drafted the laws unilaterally and would now pass them on its own—overriding Hong Kong's legal and political system. China no longer trusted Hong Kong's people or its government—if it ever had. To execute the crackdown it wanted, Beijing took matters into its own hands.

The laws sought to criminalize four broadly worded offenses: secession, subversion, terrorism, and collusion with foreign powers. There were obvious contradictions between how Beijing interpreted these supposed crimes and how Hong Kong's existing common-law system did. Common-law courts largely exist in democracies with multiparty systems; Beijing's definitions of *subversion* and *secession* were meant to preserve the one-party state and outlaw challenges to it. How the crimes would be tried and the sentences they would carry were also completely up to Beijing. Even the pro-Beijing loyalists in Hong Kong who were let in on what was happening raised their concerns. Jasper Tsang, the former Legislative Council president who had advised Carrie Lam at the start of the protests, was worried that Chinese experts rather than Hong Kong ones were writing the law. "I can assure you," a mainland official representing the drafting committee told him, "we have taken into consideration all common law characteristics."[5]

The pretense of due process started on May 18, during the 18th Session of the Standing Committee of the 13th National People's Congress.

Delegates listened to and reviewed the "Report of the State Council on the Maintenance of National Security in the Hong Kong Special Administrative Region." A state media readout followed, saying there were "obvious deficiencies" in Hong Kong law enforcement that needed to be addressed.[6] Several days later, on May 21, Hong Kong outlet *HK01* broke the news. The short article was titled "The Four Main Points of the 'Hong Kong Version of the National Security Law' Are Exposed!"

It was one of the exceptionally rare situations when an exclamation point in the headline was appropriate. Until then, there was still a vague hope that dialogue could provide a path to reconciliation. There was still clamor for an investigation into police behavior and into the whole extradition crisis. Not only would there be no concessions; Hong Kong—and the world—now knew that Beijing had been working quietly for months, rewriting the rules that governed the city. It laid bare how negligible Hong Kong's autonomy was. The National People's Congress said the law would be in place by July 1, the twenty-third anniversary of the transfer of sovereignty from Britain to China.

The shock was followed by a solemn recognition of what was unfolding. Dennis Kwok, a lawyer and pro-democracy lawmaker who was among the first to raise the alarm on the extradition law, processed the implications as he was speaking to us that day: "I think it means the end of 'one country, two systems.' When the world is not watching [because of COVID], they are killing Hong Kong, killing 'one country, two systems,' and using social distancing rules to keep people from coming out to protest. This is the most devastating thing to happen to Hong Kong since the handover."

———

THERESA MOVED OUT OF THE RICHMOND STUDIO SHE'D SHARED WITH FINN in May 2020. It felt to Finn like he finally had some relief. Since pandemic restrictions had kicked in at the end of March, Finn worked from home, navigating the small space with his soon-to-be ex-wife. Theresa drank constantly, finishing bottles of wine on her own. Sometimes she burst into tears. There was no separation in the studio except for one makeshift divider. He struggled to concentrate on his job. He couldn't focus on Stand with Hong Kong's lobbying work either, which was growing more important with news of the impending national security law. Finn's escape was taking long walks by the Thames. These solo rambles were one of the few activities still permitted under the COVID-19 protocols. Even after Theresa moved out, Finn continued his ritual, walking down the river past a string of restaurants, including the Nandos where they had eaten their last meal together, down toward gardens that were dark and silent in the winter night.

Around 9 p.m. on June 2, Finn was out on one of his strolls, a white windbreaker protecting him from the still-cold air. He believed that three men were tailing him, but he couldn't be sure. In the darkness he could only guess that they were of South Asian descent. They wore hoodies and surgical masks, obscuring their identities. Finn was about to pass a lamppost and thought he would stop under its fluorescent yellow light, just to see if the men might stop, too. As he did, they rushed him, pummeling his head and face. They said nothing but continued the beating wordlessly. There were no racial slurs, no demands to hand over his cell phone or wallet.

Finn didn't know how long the assault went on. He soon fell unconscious, lying bloodied by the river in London's safest borough.[7] When he came to, he realized the men had left all his possessions intact. Finn called an ambulance himself. He sat bruised on a hospital bed as a doctor stitched a wound above his left eye and glued other cuts and lacerations on his face. He had never felt so alone.

CHAPTER 16

EXILE OR JAIL

RAIN POURED DOWN ON THE BLACK WATCH REGIMENT ON THE NIGHT of June 30, 1997, as the British soldiers, with solemn precision, marched in Hong Kong for a final time. The pipe band blared "Auld Lang Syne" as the gathered crowd, among them a drenched Prince Charles and Chris Patten, Hong Kong's last British governor, sang the lyrics to the melancholic Scottish folk song. The city was setting off, a TV commentator remarked over the live broadcast, on "a slow march into a new order." It took twenty-three years for the full weight of that new order to arrive, and it came with the enactment of the national security law at 11 p.m. on June 30, 2020.

Details of the law, formally titled the Law of the People's Republic of China on Safeguarding National Security in the Hong Kong Special Administrative Region, were far worse than even the most pessimistic of observers predicted. The four crimes—secession, subversion, terrorism, and collusion with foreign forces—encapsulated actions that were essentially speech crimes. Under the definition of "terrorism" was "dangerous activities" that could "jeopardize public health, safety or security." "Subversion" could include "undermining the performance" of the Hong Kong government. Provoking "hatred" against the government was a crime, too. It was illegal not only to commit these acts but also merely to incite someone to engage in them. Those found guilty could be sentenced to life in prison.

To investigate these crimes, police now had new and expansive powers, able to conduct covert surveillance and freeze assets without a court order. The law created a new authority, the Committee for Safe-guarding National Security, a body that did not have to disclose its work and was not subject to judicial review. Chinese security agents were allowed to operate officially in the territory for the first time. Judges who handled national security law cases were to be handpicked by the chief executive. Defendants were no longer guaranteed a trial by jury. Bail would not be granted unless defendants could prove they would not "continue to commit acts endangering national security," a negative that was, of course, nearly impossible to guarantee. The law included a section asserting extraterritorial jurisdiction, meaning that people could fall afoul of it anywhere in the world.

The law threw in an especially perverse twist. The 2019 movement started when Carrie Lam tried to introduce a bill that would allow extraditions to the mainland. Protesters stopped her effort—their sole tangible victory. The national security law, which they were now power-less to resist, declared that suspects in the most serious cases could be sent to mainland China to face trial.

Any ambiguity was not a flaw, but part of the design. With the law so unclear, "real effects of intimidation and deterrence" could be deliv-ered, said Stanley Ng, a pro-Beijing lawmaker who also sat on China's National People's Congress. "You can see the rebels in Hong Kong are now in turmoil," he said triumphantly.[1]

The first attempts at erasure were voluntary, acts of self-preservation in a terrified city. Facebook pages of pro-democracy and pro-independence parties immediately filled up with posts announcing their disbandment. Those that didn't fold saw their ranks deplete in real time as droves of people fled from even the most innocuous of civic groups. Workers at cafés sympathetic to the pro-democracy cause scrubbed their walls of protest memorabilia and signs of support for the movement. "Liberate Hong Kong" flags, sticky notes scribbled with messages of solidarity, and tchotchkes collected through the more than half a year of protests were piled into trash cans along with half-eaten burgers and empty cups of bub-ble tea. On social media, activists living abroad posted that they were sev-ering ties with the friends and organizations in Hong Kong, hoping that would minimize the risk of association. Bookstores paid attention to any unfamiliar customers, worried they could be undercover agents. The Hong Kong Alliance, whose existence since 1989 underscored Hong Kong's relative freedoms, raced to digitize a museum commemorating June 4, afraid that the artifacts would soon be seized.

Immediately, the new law changed the nature of protest. Authorities for the first time in seventeen years banned the traditional July 1 march organized by the Civil Human Rights Front. A few from the Front took to the streets anyway, and thousands joined, but the showing was fractured and directionless. Small groups gathered, shouted a few slogans, and hurled some abuse at police while hiding around corners. The desperate, disheartened energy reflected a city reeling from a blow it had yet to fully absorb. Police moved swiftly to end the unauthorized demonstration, chasing people as water-cannon trucks raced up and down the streets. Among the 370 arrested were at least 10 suspected of violating the new law. A twenty-four-year-old cook who crashed a motorcycle into police officers while flying a flag with the slogan "Liberate Hong Kong, Revolution of Our Times" became the first person formally charged for a national security violation. Before the law, his crimes would have likely been a traffic offense, perhaps with an additional charge of assaulting police officers. Instead, he faced charges of terrorism and inciting secession. Authorities later ruled that uttering the slogan itself was subversive.

Hong Kong began its time under Chinese sovereignty asking for the very modest demand of a democratic system, as promised in the Basic Law. That door closed, definitively, in 2014. Still, Hong Kong held on to its other liberties—freedom of the press, speech, protests, and the rule of law—even as Beijing tightened its grip. The national security law put an end to all of it. The law prompted a wholesale reengineering that would soon creep into all sectors of society, from kindergarten classrooms to corporate boardrooms. The law was crafted to extinguish not just political opposition but also the bonds among Hong Kong people themselves, now encouraged to report each other for playing songs like the protest anthem "Glory to Hong Kong."

Zhang Xiaoming, the deputy director of the Hong Kong and Macao Affairs Office, described it as Hong Kong's "birthday present," the law a "guardian spirit" that would protect the city. Beijing wasn't just mocking Hong Kong. They were telling Britain, their co-signatory to the 1984 Sino-British Joint Declaration, and the United States that the Chinese no longer needed to abide by any promises they made from a position of weakness. China was saying that it was a world power on its own terms, unafraid of repercussions. A journalist asked Zhang if China was worried about retaliation from the US, including sanctions. "Of course we're not afraid," he replied. "The era when the Chinese cared what others thought and looked up to others is in the past, never to return."[2]

———

INTERNATIONAL CONDEMNATION WAS SWIFT AND IMMEDIATE. A SPECIAL weight was attached to the words of British prime minister Boris Johnson, who declared that China was in "clear and serious breach" of the Joint Declaration. Johnson's government went a step further. On July 1, 2020, Johnson announced that his government would upgrade the British National (Overseas)—BN(O)—status to offer a pathway to residency in the United Kingdom. Some 3 million Hong Kongers were immediately eligible. The scheme would later be extended to cover 5.4 million people—72 percent of the territory.

It was a stunning decision for an immigration-skeptical government that had just left the European Union. From the time that Thatcher and Deng met at the Great Hall of the People in 1982, Hong Kong people wanted an insurance option if things were to go wrong. The British government had resisted any mass immigration scheme over the following three decades, unmoving during the negotiations over the Joint Declaration, after the Tiananmen massacre, and in the lead-up to the handover. That finally began to shift at the height of the unrest in 2019, when Chinese troops were gathering across the border in Shenzhen and publicizing their movements. It seemed possible that Chinese tanks might drive into Hong Kong, a doomsday scenario that the British government seriously began preparing for. One of the most feasible options was using the BN(O) passports to create a pathway for fleeing refugees. The crushing of Hong Kong ended up coming from a law, not tanks, but the

British government was prepared and quickly put its proposal to work. It met negligible opposition, including from the British public.

The BN(O) offer was a possible answer to a dilemma that had been gnawing at the heart of Hong Kongers since the news of national security law first broke in May: stay or flee. Those arrested like Tommy had started making plans long before, frightened enough by the existing laws against rioting, arson, and their other crimes. The severity of the new law prompted tens of thousands more to contemplate a life in exile. Middle-class parents started putting their apartments up for sale, unwilling to put their children through the brainwashing that China could now impose on the young. Lawyers who had spent their careers defending political prisoners looked to convert their qualifications. A new generation was running from the Chinese Communist Party.

One group faced this choice more urgently than most: the cadre of high-profile activists explicitly targeted by China since the earliest days of the pro-democracy movement. They were Beijing's most despised and knew the law was coming for them. Jimmy Lai, in his seventies, and Benny Tai, fifty-five, chose to stay. Reverend Chu was shocked by the implications of the law but figured he was at low risk because he had kept out of the spotlight in 2019. "I am a civilian," he said, "no longer a special person." These men had lived full lives. Others, far younger, weren't as stoic. One in particular, just shy of his twenty-fourth birthday, badly wanted another path.

Joshua Wong had curated an image over the past decade as a fearless international dissident, debating chief executives, climbing over fences, screaming into bullhorns, holding court with foreign ministers and senators. When the national security law passed, however, he was terrified. Joshua did not have his passport, which had been confiscated by the police while they investigated charges against him. Some of his colleagues, including Nathan Law, who rose to prominence alongside him during the Umbrella Movement, had their travel documents in hand and flew out of Hong Kong ahead of the security law. Somehow, no one stopped them. Joshua couldn't leave and feared he was a sitting duck.

If his iconic status was a vulnerability, Joshua reasoned, it might also be his ticket out. He wanted to take his chances not with Britain but with the most powerful democracy in the world. By the end of June, Joshua had a plan, formulated largely by his closest friend in Washington. Their idea was not without precedent. The astrophysicist Fang Lizhi, after all, had lived in the US embassy in Beijing in 1989 after the June 4 massacre until his negotiated release to Britain. Fang died a free man in Arizona, not in a Chinese jail. More recently, in 2012, Chen Guangcheng, a Chinese civil-rights activist, was also given refuge at the US embassy in Beijing. Then-secretary of state Hillary Clinton helped negotiate his release to New York City, what she called "an example of American values in practice."[3] Chen was now a US citizen.

Joshua believed he would be the latest activist to be granted such exceptional protection by the United States of America.

––––––––––

A FULL MONTH BEFORE THE NATIONAL SECURITY LAW WENT INTO EFFECT, Washington was planning a seismic recalibration of its relationship with Hong Kong. On May 23, 2020, Secretary of State Mike Pompeo convened his closest advisers over a secure phone line. It was the start of the Memorial Day long weekend, but the matter at hand was more pressing than any weekend barbecue. Pompeo was preparing to announce that America no longer considered Hong Kong sufficiently autonomous to warrant separate treatment under US law. Beijing had already announced it would be unilaterally passing the new national security law. Pompeo wanted policy suggestions on what should follow the announcement.

The advisers threw out a long list of punishments: sanctions against top officials, scrapping training programs with the Hong Kong police, stopping the export of defense equipment to Hong Kong. There were also ideas on how to help Hong Kong people. Miles Yu, Pompeo's China policy adviser, suggested that Washington create a special immigration pathway for Hong Kong residents.[4] Britain had the BN(O); Canada and Australia were also working on lifeboat schemes. It wasn't just charity. These schemes, some later suggested, could be tailored to Hong Kong residents with university degrees or with specialized skills. Western countries stood to benefit from fleeing Hong Kong talent.

The policy recommendations reached President Trump, whose National Security Council had also prepared three lists of options in response to China's strangling of Hong Kong. Matt Pottinger and Ivan Kanapathy at the NSC described it as a "Goldilocks and the Three Bears"–style menu, after the fairy tale: one a list of "hot" options (a maximalist approach), the second "cold," and the last an in-between. The "hot" list included measures that had nothing to do with Hong Kong but were things that China hawks could push now that Beijing's violations were laid bare. One of those was closing the Chinese consulate in Houston, where Washington claimed that spies were aiding in espionage and the theft of scientific research. Another was the suggestion that Secretary of Health and Human Services Alex Azar visit Taipei. It would reaffirm American support for Tsai's government after Beijing froze Taiwan out of the World Health Organization during the pandemic, and would mark the highest-level visit there since 1979.

Trump picked the "hot" menu. He even liked the immigration idea. "President Trump said, 'Why don't we just open up? Why don't we just let a huge portion of people from Hong Kong move to the US?' And I loved it," Pottinger said. "You know, my view was just transplant the whole damn city and make a new Hong Kong in America. [Trump] was like, 'they're going to be industrious, they'll be great. They'll make great Americans.'"[5]

In the unpredictable Trump administration, though, it was often the ones who had the last word with the president who influenced his thinking. Stephen Miller, Trump's far-right political adviser, stopped the immigration scheme from going further. He was "very persuasive," said Yu.

The White House and the State Department moved forward on most of the other measures but shied away from financial sanctions that some were calling for on banks such as HSBC and Standard Chartered or from probing connections like the one between the Shanghai and Hong Kong stock exchanges. Those were scuttled by the Treasury Department, protective of US banks and Wall Street interests.

Some in the administration were unhappy with the conservative nature of bureaucrats and those who held back further punishment. They believed that China needed to see the US response to the Hong Kong crackdown as a lesson. One senior official put it this way: "So now we're going to be thinking about Taiwan. We need to be thinking about the next steps and saying, look, if you're going to kill the golden goose, we're not going to put the goose on fucking life support. We're going to let you kill the goose. And then we're also going to make sure that you regret it."

Pompeo announced on May 27, 2020, that Hong Kong no longer had a high degree of autonomy. Trump followed Pompeo's announcement with a speech at the Rose Garden in which he promised to eliminate "policy exemptions that give Hong Kong different and special treatment."[6] Underscoring the point about unpredictability, Trump then went off script and vowed to cut America's ties with the World Health Organization. The WHO announcement completely overshadowed the Hong Kong news.

———————

JOSHUA AND HIS ALLIES WEREN'T PRIVY TO THE BACK-AND-FORTH IN Washington over their city. What they saw was a president who claimed to be tough on China and bipartisan concern for the fate of Hong Kong. Joshua had entrusted Jeffrey Ngo, the history PhD candidate at George-town University, to help him execute his asylum bid.[7] Joshua and Jeffrey had operated since 2016 as a team, relentlessly knocking on doors and making inroads with American lawmakers, winning over those who were ignorant about the goings-on in Hong Kong. Their Rolodex boasted an impressive list of staffers and officials in the administration. What was all that for, if not this precise situation?

The first part of Joshua's asylum bid quickly failed. He had arranged a meeting with officers at the US consulate in Hong Kong, hoping they would let him into the consulate premises. Instead, on June 30, they met across the road at the St. John's Building, a twenty-two-story structure where the US government had rented offices. It did not offer the protection of a diplomatic compound. It was up to Jeffrey to negotiate a different outcome.

With Hong Kong so prominently on Washington's agenda over the past year, Jeffrey knew a range of staffers on the Hill. He settled for the policy adviser to Josh Hawley of Missouri, reasoning that the ultra-Trumpian senator who had visited Hong Kong in October 2019 could snag the president's ear. Responding at 1 a.m., Hawley's staffer promised to pass the message on to his boss, but nothing changed. There was still no offer of protection by the time the security law passed. Instead, diplomats were speaking legalese, explaining that one couldn't technically apply for asylum from outside the United States itself. Joshua and Jeffrey knew that. They were asking for the same pathway to safe haven that had been granted to Fang Lizhi and Chen Guangcheng.

Jeffrey had another card to play. For years, he'd worked behind the scenes for Joshua, writing op-eds in his name and even editing his tweets. Jeffrey knew he had to be concise this time and unambiguous. He drafted an email addressed to Pompeo himself, signed by Joshua: "I hereby formally request political asylum and seek protection from the U.S. government. . . . I request U.S. protection so that I may apply for asylum, including as necessary traveling to the US for the purpose of applying for asylum. This is in no way an easy decision but I hope you will kindly consider this request."

The email landed in the inbox of Mary Kissel just after noon on July 1 in Washington. Kissel knew Joshua and Jeffrey personally. More than a decade earlier, she had worked at the *Wall Street Journal Asia* in Hong Kong, where she rose from a foreign correspondent to the editor of its right-leaning editorial page. She moved back to the *Journal*'s headquarters in New York and was among the most vocal critics of China's human-rights record on the newspaper's editorial board. The Harvard graduate's consistent hawkishness on China—advocating for the Uyghurs, for Hong Kong's democracy movement, for closer US-Taiwan ties—earned her a place in the administration in 2018 on the seventh floor of the State Department, where the secretary and his immediate staff sat on the south side of the building with windows looking out to the Lincoln Memorial and Potomac River. Kissel printed off the email and handed it to the office of David Hale, the highest-ranking foreign-service officer at State. Joshua's request was now as close as it could get to the highest levels of the US government.

Within the next forty-eight hours, Pompeo summoned his half-dozen or so top officials to discuss Joshua's request. They immediately ruled out sheltering him at the consulate. Plans were already underway to close the Chinese consulate in Houston, part of the package of actions that Trump chose in May. The announcement was coming soon, and Beijing would likely retaliate. If Joshua was hiding in the Hong Kong consulate, it was possible—unlikely, but possible—that Beijing could close the whole place. Instead of negotiating for Joshua's release by trading him for an existing Chinese citizen held in the US, Beijing could also simply do what it did when Canada held Huawei executive Meng Wanzhou on an extradition request from the US: snatch American citizens off the streets of Hong Kong and hold them in arbitrary detention, like they did with the two Michaels.

The only route that seemed viable was covertly extracting Joshua out of Hong Kong in an undercover operation. This had been done before. Within the National Security Council, there was someone with expertise in such missions, successfully getting dissidents out of places including Myanmar and North Korea. If they were to extract Joshua, it would be over water. Hong Kong's unforgiving geography—sharing a land border only with mainland China—meant that the most realistic way to evade authorities and escape was by boat, sailing across the Taiwan Strait or down south toward the Philippines. There was concern that any activity like that could bump into the Chinese Coast Guard or be uncovered long before Joshua even made it to the pier. With American involvement, it could snowball into an international incident.

Options dwindled. Soon the officials came to believe that they had none left. Pompeo with his advisers decided that there was no way to facilitate Joshua's protection. At the heart of the decision was realpolitik. It was not 1989. Some believed that Washington had little to offer Beijing, unlike in the wake of Tiananmen, when China was desperate for international legitimacy after massacring its own people. On the issue of Joshua's fate, there was unanimity among Pompeo; his assistant secretary for the East Asia and Pacific bureau, David Stilwell; and the US consul-general in Hong Kong, Hanscom Smith. Joshua, they decided, would not be let into the consulate or extracted from Hong Kong.

"You've got national interest and personal interest, and some ways you try to find a balance between the two," said one senior official involved in the process. "In the end, you know, on the 7th floor of the State Department, national interest won out."

It wasn't a unanimous decision within the Washington foreign-policy establishment. The National Security Council said in a memo to State that Joshua should be protected, but "respected" that it was State's decision. Matt Pottinger at the NSC explained that although he was upset, aware that the rejection of Joshua's asylum bid would mean his eventual detention in Hong Kong, he deferred to Pompeo and his department because he believed they had a "fuller picture" of the facts.[8] Yet the decision continued to sit uncomfortably with Pottinger's deputy, Ivan Kanapathy, who then had the Hong Kong portfolio at NSC. Kanapathy believed that saying no to Joshua because of fear of what Beijing would do in response was the "absolute wrong" reason. "If you can't do what I think a lot of people would say is the right thing [because] you're afraid they're going to do the wrong thing, then you've already lost," he said.[9]

Realpolitik aside, the process was badly handled. No one told Joshua or Jeffrey that a decision had been made. With false hope that there was still a chance to save his friend, Jeffrey redoubled his efforts over the next months. "At the back of my mind, I just thought it would somehow work," he said.[10] In July, Jeffrey turned to more contacts on the Hill, broadening his ask to Senator Marco Rubio and Speaker of the House Nancy Pelosi. Both had worked with Joshua since he was a teen. This bipartisan group agreed that Joshua was worthy of protection and made their own calls to State in those weeks, pushing it at the "highest levels," according to one Hill staffer. In late July, Nathan Law, Joshua's close ally who had slipped away to London just before the national security law passed, met with Pompeo in private. He raised Joshua's plight directly and emotionally to Pompeo. Nothing changed. It was a "slow-motion tragedy that wasn't particularly climactic," one State Department official involved said. "It dragged, and it lingered, and then the inevitable happened."

It set a precedent for further requests. Later that year, four Hong Kong activists seeking asylum at the consulate—including an American citizen and the teenager shot on October 1, 2019—were turned away.[11] The four went into hiding, spending more than a year being secretly moved between safe houses. Sometimes they were stashed inside large boxes. They appeared to be preparing their escape to Taiwan when police apprehended them in July 2022 and perp-walked them in front of the media. Their disheveled hair reached past their thin shoulders.

———

GWYNETH LAUNCHED HER STREET CAMPAIGN FOR THE PRIMARY ELECTION in June, just weeks before the national security law went into effect. She wore a black jumpsuit, picked to portray herself as tough rather than girlish. Her campaign team forced her to wear some makeup, which she hated.[12] They urged her to slow down when she spoke and to stay on topic. Gwyneth didn't really bother with specifics on policy. Her platform was simply that of resistance. It was about using "our life, our future and even our flesh" to fight the state's totalitarianism, she said. "We have to be willing to sacrifice everything for the future of others . . . regardless of the cost." Her campaign slogan encapsulated the message: "In the same breath, we share our fate."

Gwyneth's transition from journalism to politics was not unprecedented. Emily Lau, the reporter who had forcefully questioned Margaret Thatcher at her press conference on the handover agreement, went on to have a lengthy career as a pro-democracy lawmaker. Claudia Mo, who had covered the Tiananmen Square massacre, helped found the liberal Civic Party in 2006 and was running in the same primary as Gwyneth. Yet not everyone was comfortable with her decision. In a long *Stand News* profile, a former colleague described her as "a blunt and vulgar person" who "ate snacks, poured her own water, used foul language, and even applied makeup while being interviewed." He questioned Gwyneth's switch from being a critic of politicians to being one herself. Ultimately, he concluded that Gwyneth had taken "a bungee jump from the moral high ground."

Almost immediately after the national security law passed on July 1, Hong Kong government officials warned that the primary could be in violation of the new law. They offered few specifics. Tai pushed back, pointing out that his scheme rested on provisions in the Basic Law itself. Still, there were divisions among those who had signed up as candidates. Some moderate pro-democracy politicians were getting cold feet. Gwyneth's attitude, in summary, was "fuck it."[13] She preferred strategy over emotion, focused on making sure that people turned up to vote and were not afraid. Joshua, despite his ongoing efforts to seek asylum, continued to stand in the primary too. It provided a cover of normalcy.

The night before the vote, Joshua officially endorsed Gwyneth. He posted a photo of himself with Gwyneth and Brian Leung, taken the previous September outside the headquarters of the *Washington Post*. "Journalists," he wrote, "have faced no less risks than any other politician on the streets where bullets fly around like rain." Gwyneth's interviews had given her an "even deeper understanding and awareness of how to walk with the protesters, compared with many allies, including me."

On July 11, 2020, the primary went ahead. Polling stations were not libraries or community centers, but average businesses in support of the democracy movement that had offered up their space. Voters in the Kennedy Town neighborhood cast their ballots in My Secret, a cramped lingerie shop displaying flesh-tone bras with oversized padded cups.[14] The quirks did not undercut the legitimacy of the exercise in the eyes of many. Over that day and the next, 610,000 people voted in 90 degree heat. They guessed that their chosen candidates would probably be disqualified from running but turned up anyway. It was a way to telegraph to the world that Hong Kong had not given up on its dream of democracy. The primary was among the last forms of expression the city had.

Both Joshua and Gwyneth won the most votes in their respective constituencies. So did Winnie Yu, a nurse who was the face of the medical workers' strike aimed at closing the border with the mainland when COVID hit, and Jimmy Sham, the convenor of the Civil Human Rights Front. They were inextricably tied to the movement and were picked to continue its momentum.

The condemnation came quickly, more specific this time. China's Liaison Office in Hong Kong said the vote was "illegal" and would undermine the upcoming Legislative Council elections. The Hong Kong and Macao Affairs Office in Beijing added to the chorus. The pro-democracy groups "are actually trying to use the so-called 'public opinion' to harm the country and disrupt Hong Kong, turning Hong Kong into a base for 'color revolution,' infiltration and subversion activities against the country," it said. The whole primary, Beijing suggested, could be in violation of the new law.[15]

The winning candidates responded with the same bravado they always showed publicly. Days after the election, Joshua, Gwyneth, and fourteen other contenders held a press conference. All were under thirty except Eddie Chu, the localist lawmaker who had taken on Carrie Lam at Queen's Pier. They were dressed in black T-shirts, their faces obscured by surgical masks because of the pandemic. In front of a row of microphones, they promised to uphold Tai's strategy and vote down the budget if elected. After they finished answering reporters, the sixteen candidates put their arms around one another and huddled close, posing for photos as news cameras clicked. They smiled behind their masks, wrinkles creasing around their eyes. Each was instantly recognizable. Some had been fighting for democracy since their teens; others were relative newcomers like Gwyneth. It was a portrait of defiance.

The group believed that they knew what was coming—disqualification, marginalization from politics. Only a few were prepared for how far Beijing would go.

On July 30, Joshua, Gwyneth, and nine others were disqualified from running in the Legislative Council elections. Gwyneth celebrated. She and her fellow candidates wanted to prove that the system and its promise of fairness were hollow, and they had succeeded. Joshua was still outwardly defiant. Beijing, he said, had shown "blatant disregard" for the will of Hong Kongers. "Our resistance will continue on and we hope the world can stand with us in the upcoming uphill battle," he wrote on Twitter. Inside, he was growing more fearful. Since the primary election, convoys had followed him around Hong Kong. He spent every night anticipating a knock at the door.[16] In disqualifying him, election officials said that Joshua had been "soliciting interference by foreign governments in the internal affairs" of the PRC. It mirrored language in the national security law exactly. Jeffrey tried again to lobby for Washington to grant Joshua asylum.

Joshua was arrested in September 2020 when he reported to a police station for another case against him, charged with "illegal assembly." He was released on bail but pled guilty in late November to organizing an unauthorized assembly and inciting others to take part. Joshua was immediately remanded to custody and remained in detention as cases piled up against him.

CHAPTER 17

THE FIVE

A s far as Tommy's family and most of his friends were con-cerned, he had vanished. He didn't come home, dropped off social media, and stopped responding to calls and messages. Tommy had told his friends months earlier that one day he might just disappear. "Don't be surprised," he told them. "I am planning to run away." It was hard to tell if he was joking until the days stretched to weeks, then months. His friends would ask each other how many days it had been since they'd heard from Tommy, but all had lost count. His lawyer was waiting for him at the courthouse for a scheduled hearing in June, but he never showed up. The judge issued an immediate warrant for his arrest. A new charge of skipping bail was added to his case file.

Tommy had reason to take extreme precautions. His first escape attempt, the one he had started planning before the new year, had failed. He showed up to a dock in Sai Kung late one February night and boarded a small speedboat driven by a man he didn't know, crammed in with two other protesters. The network of "parents" he knew only from Telegram had put him in touch with a boatman who'd take the three fugitives out of Hong Kong waters and transfer them onto a larger fishing vessel. That more seaworthy boat would take them across the Taiwan Strait. The "parents" asked for $2,600 for the journey, promising that others had successfully made it out this way. As they set off, the wind picked up, threatening to blow the speedboat off course. The conditions unsettled the pilot, who was already starting to rethink what he'd signed up for. About twenty minutes into the trip, lights coming from another vessel broke through the pitch-black darkness. It was enough to spook him, and he turned back. The four went on their separate ways and never saw one another again. The middleman who helped organize the escape attempt returned Tommy's money, then disappeared off Telegram.

This network of anonymous intermediaries was all that was available to Tommy. He did not have ties to Washington. Unlike Operation Yellowbird, there were no movie stars or pop idols willing to openly use their star power to assist demonstrators. The triads still had resources to facilitate rescues, but they had shown clear loyalties to the mainland when they came together for the Yuen Long attacks on July 21. Tommy had a friend with triad connections but didn't trust the organized-crime syndicates not to sell him out. Tommy was dejected but had to keep trying.

In May, someone on Telegram told Tommy that he knew some others who, like him, were desperate to escape. He would group them together and pool their money so they could buy their own boat. They could then sail themselves to Taiwan. Only the fugitives would be on the boat, no one to throw them off course. To address the obvious issue—none of them knew how to operate a boat—they'd find a sympathetic boat captain who'd help them learn. Navigators would map out their path on an app.

It sounded feasible. Tommy was in. To ensure that nothing threw off the plan, he went underground. Tommy took up residence in a friend's film studio, among the computers, speakers, and cameras. He subsisted on a diet of instant noodles and cheap takeout delivered by the only friend who knew his whereabouts. He drifted from one day to the next. Tommy was beset with nightmares. His sleeplessness worsened after he popped downstairs one day to have a cigarette, and a police car pulled up to the curb. Tommy was sure he'd been caught, but the officer who got out walked right past.

Tommy tried to prepare for his journey like any Gen-Z kid would. He turned to YouTube, watching hours of boating videos. Two weeks before they were set to depart, a middleman reached out to Tommy, telling him to show up for a practice session. For the first time he met two of the four men who would join him on the escape, but he couldn't see their faces behind the surgical masks. One introduced himself to Tommy as "Zebra." The other, a little younger, said that his name was Aaron. Zebra would be the one to pilot the boat, the trainer said. He didn't have any experience but knew how to drive a car, which was better than nothing.

Before he disappeared, Tommy had one last Sunday lunch with his grandmother. It was his favorite ritual. The television was on for some background noise, turned to a news channel. The anchors were discussing how people were planning to leave Hong Kong, fearing a reign of terror once the national security law came into place. The cue was enough for his "mama." She—once again—launched into the story of how she came to Hong Kong as a Freedom Swimmer, escaping with a group of people she didn't know, making the journey although she couldn't swim. Tommy stayed silent. He didn't want to tell her what he was planning. He listened more intently than usual, haunted by the parallel. He was grateful for every moment he could steal in her company, knowing that it might be the last.

————

EARLY ON JULY 17, THE FIVE MEN ARRIVED ONE BY ONE AT TAO TAO Restaurant, a shabby dining establishment popular with fishermen and day trippers, steps from the Hebe Haven harbor on the Sai Kung peninsula. With knowing nods and whispered questions, they established their identities. The five gathered around a large round table sitting on green plastic stools, acting as though they knew one another well and were excited to reconnect for a day out on the water. They had brought plenty of props: a cooler, some fishing gear. On that warm Friday morning, they seemed to blend in with other groups venturing out for a weekend adventure.

Inside, Tommy was panicking. He wolfed down a Spam-and-egg sandwich between soft white bread, not knowing when his next meal might be. He feared that he, or one of these strangers, had been tailed by the police. In the scenario that replayed in his head, officers were watching them from afar as they prepared to leave. Then, as they were ready to cast off, confident that they were safe, the officers would swarm in and haul them all to jail.

After they finished eating, the five walked down to the water. The cerulean sky stretched out to the horizon. Tommy carefully stepped off the dock into the boat, a rigid inflatable Zodiac. He hoped, again, that his feet were touching Hong Kong for the last time. The motor clamored to life, giving off a plume of gasoline fumes. Zebra began to steer, slipping the boat past ferries laden with tourists headed to the nearby beaches and moored yachts. As they exited the harbor, Zebra opened up the throttle. A ribbon of white wake churned behind them as they accelerated. The hull of the boat smacked the waves. All five were silent. It was too loud to talk over the motor and wind.

The four tried their best to manage the jobs that Zebra assigned them. Tommy was tasked with keeping the supplies in order. Aaron, who was eighteen, had purchased six life jackets for the journey. He didn't know how to swim, so he needed to be extra cautious. If things went wrong, he planned to wear two.

Tommy struggled to handle his assignment. As the boat flew across the waves, the wind picked up the life jackets and sent them fluttering into the water. Only two remained. Tommy tried to sprawl across the bags the men had packed, but it was a useless effort given the heaving of the boat. Plastic bags full of chips, their rations for the trip, went flying overboard, as did one of Tommy's green sneakers. They didn't want to risk turning back. The boat charged ahead, leaving a trail of flotsam bobbing in the water. Tommy had failed in his one and only responsibility. "It wasn't easy, man!" he argued. Then he shrugged it off. There were more important things than the chips.

They raced across the South China Sea, scanning ahead for authorities. They passed two men fishing in a rowboat. Then massive tanker ships from Singapore and China, stacked with containers that made their own boat look minuscule. Far from shore, the sightings became more infrequent. Ray, a quiet and unassuming IT worker, swore that he saw a Chinese Navy vessel, but it was a false alarm. Out in the open ocean there was no respite from the sun. Their skin baked. The collective nervousness morphed into agitation. Zebra's insistence on keeping the boat at top speed grated on the others, who were enduring the constant pounding of the waves. One of the men shouted to slow down while he tried to peel the identifying numbers off the bow of the boat. Zebra refused. The other man screamed at Zebra: "I'm going to beat you up after this!"

To navigate, they used their phone GPS and an app. Tommy found it difficult to keep track of how many hours had passed. In his mind he pictured his friends in the boat with him instead of the strangers. Tommy was sore from repeatedly slamming against the hull as the sun began to move low in the sky and slip behind the horizon, casting golden streaks across the water. Ray pulled out his phone to capture it on video. In the darkness, the GPS showed they had made it out of Chinese waters and into Taiwanese territory. The frustrations from earlier dissipated. Zebra finally eased back on the engine. Only then did Tommy begin to relax. The first leg of their implausible, extraordinarily risky plan had worked. They dialed up a contact in Taiwan on a satellite phone and told them to alert the coast guard to a boat in need of assistance. In a spontaneous, puerile celebration, the group grabbed Tommy's remaining shoe. They took turns peeing on it, then kicked it overboard.

The five shared the few snacks that Tommy had managed to keep inside the boat. For the first time, they told one another a bit about themselves: why they had decided to take such a drastic measure to escape home. They realized they had been at the same protests and rallies. Maybe they had even helped one another on the streets. Floating far from the glow of Hong Kong, the night appeared to this group of city dwellers almost unimaginably dark. The five lay on their backs and looked up at the stars. Tommy thought it was one of the most beautiful sights he had ever witnessed.

A Taiwanese Coast Guard vessel carrying about ten sailors arrived around two hours later. At first, Zebra kept up the charade that they were fishing. Others, fearful they would appear suspicious, quickly interjected. "We are protesters from Hong Kong," Aaron blurted out in Mandarin. "We are seeking asylum." More like a motorist who needed help with a flat tire than wanted men on the run, Aaron had a quick question. Would they mind, he asked the sailors, if they brought them onshore and allowed them to make a few calls? The puzzled officers conferred among themselves. Their radios crackled as they discussed what to do. Some were on edge. Tommy was not. He sat on the back of the boat, munching on spicy potato chips. We are in Taiwan now, he thought to himself; *there is no way they are going to push us back to Hong Kong.*

Tommy was right. He was unaware, though, that this was only the beginning of their long endeavor.

The coast guard latched the Hong Kongers' boat to their vessel and began towing them toward land. When the five clambered ashore, they realized that the sailors were carrying automatic weapons. The place where they had landed seemed largely abandoned, dark except for some large floodlights. This, their map indicated, was Pratas Island. Located some two hundred miles southeast of Hong Kong, the island is a tiny, U-shaped rock controlled by Taipei but situated closer to China than to Taiwan. China insisted that Pratas was theirs. Beijing's aggressive moves in the South China Sea and belligerence toward Taiwan had made Pratas Island a geopolitical flashpoint of global importance. The only inhabitants were Taiwanese Coast Guard officials and Marines on the front line of a simmering conflict.[1] Now it also included the five Hong Kong protesters.

A military official peppered the men with questions: "Why did you come here? Are you spies?" They mostly told the truth, choosing to omit only certain details to avoid implicating those who had helped them back in Hong Kong. Satisfied with their answers, the official sent the five to board a small boat that ferried them out toward a hulking military ship that sat offshore. As they pulled up alongside the ship, the smaller craft pitched and rolled. One by one, the men grabbed tightly onto a ladder and scurried up it to the massive deck. The unexpected additions to the manifest were sent to the medical bay and told to stay put. It was disorienting. They had no idea where they were going. There were no portholes to look out of to try to position themselves. A sailor wordlessly delivered them meals, then disappeared again. They were allowed to keep their phones, so they listened to music and smoked. Some took selfies. The ship sailed for hours. Tommy ate three times before it finally came to a stop.

When the ship eventually docked, the five descended a massive staircase onto the dock below, tired, raggedy, and sunburned. Dozens of law-enforcement and military officials watched the Hong Kong castaways as they disembarked. Tommy walked gingerly across the asphalt. He was still barefoot, his shoes drifting hundreds of miles away.

————

IT SEEMED AT FIRST THAT TOMMY AND THE REST OF THE FIVE HAD SLIPPED into Taiwan largely unnoticed. China's first overseas targets after the national security law went into place were not the five, but six prominent activists whose locations abroad had long been publicized. Chinese state media reported on July 31 that these six activists were "wanted" for violating the new law and that warrants had been issued for their arrest.

The six included Nathan Law, who had by then made his residence in Britain public. Others were young Hong Kong activists who promoted independence. Among them was an American citizen: forty-two-year-old Samuel Chu, Reverend Chu Yiu-ming's son and the managing director of the Hong Kong Democracy Council. He was the first foreign national targeted under the new law.

The Hong Kong Police refused to confirm the existence of this wanted list, but the broadcast over Chinese state media was clearly designed as a warning. At first, it seemed almost anticlimactic, more an indication of the limits of Beijing's reach. These "warrants" had limited practical purpose, given that the six dissidents were in the UK, the US, and Germany—all countries that had scrapped their extradition agreements with Hong Kong when the security law came into force. Beijing had made clear that the six were now exiles, but they knew that before the warrants. The only pressure that authorities could exert was on their families still in Hong Kong.

Reverend Chu and Dorothy were in Hong Kong when they heard their son was now wanted. Samuel had not consulted his father before he took up the Hong Kong Democracy Council role. The two lived many miles away from each other, Samuel's life largely between Los Angeles and Washington and Chu's in Hong Kong. The reverend was completely removed from his son's work. Chu worried for Samuel but not for himself. When friends told him to consider leaving Hong Kong, Chu wondered if it was really necessary. No police officers were knocking on his door; no one was threatening him. He and Dorothy decided to wait and see.

In the early hours of August 10, officers arrived at the home of Jimmy Lai, the founder of *Apple Daily*, and his sons, taking them away in cuffs. They arrested four other media executives at Next Digital, the parent company of *Apple Daily*. More than two hundred officers entered the media outlet's headquarters, rifling through reporters' desks and papers. The reporters dutifully live streamed the whole affair, capturing the dissolution of the free press in Hong Kong in the name of security. By the end of the operation, authorities seized twenty-five boxes of material. The newspaper defiantly kept running.

In total, ten people were arrested in a twelve-hour police operation that day—the first in Hong Kong to be specifically generated by the law. Jimmy Lai was an obvious target, but it was hard to make sense of the collection of names or piece together why the others had been rounded up. Some were famous, such as Agnes Chow, the twenty-three-year-old activist who was one of the faces of the Umbrella Movement alongside Joshua Wong and Nathan Law. Others seemed random. Who, for example, was twenty-nine-year-old Andy Li Yu-hin? Most reporters could link him only to an independent election-observation mission that had sent volunteers to the District Council elections that past November.

An article from *Ta Kung Pao* hinted at his significance to Beijing. Andy Li, the paper revealed on China's behalf, was a member of the "laamcau team." It was now better known by its English name, Stand with Hong Kong. Its work in lobbying foreign governments under the "laam caau" philosophy, the paper said, citing "legal experts," has "clearly violated the national security law."[2]

Within twenty-four hours, a different pro-Beijing media outlet identified another overseas activist wanted for violations of the security law. He was a twenty-six-year-old man who had moved to the United Kingdom in January 2019. The paper provided his name as Lau Cho-dik, leaving out his English name: Finn.

The revelation that two of their main leaders had been identified threw the rest of Stand with Hong Kong into a tailspin of anger and distress. Some screamed at Andy for not being careful enough with his security protocols, given his background in IT. All of his electronic devices were now in possession of the police, who had the additional resources of the National Security Department and mainland Chinese officials to help them bypass encryption. They were livid, believing that Andy had put their identities and those of their families back in Hong Kong at risk. Finn urged them to stay calm, reminding them it was Andy—not them—who was now facing charges that carried up to life in jail. Soon, Finn's teammates started to attack him, too. They said Finn's issues with depression and anxiety were clouding his judgment, as was his divorce.

Out on bail, Andy panicked. His passport had been confiscated by police. He began desperately searching for ways to leave. Some seemed outlandish, particularly an offer from someone who claimed he had contacts within the French military who could send a plane to Hong Kong for this covert mission. In the end, Andy, through "a friend of a friend of a friend," found someone arranging a boat from Hong Kong to Taiwan. The boat would be full of fugitives, no middlemen, who wanted to escape the city. Andy would be the twelfth addition to the boat. He sent his last good-byes, including to Finn. He thanked him for everything and set off before dawn from the Po Toi O pier on August 23, 2020, heading for Taiwan.

It was the exact way that Tommy and the others successfully escaped. But hours after it departed, the boat was intercepted by the Chinese Coast Guard. A Hong Kong government aircraft was circling the water above.[3] Andy Li and the others were captured and held, incommunicado, on the mainland in Shenzhen. They became known as the "Hong Kong 12." Finn prayed that he could trust his friend not to give up the rest of the group.

Days after the twelve were seized, *Ta Kung Pao* came forward with yet another "scoop."[4] The paper, in what it claimed was an investigative report, said that it had discovered the "power behind the throne," the man who had helped "more than 200 rioters" flee from Hong Kong to

Taiwan. That large-scale smuggling operation, *Ta Kung Pao* said, was the handiwork of a Taiwanese pastor with connections to Lee Teng-hui, the former president who helped usher democracy into Taiwan. It was not clear, the paper said, which "underground organization" the Taiwanese pastor had worked with in Hong Kong to pull this off. All they knew was that his concern for the protesters was sparked by a fellow pastor: Reverend Chu Yiu-ming.

Once again, it was a newspaper that alerted Chu to something that would alter the course of his life. Chu had played no role in the boat escapes and didn't even know the Taiwanese pastor; he was "irrelevant" in all of this. Perhaps authorities were just fishing, given his role in Operation Yellowbird transporting Chinese dissidents into Hong Kong. Dorothy was worried—had been since Samuel was named for violating the security law—but knew that Chu hoped to stay.

A few days after the article was published, Dorothy heard Chu having a conversation in the bathroom. It was a friend calling from the United States. He emerged, harried. "Let's leave, let's leave," he said suddenly. Dorothy's friends had said the same to her. Yet they were not prepared. Chu had paid for his involvement in the 2014 protests with a trial and suspended sentence, then stepped back and tried to live a quieter life. What more was left to give?

Chu and Dorothy packed only two suitcases. "My heart is hollow," Chu said to Dorothy as they were at the airport, waiting for an evening flight to the US. She felt helpless. Their whole family, Chu said, "had to accept an old man in exile and a wanted son." A friend offered them a place to stay for a few months. The day Chu arrived, he fell sick with acute gastroenteritis. The friend they were staying with tested positive for COVID, so Chu and Dorothy had to move. Now almost eighty years old, Chu was living the same "wandering life" as in his youth. "I wonder," Chu thought, "whether I will end up dying in a foreign country."

———

WHATEVER TOMMY AND HIS FOUR BOAT MATES PICTURED WHEN THEY thought of life in Taiwan, it was not this. When they disembarked from the ship, they were brought to the fourth floor of a dormitory belonging to the Coast Guard Administration's Offshore Flotilla 5. The low-rise building was in the Qianjin District of Kaohsiung City, an industrial area on the edge of a harbor filled with working boats. Taiwanese authorities almost immediately confiscated their phones, worried they would take to social media to announce what they had done. The five had little leverage against their heavily armed chaperones, who also denied them access to computers. They were left confined to their rooms for most of the day, let out only for about an hour to smoke and play table tennis in a common area. In their rooms, they passed time watching TVs that carried commercials during the day and local comedy programs at night. They couldn't understand the context of the jokes. It was hard to deviate from the monotony. Guards were stationed outside their rooms overnight.

Tommy read copies of Lai's *Apple Daily* newspaper, also distributed in Taiwan. He clipped articles he found interesting. He tried to draw as well, sketching what he saw on TV. He drew a baseball player winding up to deliver a pitch, capturing the explosive energy of the moment although he had no idea how the sport was played. The rhythm of the pencil against paper provided some small solace. He hated the food and that dinner came so early. He was hungry by the time he went to bed. Tommy hated being kept alone, isolated in his room like a prisoner in solitary confinement. The five asked their guards to let them pair up for their sanity. Tommy ended up bunking with Ray, who had found an escape listening to his iPod until it, too, was confiscated over security fears.

The Taiwanese government had anticipated a rush of immigration from Hong Kong, just not in the manner Tommy and the others arrived. Even before the passage of the security law, the government in Taipei had approached US officials with concerns that they wouldn't be able to handle such an influx. Taiwan did not have a system set up to process asylum claims. The self-governing island had also long been suspicious about Chinese agents slipping into Taiwan, and accordingly had tight immigration controls. President Tsai had won a resounding victory in large part because of what was happening in Hong Kong, but there were limitations to her government's generosity. There were worries about the arrival of Hong Kongers who could create an "unwelcome political complication with their already fraught relationship with the mainland," according to a former US official based in Taipei. The five were even more problematic than typical immigrants, given their lack of documents and the way in which they'd arrived. Taiwan wanted to get them moved on as soon as possible.

As the days stretched on, it was clear to Tommy and the others that they were not welcome. Many of the guards treated them rudely. They were given five pairs of paper disposable underwear that wore down to sheer mesh. Eventually, they stopped wearing them altogether. They got proper boxers only when an older guard took pity on them and purchased some. They suffered from anxiety-fueled insomnia. A doctor arrived and doled out antidepressants.

The question now was who would take them, and when. Taiwanese officials interviewed the young men on August 25. Andy Li, as well as his eleven boat mates, had just been captured, and word of the five's arrival was made public in an article published by a pro-Beijing newspaper. Taiwanese officials, perhaps spooked by the sudden developments, told the men that they could not stay. The information further deflated Tommy. He thought for certain that Taiwan would understand what Hong Kongers were facing and be willing to help. As a backup, Tommy said he would go to the United States. He couldn't really articulate why. He had an idealized version of America in mind, a country where he thought he could be anyone he wanted, pursue anything he wanted—be free.

The Taiwanese government approached the State Department about the five. This time, the answer came a little easier. Unlike Joshua's asylum bid, the issue didn't even rise to the upper ranks of the bureaucracy. With the five already out of Hong Kong, the US was happy to vet them and then take them in under a rarely used humanitarian parole pathway.

Within a few months, diplomats at the American Institute in Taiwan, the quasi-embassy that represented US interests, were deployed to speak to the five and provide updates on their case. Tommy and the others took a liking to one, a young Asian American political officer whom they found friendly and relatable. The diplomat didn't tell them that officials at the State Department were screening the men and their backgrounds. He probably knew more about them than he was letting on, including details on what they had done on the front lines and how they were arrested. The diplomats tried to assure the restless young men. Your case is already inside Washington, he told them during one early visit, so don't worry.

Impatient and with too much free time, the five started scheming. If someone else knew they were there, maybe they would be willing to help them get out. Their first plan to attract attention was the product of watching too many movies. They wrote messages explaining their situation on small pieces on paper, then froze them in water. When they went to play their daily table tennis games, they surreptitiously tossed the ice out the window. The hope was that the cubes would melt and the messages would be found by the old men who fished nearby each day. If any of the fishermen did find their soggy cries for help, they didn't do anything. The five remained stuck, caught in political purgatory with no foreseeable end.

Tommy and the youngest of the five, Aaron, decided to push a little further. It was now September 2020. They had been waiting months for a resolution. If Taiwan was not going to set them free, they decided, they were going to fight for freedom for themselves. Someone would surely be sympathetic. They just had to get their message out.

The two first began probing the dormitory defenses by changing up their footwear. They ditched their usual flip-flops for sneakers when they went out for their social time. (Tommy had finally been given a new pair.) None of the Taiwanese officials guarding them took notice. So they wore them the next day as well. Planning their escape was a bit like being back in Hong Kong on a nightly protest mission. They had teammates again, working toward a common goal, strategizing and dividing tasks.

"How's your day?" the guard asked Tommy and Aaron on September 19. "Everything good, you need anything?" They were fine, they replied. As soon as the man had passed, they pushed open the door to the stairwell and raced down the steps. They slammed through the exit door into a courtyard, then slowed to a walk to try to appear as if out for a casual stroll. They looked over their shoulders. No one had given chase. Step by step, the two got closer to the road.

Suddenly, a guard's voice boomed behind them. "What are you guys doing?" he shouted. Tommy and Aaron bolted. The two sprinted down the street into a seafood restaurant. Aaron was carrying a note that explained that there were five Hong Kongers held in the nearby facility who needed help. He stuffed it in the hands of a bewildered worker before he and Tommy dashed out back to the street.

Aaron and Tommy saw a taxi drive by and frantically started giving chase. When they caught up to it, the two, winded from the running, flung the door open and climbed in. Just then, a hand roughly grabbed Aaron's head from behind. The escape was over. Tommy tried to draw away the officers who had caught up with them by running around the car in circles. He looked ridiculous, like a child on a playground trying to avoid being caught during a game of tag. Curious pedestrians nearby who saw the ongoing commotion took out their cameras to film and take pictures. "Delete those!" an officer shouted at them. This was a matter of national security, he warned. "Delete them now!" Officials brought the two back inside and sent them to their rooms. Upstairs, they found their other three companions laughing. They had taken bets on how long it would be before Aaron and Tommy were caught and returned.

The two didn't think they had failed. They made it out of the dormitory, so, technically, they had escaped. They were just caught afterward. They were not punished, either, and had secured a small victory for the group. The next day, instead of the usual bland congee and fatty pork on rice they were used to, they were served bags of burgers from a nearby outlet of Dain Dain, a popular Taiwanese fast-food chain. Maybe the guards finally realized they were miserable. It provided a little bit of a morale boost.

The escape underscored to the State Department and Taiwanese officials that they had to move faster to avoid another incident. The next month, the State Department reached out to a potential sponsor for the five who could help resettle them, find them homes, and facilitate their entry into the United States. They contacted the Hong Kong Democracy

Council's managing director, Samuel Chu. He seemed to know more about such a process than even the diplomats. After all, Samuel had spent his childhood roaming around safe houses on the fringes of Hong Kong, hearing his father have parallel conversations with displaced, frightened young refugees. As far as State was concerned, Samuel ticked all the boxes. He was about to join the family business of dissident resettlement.

CHAPTER 18

DISAPPEARANCES

W E WOKE UP BEFORE DAWN ON JANUARY 6, 2021, TO A CHAOTIC string of messages on our social media feeds. Posts were spreading from Facebook to Twitter, then among WhatsApp and Signal groups for journalists, detailing arrest after arrest in Hong Kong. Some of the posts had videos attached. One showed a pro-democracy lawmaker opening the door of his apartment to find half a dozen police officers in navy-blue windbreakers demanding to be let inside. "You allegedly violated the national security law and committed a crime of subverting state power," one sternly told him through his security gate. He opened the door to let in the stream of officers, who, after searching his home, locked him in handcuffs and led him away. The speed at which new names were appearing made it difficult to track. It was one of the many mornings we'd spend scrambling to take stock of what was unfolding, stunned at the scale and the implications. The crackdown on Hong Kong was accelerating.

By afternoon, police had arrested fifty-three people—Benny Tai, former pro-democracy lawmakers, activists, trade unionists, and an octogenarian American lawyer who hobbled from his office, a walking stick in hand, surrounded by officers. Gwyneth Ho was among them, taken from her parents' home in Yuen Long. Two more, Joshua Wong and an outspoken radio DJ, were approached by officers while in jail and told they were under arrest and facing new charges. Joshua was already serving a 13.5-month prison sentence. More than a thousand officers were deployed for this special operation. They searched seventy-six locations, including Joshua's home and the offices of a public-opinion research institute, and froze tens of thousands of dollars in funds.[1] Those who still had their passports had them confiscated by police, removing the option of exile. It was a sweep befitting a criminal enterprise, something that a triad or a gambling ring might have experienced. Their alleged crime, though, was a little more questionable. All were arrested for their participation in the pro-democracy primaries back in July 2020: Tai's "35 Plus" scheme. Forty-seven were arrested as candidates and six, including Tai, as organizers. Never mind that some of the candidates were later disqualified. Never mind that the Legislative Council election itself had been postponed, authorities conveniently citing COVID as the excuse. As far as the police and the government were concerned, the group now stood accused of a "vicious" and premeditated plan that aimed to sink Hong Kong into an "abyss from which there is no return."

"This is severe, and we will prosecute accordingly," John Lee, the ascendant secretary for security, said in a press conference.[2] He, not Carrie Lam, was at the forefront of the dark public messaging around the case.

In one fell swoop, the police had arrested almost every prominent opposition voice in Hong Kong, from the moderate to the radical, from the ones who pushed the "redline" of independence to the ones who stayed firmly within the rulebook of the Basic Law. Observers and reporters short on word count tended to describe those arrested as part of the city's pro-democracy movement. While true, it flattened them and their ideology. They were some of the champions of Hong Kong's progressive values: noted gay-rights activists, pioneering labor leaders, feminists, medical workers, and the city's first ethnic-minority social worker, all caught in a dragnet deployed to stifle democratic development and pluralistic politics. It marked the most dramatic onslaught in Chinese president Xi Jinping's transformation of Hong Kong into a city gripped by fear under authoritarian rule.

———

SINCE LATE DECEMBER 2020, A TUTOR HAD VISITED TOMMY AND THE other four men in the Taiwanese dorm, helping them brush up on their English. She brought a stack of a worksheets that described Boston. They learned about landmarks like Faneuil Hall and Bunker Hill, and learned how to ride the MBTA. The lessons were rudimentary, but the men took it as a hopeful sign that they might be heading out soon. They started seeing doctors for medical checkups. The days were dragging on in this limbo when Tommy realized it was December 31, 2020. He had now been held in the military facility in Taiwan for six months. Emotionally and physically, he was so far away from the beaches of Sai Kung. He yearned to laugh and drink, to talk about stupid shit with his friends, to be unburdened of his emotions. Inspired by one of the other five, Tommy decided to shave his head and rid himself of the permed curly locks that defined him, in anticipation of the new year. He sat silently listening to the hum of the razor, watching the black hair fall in ringlets around him.

On January 13, 2021, they packed up their few belongings. The five piled into a car that drove them north from Kaohsiung to Taipei, almost the entire length of Taiwan. It was the first time Tommy had been out of the compound since his and Aaron's foiled dash to freedom months earlier. The others hadn't left at all. They peered out the windows, looking at the changing scenery across the island that they thought would be their refuge. The car stopped only for them to use the restroom.

Like Tommy, some in the group didn't have passports. Even with travel documents, they had not formally entered Taiwan and couldn't go through immigration like regular passengers. In the largely deserted Taoyuan International Airport, still quiet because of COVID travel restrictions, they were ushered past the immigration checks and brought into a special area of the terminal. The lack of usual airport procedures gave them the feeling of being a group of VIPs. Officials from the Mainland Affairs Council, the Taiwanese government division that handled relations with mainland China and Hong Kong, were gathered at the gate to see them off. Each of the five received a red envelope containing $2,000. Taiwanese officials had also quietly collected $100,000 in donations for them. The government didn't want to be seen as having anything to do with it, nor did the US State Department. Instead, the money was handed over to Samuel Chu's Hong Kong Democracy Council, leaving it to the group to distribute the funds. Both governments continued to maintain deniability. The American Institute in Taiwan declined multiple interview requests. A spokesperson for Taiwan's Mainland Affairs Council replied to a two-page list of questions from us with just two lines: "The spokesperson's office expresses gratitude for the efforts made by various sectors which have assisted Hong Kong people. There is no other relevant explanation." A spokeswoman later nervously told us that the case was "very sensitive" and it was "hard to explain" why her department couldn't say anything. The handouts felt like hush money.

As the five boarded the plane, officials handed them back their phones for the first time since July 2020. Once airborne, they badgered Zebra to use his credit card so they could purchase in-flight WiFi. They wanted desperately to reconnect with the world. Turning on their phones for the first time, freshly powered up, came with a rush of joy. After scrolling through Instagram, Tommy spent the hours in the air running over and over in his head what he would say when he got the chance to call his family. He practiced a few casual quips and rehearsed some jokes that might make them laugh. Nothing too serious—that wouldn't be his style. He felt guilty that he had disappeared without telling them, but he told himself there was no other way. He thought about how much they had worried about him, not knowing where he had gone or what had happened. A lighthearted hello would provide some comedic relief. Maybe a "What's up?" Tommy called his family just after he landed in New York. When his mother answered, the lines he prepared stuck in his throat. Tommy broke down crying before he could speak.

After they arrived at John F. Kennedy Airport, volunteers drove the five to a house in Virginia, an Airbnb. Tommy snapped a picture of himself and posted it on his Snapchat that first night in the US. His account had been inactive for nearly a year. Prudence and others who saw the alert thought that the account must have been hacked and were unsure about opening the post. When they did, it was unmistakably Tommy, still with his odd sense of humor. In the picture he was in bed, resting on a pillow propped up against the headboard, scowling slightly. He had

a blue blanket pulled up to his chin. A cream-colored knit beanie covered his shaved head. Across the post, Tommy had written "gd night."

Prudence rushed to call Tommy, wanting confirmation from his voice
that it was really him. They spoke for hours. He sounded so casual ("Oh,
I just got on a boat to Taiwan, and now I'm here! Easy!") until he admitted he was imagining her and their other friends with him as he sailed
across the Taiwan Strait. It hurt her to contemplate what Tommy had
been through. "Why did he have to suffer so much, all by himself?" she
thought.

———

THOSE ARRESTED UNDER THE NATIONAL SECURITY LAW FOR PARTICIPATING
in the primary were interrogated by police; then all but one were
allowed to return home. They were on borrowed time. At the end of February, all but six and the two already in jail got calls from the police telling them they needed to report to various police stations. They guessed
at the implication of the orders and prepared accordingly. One went to
a tattoo artist to get a Buddhist mantra inked on his forearm. Another
purchased pink-rimmed glasses to replace her contact lenses, left her
two cats with a friend, and swapped sneakers for wool slip-on shoes.
Others sold their furniture. Gwyneth played *The Legend of Zelda*, a Japanese action-adventure game, and tried to unlock all the side quests,
not content with just completing the main game. She was a little numb.
Gwyneth had known from the moment that she decided to run for
office that this would be the eventuality. For the past ten years, she said,
everyone had been declaring "the death of Hong Kong." But "we are
not at the very bottom of hell yet," she said months before her arrest.
"There's still a long way to go."

On February 28, they entered various police stations. Most posted
a final message on their public Facebook accounts. Gwyneth's was
uncharacteristically short. "There's not much time, typing briefly
[here]," she wrote. The post started with a few lines on how best to
translate the word *unapologetic* from English into her native Cantonese.
She came up with a phrase that loosely translated to "neither humble
nor arrogant."

Gwyneth continued: "I have realized that the cost of exile is greater than anything I can bear. So a decision that, to you, looks like a lion choosing the zoo, to me, is a tradeoff I had made after recognizing what I can bear.

"I seek peace of mind more than safety, and the two are sometimes the opposite. I wish you all the best of luck to find your path towards peace of mind, and then press forward."

They were immediately detained. Their case became known as that of the "NSL47," the most sweeping use of the security law since its imposition. Less than two years after a million people had marched on the streets, sparking the biggest protest movement in the city's history, every prominent opposition voice in Hong Kong had been jailed, had fled, or had been silenced. Authorities had said that the national security law was meant to restore calm to Hong Kong. The true intent of the legislation was now apparent: to remove every opposition voice. With the strongest and bravest of Hong Kong in jail, what was left for the rest of the movement? As one of the jailed forty-seven wrote before walking into the police station, "I do not fear my own fate. I only fear that there will be no one to replace me."

———————

THE BAIL HEARINGS FOR THE FORTY-SEVEN DEFENDANTS BEGAN THE NEXT day. They appeared to follow the protocol of any usual court hearing in Hong Kong. Lawyers still referred to the judge as "Your Worship," and the prosecutors presented evidence as though they were genuinely making a case before an impartial magistrate. Yet the spectacle put on full display the rot that had seeped into Hong Kong's once-lauded legal system. Government prosecutors insisted that all forty-seven should be tried together, like a mob. All the defendants were crammed into a courtroom at the West Kowloon Magistrates' Court, turning it chaotic because of the number of lawyers and defendants. It wasn't large enough to hold their families, who were stuck in overflow rooms, watching through a small screen. Journalists had to arrive hours before the proceedings started to get a seat. There was only so much we could report. The details of these hearings operated under an article called

"9P," a holdover from the British that restricted reporting on bail hearings, theoretically to protect the defendant in case of a trial by jury. Defendants pushed back. Their lawyers pointed out that it was almost impossible that such a case would be tried by a jury. But the restrictions held. In a proceeding that used parts of the old system alongside the national security law, the forty-seven were about to be introduced to the perverse meaning of justice in the new Hong Kong. Their resilience, their suffering, and their pleas would happen largely in secret, known only to those in the court.

Gwyneth and others tried to start the hearings with a little bit of lightness. When her mic was switched on and before the hearings officially started, Gwyneth hummed a song from the Cantopop boy band MIRROR. "So say I love you . . . ," she sang, to a mix of laughter and confusion. Some shouted messages of love to their families. They knew they were not alone. Dozens were gathered outside the courts, intermittently screaming protest slogans, hoping that the defendants inside could hear them. Still, as the hours of procedure and back-and-forth between judges and lawyers passed, the group—their ages ranging from twenty-three to sixty-four—grew tired. All but those who were already serving time in prison were wearing the same clothes from the time when they'd walked into the police station. The discomfort grew more intense as the hearings dragged from one day to two, then three, then four. Multiple defendants were taken to the hospital after passing out from exhaustion.

The national security law flipped the presumption of innocence in common-law courts on its head. For the defendants to be granted bail, they had to demonstrate that they would not "continue to commit acts endangering national security." Through their lawyers, they promised to stop speaking to reporters, to quit their political parties, to shut their social media accounts, to never stand for election again— bargaining away their basic freedoms so they could stay close to friends and family for a while longer. Many of the accused recounted stirring stories of hardship and poverty from when they were growing up that had led them to activism and politics, working for a better, more equitable Hong Kong.

At the end of the grueling hearings, some dismissed their lawyers and addressed the court directly. Alvin Yeung of the Civic Party, one of the first to sound an alarm over the extradition bill and a lawyer himself, stood up and gave a statement. His roots, he told the judge, were still in the law. Yeung told the court he believed in the judiciary. He submitted his voting record to show that he was not totally opposed to the government and had in the past agreed with some of his pro-Beijing counterparts in the legislature. Yeung spoke of his mother, a cancer survivor who raised him alone. "I was her pride," he said, crying, "but now I am her biggest worry." Another lawmaker from his party told the judge he had purchased a home on the mainland, implying that he couldn't be entirely opposed to China. The court could keep it and his home in Hong Kong, he said; he would gladly return to public housing in order to gain bail. "I am willing to do anything," he said, "anything to hug my family."

On the last day of the hearings it was Gwyneth's turn to address the court. Identified just as "D33," she stood up and began to speak. She was fine, she said, with conditions that included home detention and curfew, but she would not, under any circumstances, agree to having her freedom of speech curtailed: "I also believe a real, independent court will never ask civilians' freedom of speech in exchange for their freedom." If the court allowed her bail but limited her ability to speak, "I don't want to be a part of this."

The fifty or so hours of proceedings led all the defendants back to the same point. Only fifteen were granted bail, and the government immediately appealed the decision, sending them back into custody pending appeal. It was a sham. Before the court turned off their microphones, one of the defendants shouted, for all to hear: "Hong Kongers, never die!"

A FEW MONTHS AFTER HIS NAME WAS PUBLISHED BY PRO-BEIJING MEDIA, Finn decided it was pointless to keep hiding. He wanted to get some control back over his life, which had spun so far off course in the past sixteen months. Finn propped his phone on a tripod, angled it toward a blank white wall where he'd hung Hong Kong's colonial flag, and began recording. "Greetings," he said. "This is iwantlaamcau, Lau Cho-dik, Finn. Yes, this is actually what I look like." Finn went on to explain his background: an "ordinary guy who loves Hong Kong" and a chartered surveyor, without any connections to political parties when he posted the doctrine that became the ethos of the movement. He tried to be honest about what the movement had cost him. He didn't mention Theresa but said that everything he'd been through had left him with severe depression. Stepping out of the shadow of anonymity, he said, was to show detractors that he had risen above all that and would keep fighting. "It was never our aim to become refugees," he said. "Hong Kongers scattered across the world must demonstrate our unique role and strength in impeding the Chinese Communist Party, creating our own future. . . . May glory be to Hong Kong."

Finn made his public declaration amid bitter argument among members of Stand with Hong Kong (SWHK). Detained on the mainland, Andy Li had told authorities what they wanted to know about the group. People heard screams from the single cell he was held in. His information led to the arrest in Hong Kong of his teammate Waylon Chan, who was charged both for helping Andy escape and under the national security law for his involvement in Finn's group. The other still-anonymous members were livid, blaming Finn for risks to their own safety. Telegram, once a tool for organizing, descended into a platform for gossip. They accused him of being too emotionally wrought to make sensible decisions. Finn tried to come up with a solution, splitting his two teams so one could operate under his name and the other anonymously, behind a PR agency. He said the two could split in half the money crowd-funded for Hong Kong advocacy. It wasn't enough to placate his former teammates, who brought their fight to the public domain that first made them famous: LIHKG. Beijing's crackdown had done more than silence the city. It left the diaspora activists who still had their voices in turmoil, fighting over large sums of money they knew would be impossible to raise again. Even as he spoke of strength in his "coming-out" video, posted to YouTube, dark circles were still visible around Finn's eyes, his cheekbones more gaunt than usual. As grievances hardened, Finn quit

Stand with Hong Kong. The teammates he had started this work with were either in jail or wanted nothing more to do with him.

One of the few people Finn felt he could turn to in those days was Catherine Li, the bubbly young woman he'd met at the double-decker bus protest in London. After that interaction, Finn had recruited her to SWHK, impressed with her ability as an organizer. Catherine was one of the few in the group around the same age as he, so the two became friends. When conflict broke out in the group, Catherine felt like she was caught in between, not exactly happy with how Finn had handled things but also sick of the personal attacks and the weaponization of his mental health. She was embarrassed at how public the infighting had become, displayed on online forums for any Hong Konger to see. The real enemy, she believed, should be the government, not each other. Catherine continued speaking to Finn. In late January, SWHK kicked her out of the group for not explicitly taking sides. She felt like she'd lost the nearest thing she had to a family in this foreign place. She turned to Finn for support, and the two grew closer that winter, helping each other through the isolation of a second COVID lockdown across the UK.

Catherine's twenty-fifth birthday fell that April in 2021. Finn asked what she wanted to do to celebrate. Because he was now recognizable, Catherine suggested they do something more low-key than celebrate in London, perhaps a trip somewhere remote. She suggested going to Hastings, a seaside town on Britain's southeastern coast. On the trip, Finn surprised Catherine with a present: a book titled *Hong Kong Protest Music*. Catherine thought it was the perfect gift, the encapsulation of the two things that drove her and a nod to how they'd met back in June 2019. Catherine was especially touched that Finn supported her aspirations of a career in drama, something she hadn't even told her parents. Finn had goals of his own. He told her he wanted to leave the UK and start afresh, perhaps in Canada or the US. There wasn't much point to staying in London, Finn said. He barely had any friends after the divorce and the collapse of SWHK, only painful memories.

It felt like their friendship had an expiration date. Catherine accepted that and wanted to enjoy the time they had together. In June, she too "came out" as an activist, tired of hiding behind a pseudonym. She did it in style: at the *Top Model* search and fashion competition, in a yellow hard hat strapped with goggles, a respirator around her neck and an umbrella in her hand. *Stand News* interviewed her. Catherine had accepted the risks that came with her decision—ostracism from her family, never being able to return home—so hanging out with Finn was now the least of their concerns. With the COVID lockdown over, the two explored Britain as it came back to life that summer: watching the EuroCup final at a pub in Croydon over pints of beer; traveling to the cathedral city of Ely, where a Hong Kong chef had set up a booth at a weekend market; taking a trip to York. Spending time with Catherine was effortless, Finn thought. Nothing needed to be explained—especially not his love for Hong Kong and his need to keep working for the movement, as thousands more Hong Kongers arrived to the UK daily under the BN(O) passport scheme.

In mid-October, Catherine and Finn were having one last dinner at her apartment. He was due to leave to Canada the next day, where he'd explore the possibility of relocating. At some point that evening, Catherine took out her guitar and played a song for him, one she'd been working on with the composer of "Glory to Hong Kong." Finn watched wordlessly, chin propped on a closed fist. In the months since they'd been spending time together, his headaches had eased. He found himself sleeping better. Some fullness had returned to his cheeks. Finn had made wrong choices for love more than once. Looking at Catherine—bangs framing her soft features, protest artwork hanging on the wall behind her—he knew he would regret leaving her. It felt to Finn like she had saved his life.

Finn returned from Canada in December to spend Christmas with Catherine. He stayed at her apartment. They shared their first kiss soon after. Finn couldn't remember the last time he was this happy. He never moved to Canada. A few months later, the two officially started dating, proudly walking hand in hand as they stood in front of large crowds of Hong Kongers, leading them in chants of "free Hong Kong," promising to never give up on the dream of democracy.

TOMMY COULDN'T TELL IF HIS APARTMENT IN JULY 2021 FELT MUCH BIGGER than the Yuen Long public-housing estate he grew up in because of its size or the absence of clutter. He lived with Ray, his roommate from Taiwan, who spent much of his day in his room working remotely for a sympathetic Hong Kong company. The other three men had scattered. Two went to California and the other to Virginia, where he was living with a group of Hong Kong exiles in an apartment outside of Washington. Tommy and Ray's new home was just off 18th Avenue in Bensonhurst, Queens, where faded red, white, and green Italian flags were slowly being replaced by Chinese signs and shop fronts, the sound of Italian giving way over the years to Cantonese and Fujian-accented Mandarin.

Anyone entering the apartment was first greeted by a sign on the front door that read "No Stupid People." There was a mattress in the living room covered in a light-blue sheet that served as a makeshift sofa, although Tommy and Ray did not like having people over, slightly embarrassed that they "had nothing," in Tommy's words. Inside, a small dresser in the middle of the living room doubled as a dining table. Ray and Tommy had found it on the curb, in near-perfect condition. They were amazed by their luck and they seemed to have plenty of it. Bags stuffed with clothes lined the wall. They were donated from good Samaritans who had heard the extraordinary story about the "boat kids," five young men who had raced across the sea from Hong Kong to Taiwan and were somehow granted asylum in the US. Setting foot on the boat was one of the last decisions in which they had agency. Since then, the confluence of circumstances and events beyond their control, decided by unknown people, landed two of them in Queens.

Under his bed—the frame also scavenged—Tommy kept a green hard-shell suitcase given to him by the government of Taiwan. Like many people whose moves to foreign lands were made of necessity rather than choice, he had collected a stack of important papers: his I-131 form for a US travel document, his I-94 entry record, and other assorted sponsorship documents. They were his way to prove he belonged in the US, but also souvenirs of an improbable situation, physical reminders of a journey that even Tommy himself had difficulty believing at times. There were also the newspaper clippings from *Apple Daily*. Back home in

Hong Kong, the paper, like much else, was now gone, forced to close in June 2021 after police arrested its top editors and froze its assets. Hong Kongers gathered outside the newsroom holding their cell phones aloft with the lights on as the reporters inside the building did the same. A million copies of the final edition were printed. They sold out.

Most important among the scraps and mementos was a torn boarding pass for flight CI12, a China Airlines flight from Taipei to New York that boarded just before 5 p.m. (China Airlines is the flagship carrier of Taiwan.) It was, his friends back home told him, a second chance at life. He agreed, but the transition hadn't been easy. When he had first arrived, he wasn't sure where to go or what to do. He spent some time in Pennsylvania, working at a sandwich shop, and had briefly lived with his uncle, but he eventually returned to New York. He got hooked up with a job serving sweet bubble tea in Manhattan's Chinatown. There was some discussion with sympathetic Hong Kong–born Americans about taking him on at their interior design firm, which would allow him to do some creative work. When he wasn't working, he visited museums, wandering alone among the sculptures and paintings. He watched Netflix to try to learn American jokes as quickly as possible. Everyone in Hong Kong knew him as the humorous one. Tommy wanted to make people laugh again, although he carried so much sadness.

Sometimes, out to dinner or on a date, Tommy felt content and at peace. Then, like a jolt, he'd remember everyone he was missing and what was happening back home, and the sadness returned. When he spoke with his friends still living in the city, they rarely mentioned the protests. Many of his friends wanted to avoid reflecting on what happened and seemed content to return to their lives—shopping trips, hot pot, and gossiping about Cantopop stars. It was as if they had all imagined the demonstrations. He understood. He did it himself sometimes. "Everyone deep down, they know, they just don't want to talk about it," he said. "I don't think that is a better way. But that is the easier way."

One day that summer, Tommy grabbed his skateboard and headed with Ray and some other friends to a skate park near their apartment. The skateboard, too, was a lucky find from the basement beneath their building while they were rummaging through items left behind by previous tenants. His last attempt at skateboarding had left him with a swollen, purple foot, likely a sprained ankle. Dressed in a mandarin-collar linen shirt and beige pants, he was keen to try again. He stood at the top of a concrete ramp, hesitating a bit before dropping in. Within seconds, he fell on his knees, caught himself on his hands. He got up, laughing, picked up the skateboard, and started over.

———

AMONG THE MOST VENGEFUL DISAPPEARANCE OF ALL WAS WHEN THE authorities came for the Hong Kong Alliance, thirty-two years after its founding in 1989. It was just after sunrise on September 8 when Hong Kong police officers began rattling the door at the chambers of Chow Hang-tung, a young Cambridge-educated lawyer and activist. Chow was Gwyneth Ho's lawyer and had also been the Alliance's vice chairman since 2015. She had spent the night in the office working: she was scheduled to represent Gwyneth during a bail hearing later that day. "It looks like they've really decided to take action today," Chow said with a slight laugh during a live stream as officers attempted to enter.[3] She oscillated between contemplative and humorous as she documented her final moments of freedom on social media. "The worst thing about being arrested is that I've not changed into a new set of clothes or brushed my teeth," she wrote in one post. "Will my breath overwhelm the national security police?" Officers took Chow away and rounded up three other Alliance leaders. Most of the group, well into their sunset years, voted to disband that September. One of the remaining leaders of the group, out on a suspended jail sentence, said he planned to visit Szeto Wah's grave to explain the decision. Police from 2020 onward banned the annual candlelight vigil commemorating the massacre that the Alliance had organized each year. The authorities were not even brave enough to admit the real reason, blaming COVID.

Not content with just stamping out the possibility of future remembrance of Tiananmen, authorities set about rewriting the past as well. The Pillar of Shame, the most prominent public memorial to the Tiananmen massacre, was like a barometer of the territory's differences from the mainland. It served, creator Jen Galschiøt wrote in 1997, as a test of the authorities' "guarantees for human rights and freedom of expression in Hong Kong."[4] The vivid orange cenotaph of pained, contorted bodies had been prominently displayed at the University of Hong Kong since 1998. Across its base read an inscription: "THE OLD CANNOT KILL THE YOUNG FOREVER." Students and activists gathered every summer before the June 4 anniversary to ceremonially wash the structure. It was an emotional tribute that marked the beginning of a string of events in the city to mourn the dead and celebrate the birth of Hong Kong's democracy movement.

Two days before Christmas 2021, while most students were away from campus, workers began removing the pillar from its perch under cover of darkness. Security guards tried to block reporters from filming. The statue was tightly wrapped in blankets and plastic. Workers guided it out of the campus tipped on its side. Their heads bowed slightly, they looked like mortuary attendants preparing a body for burial. The statue was loaded into an old shipping container and dumped at a nature preserve far from the city center, an undignified disposal.[5] Students rushed to photograph the emptiness that stood in its place.

The following day, the Chinese University of Hong Kong removed its Goddess of Democracy statue, a bronze replica of the one that had stood in Tiananmen Square and had been on campus for more than a decade. At Lingnan University, a relief sculpture memorializing the crackdown was torn down as well. The universities hid behind a litany of public-relations drivel and unbelievable excuses when asked about their actions. Administrators at the University of Hong Kong said they were worried about "the potential safety issues resulting from the fragile statue."[6] Campuses were no longer permitted to be incubators of activism, and many professors and administrators had no problem falling in line with the new marching orders. Arthur Li, chairman of the Council of the University of Hong Kong, who had compared student protesters to Nazis, offered up the fiction that the statue wasn't even created to honor Tiananmen victims but was a memorial to the victims of the Oklahoma City bombings.[7]

Later that same week, police arrested six current and former executives of *Stand News* in predawn raids and froze the outlet's assets, accusing them of a conspiracy to publish seditious material. The outlet that had documented some of the most defining moments of the demonstrations and helped launch Gwyneth to political stardom promptly announced it would close.

Hong Kong had anticipated the day when Beijing finally decided everything that the city valued no longer served the interests of the party. By the start of 2022, freedom of the courts, the press, political pluralism, academia, and thought disappeared, along with the banners, slogans, memorials, and newspapers that were the fabric of the city. Beijing took all of this away because it could, with few repercussions beyond a handful of sanctions. The city they left behind was unrecognizable, the disappearances quietly carried in the hearts of those who remained and still remembered, and those who'd fled and longed for the home they once knew.

————

REVEREND CHU AND DOROTHY LEFT THE US AFTER THREE MONTHS WHEN Chu's tourist visa lapsed, and moved to Taipei. Five decades on, they were back in the city where they first met. A friend had offered the pair space in a university dormitory. Chu spent his first six months in Taiwan dejected. He couldn't concentrate; he couldn't work. All of his aging friends—he called them "brothers and sisters"—were in jail or standing trial. He watched every news report, tracking developments in their cases. One clip showed Martin Lee, his old friend, walking to court. The sight of his white hair made Chu cry. His own physical health was also suffering. He underwent surgery in Taiwan and was inundated with sadness. Dorothy missed Hong Kong deeply too. People saw her as Taiwanese, and she once again was helping Chu with his Mandarin. But that was an "illusion," she said. Dorothy was a Hong Konger. Their whole life, their whole community, was there. "We seem to have become those old lonely people here," she said.

It was the Lunar New Year, and Daniel, Chu's elder son, called his parents on video chat. His children were on the call. Speaking with his eleven-year-old grandson, Chu burst into tears. The boy tried to comfort him. "You need to be brave," he said to his grandfather.

Chu's depression lingered. He wasn't sure it would ever fully lift, but he didn't want to be resigned to defeat. Giving up wasn't who he was. The best way to keep fighting for Hong Kong, Chu thought in the weeks and months that followed, was to keep telling the story of its struggle. He started to rifle through decades of documents, researching and writing his memoirs. "We must constantly tell the next generation these things, so they understand what happened." When even the truth is outlawed, the act of recording itself is resistance. "My life might come to an end soon," he said, "but there is still something left to do."

AFTERWORD

THE SKY OVER HONG KONG ON DECEMBER 10, 2022, WAS A SHADE OF BLUE that inspires clichés, cloudless and casting a soft winter light over the city below. The clear day meant we could see the skyscrapers of Shenzhen from where we stood outside the Lo Wu Correctional Facility, Hong Kong's largest women's prison. We were visiting Gwyneth Ho Kwai-lam. By then, she had been detained for two years, but her trial for violating the national security law hadn't yet started.

We were nervous, waiting to see her. We'd started pitching this book to agents at the end of January 2021, with Gwyneth as one of our potential characters. She was jailed a month later, the fate she had predicted but a logistical problem nonetheless. Aside from our hours of earlier conversations with her, it meant we had to rely on other sources to tell her story. Much was taken from her prolific writings. There were also interviews with her friends and roommates, and visits to court to watch her cross-examinations.

It almost felt like we knew her better than she realized we did, and were speaking for her when she couldn't for herself. There was also the fact that visits were capped at fifteen minutes—thoroughly insufficient.

In the waiting area, we watched guards in white and blue uniforms pack supplies for the inmates—scented Tempo-brand tissues, cheap shampoo, books brought in by friends, sanitary napkins. A goofy video played on loop, featuring a smiling prison guard explaining the visitation process. Eventually, a guard led us through a set of doors, up an elevator, and through more sets of heavy armored doors that buzzed as they unlocked.

When we reached the visitation booth, Gwyneth was already seated, separated from us by a glass wall. Like the other inmates, she wore a gray sweater over her yellow prison shirt. It was colder in here than outside. Her long bangs swept across her forehead. She gestured to the phone in front of us. We picked it up, and next to us a timer started: fifteen minutes, ticking down.

The connection was poor, and Gwyneth struggled to hear us, straining through the crackle. We couldn't discuss anything sensitive, so we asked questions that were a bit boring and, frankly, lame. *How was the food?* The curry was actually pretty good, she told us, although the vegetables were undercooked. The confines of lockup curtailed her cooking, but she found room for some culinary improvisation. She had learned from other inmates how to enhance the watery mashed potatoes by crumbling cheese crackers over them for some additional flavor and texture.

Gwyneth told us she could listen to the radio. It was her one connection to everything she loved, especially the boy band MIRROR and its lead singer, Jer Lau. Gwyneth had written before that one of her few fears was forgetting his voice. Pop music aside, the curious journalist was still there. She tried to keep up with the news by reading the limited papers delivered to the jail. Thousands of mainland Chinese had recently stunned the world when they held protests against the zero-COVID policies that had crippled their economy and robbed them of mobility since the onset of the virus in 2020. Some went further, shouting slogans for Xi Jinping to step down, denouncing the Communist Party. Journalists called them "blank paper" protests for the pieces of white paper held up by demonstrators—its roots tracing back to 2020 in Hong Kong, when protesters there did the same after the national security law made certain slogans illegal. Gwyneth said she was proud to see students at Tsinghua University in Beijing, her alma mater, taking part.

Some Hong Kong activists had dismissed the protests, asking why they should support anyone on the mainland when so few had shown solidarity with their movement. Their thinking frustrated Gwyneth. If she was out, she would have told them to "fuck off," she told us, laughing.

We eventually got to the question of what she missed. Not much, she said at first; "the mental preparation started a long time ago." She was kind of a homebody anyway, so the isolation of jail wasn't bothering her too much. Then after we had moved on to another topic, she suddenly had an answer. "Google Docs! Facebook! . . . Basically, my keyboard," she nearly shouted, "that is what I miss."

All she had was pencil and paper. Gwyneth held her writing hand up to the smudged glass to show us the calluses that had developed on her fingers. "Been here since 2021," she quipped. The hardening of her hands served as a sort of physical measure of her time behind bars.

As she kept talking, we glanced at the ticker counting down. The phone line cut mid-sentence when the ticker hit zero. Gwyneth looked at the receiver in front of us, and we caught a hint of disappointment. She shrugged; such was life without freedom. Gwyneth stood up, bowed slightly, and walked away. One of the last things she said to us was "gaa yau"—"add oil," the Cantonese refrain of encouragement that was synonymous with the pro-democracy movement.

We sat for a while outside the prison, watching the sun dip. It was maybe only in that moment we understood what Gwyneth felt in early 2019 when she was studying in Denmark, long before she took the decisions that brought her here. Why her, and not us? Why could we choose our own meal tonight, and not her? In her words, "you witness the state apparatus piercing each of [the young activists], yet you as a person can do nothing."

We wrote the vast majority of this manuscript outside of Hong Kong. Revisiting the 2019 movement meant remembering how we'd watched young men and women brutalized by the police in front of our eyes, their blood pooling on the asphalt at our feet. It meant rewatching Carrie Lam's hubris at press conferences, feeling disgust rising at her hypocrisy all over again. It meant remembering the times we'd choked from tear gas, ran from the police, dreamed about the din of their plastic shields against the ground. It meant reliving how we felt when we woke up at dawn to yet another mass arrest or raid, WhatsApp messages to sources now showing one tick: unread. When we stopped writing for the day, we were able to step into a completely different landscape, one that held no memory of the protests and their aftermath. It was easier to compartmentalize.

There were also more tangible reasons for departing. Questioning under caution by authorities over a pair of gas masks procured to use while covering the protests and a report filed to the national security police by a student at the University of Hong Kong over Timothy's coverage in the *Atlantic* seemed like signs telling us it was necessary to go. The national security law ultimately seeks to outlaw speech more than anything else—a book about the Hong Kong protests could fall neatly in any of the four categories. Five speech therapists were jailed on charges of sedition for producing children's picture books that told the story of wolves attempting to control a group of sheep. In the colorful pages, prosecutors saw a sinister plot. The therapists were denied bail, detained for over a year, and found guilty. We have traded Hong Kong for our ability to write freely about it.

Being back in Hong Kong at the end of 2022 was harder than remembering—mostly because so many have tried to forget. In the city we were back in the split-screen world that Hong Kong reporters live in: carefree meals with friends and boozy nights interspersed with days in court, watching show trials. The ideologically driven pandemic controls imposed for years were mostly lifted by then as Beijing shifted away from its zero-COVID policies. Well-heeled expats whose lives were blissfully disengaged from the protest movement, with the exception of some fleeting logistical disruptions, had finally abandoned their feigned concerns and felt comfortable airing a more truthful version of their feelings. Many didn't mind Beijing's crackdown; some openly welcomed it. Rugby tournaments had returned, as had concerts, presenting the illusion of a city unchanged. Hong Kong was "back!" the government's tagline proclaimed. More remarkable than the boldness of this lie was just how many people believed it.

Some five dozen organizations—labor unions, think tanks, and religious groups—have closed out of fear of falling afoul of ever-shifting redlines. Their absence means that advocacy on issues such as prisoners' rights, the minimum wage, land use, and LGBTQ+ and refugee rights has gone, too. *Stand News* and *Apple Daily* weren't the only publications to disappear. Even a self-funded transport news site, *Transit Jam*, closed in May 2023 after being targeted by pro-Beijing media. A few organizations have survived by allowing themselves to be corrupted. The Foreign Correspondents Club of Hong Kong, a place that once vigorously advocated for press freedoms, was pushed by sycophantic leadership to sell out its principles to keep the lights on for a crowd that consisted largely of businessmen sympathetic to Beijing and loafing red-faced lawyers who wanted a cheap place to drink.

What the Chinese Communist Party did to Hong Kong wasn't just erase its capacity for protest. It also, after twenty-five years of trying, crushed Hong Kong's spirit, particularly by exonerating the very people who brutalized it. It appointed John Lee, the security chief under Carrie Lam, as the city's next chief executive, elevating the former cop to the highest level of governance. Psychologists told officers who went through the 2019 protests to remember that they'd done nothing wrong, that any violence they meted out was against a group of radicals who deserved it. Forget an inquiry into the police—they have been celebrated, pinned with medals for their actions.

Reverend Chu, Tommy, Finn, and Gwyneth sacrificed their safety, lives, families, and freedoms for Hong Kong. Their actions and those of thousands more gave people strength to keep fighting. The authoritarian state wants to ensure that no one will ever make such sacrifices again—that no one will hope again.

The police and security forces were elevated for their service for Beijing, but parts of Hong Kong's establishment were punished alongside the pro-democracy camp. Mainland officials posted to Hong Kong who terribly misread the mood of the city in 2019 were shipped off. Beijing's top officials overseeing Hong Kong are now Xi loyalists with résumés that include tearing down crosses at churches in China's Christian stronghold and crushing the 2011 anticorruption protests in Wukan, a town in Guangdong Province.

The Beijing lackey punished most severely for the litany of failures was Carrie Lam. She announced in April 2022 that she would not run for reelection. Lam said the decision was "entirely based on" her family considerations. In doing so, she kept with the insulting tradition started by her predecessors of lying to the people of Hong Kong about the agency the chief executive possessed. Self-righteous and brimming with arrogance until the end, Lam used a farewell dinner with lawmakers to lambaste them for not supporting her enough during the protests. Beijing offered Lam no position as an appreciation for her service. She was a pariah, cast off without purpose. Her leadership left Hong Kong less free, more economically unequal, and ravaged by COVID-19. Unlike Tung Chee-hwa and Leung Chun-ying, she was not invited to China's top political advisory board after her term. In one of her few interviews since leaving office, Lam extolled the guidance and wisdom of the Central Government, the top girl still desperately searching for praise. In response to questions for this book, a representative for Lam's office said by email: "Mrs. Lam will not respond to hearsay, speculative or even fabricated comments."

The changes to the city have corroded their way unabated through all parts of Hong Kong. Schoolchildren are taught that Hong Kong was never a colony but was illegally occupied by the British, and also taught the virtues of the national security law. The media broadcast mandatory "patriotic content." The legislature is scrubbed of opposition. Taking the place of loud pro-democracy voices are toadies who slavishly repeat the mantras of the government and Xi Jinping. Most stunning has been the capture of the courts and broader legal system, which has managed to turn pro-democracy allies against each other, now testifying as state witnesses to "crimes" that have simply been invented by Beijing. The state appears to have managed to flip people in every one of the major national security cases, starting with Andy Li, Finn's ally, to editors who worked under Jimmy Lai at *Apple Daily*, to a close associate of Benny Tai, who is testifying against Gwyneth and the other pro-democracy election candidates.

They have co-opted these pro-democracy advocates in an effort to pull off China's greatest attempt to rewrite history since the 1989 Tiananmen protests. Just like it was back then, a narrative has already been set: the 2019 movement in Hong Kong was not a popular uprising but a traitorous conspiracy of troublemakers in league with foreign powers. *They've even admitted to it.* Now the chapter can be closed.

Some fallouts in the wake of the 2019 movement cannot be fully attributed to the Hong Kong government or Beijing. Without the same attention on Hong Kong, overseas Hong Kong activist groups have descended into bitter infighting. People named in these pages who worked together on singular goals, such as getting Washington to pass the Human Rights and Democracy Act, now cannot be in the same room together. The Washington-based Hong Kong Democracy Council that started with Samuel Chu as its managing director persists, but without him involved, after a feud that was half-public. It resembles the factionalism that happened among Chinese activist groups in exile after the 1989 Tiananmen protests. "Do not split" was a beautiful mantra that allowed the Hong Kong movement to endure against an unmoving opponent—and then fell apart, with the pieces excruciatingly hard to pick up.

For some, perhaps the biggest disappointment of all was the United States. Few movements hitched their wagon to Washington quite as much as the Hong Kong one. Some protesters flew American flags on the street, appealed to Trump's gigantic ego, even believed the president when he claimed to be tough on China. A more liberal faction appealed to Nancy Pelosi's longtime support for Chinese democracy activists, dating back to Tiananmen. So many believed that America had the ability to alter Beijing's course, but it couldn't. What it could have offered was a safe haven, but it didn't. There remains no lifeboat policy for Hong Kongers who want to emigrate to the US. Ted Cruz, who in 2019 dressed in black during his visit to Hong Kong and referred to the city as the "new Berlin," killed a bill in December 2020 that included provisions for temporary protected status for Hong Kongers and expedited certain refugee and asylum applications. Former secretary of state Mike Pompeo, in his self-aggrandizing memoirs, released in early 2023, wrote that he wished he had done more to punish China over Hong Kong—taking action against HSBC, for example, which he said is a "money laundering" front for the Chinese Communist Party. Yet he doesn't reference Joshua Wong, his asylum bid, or broader immigration pathways for Hong Kongers. Pompeo declined repeated interview requests for this book.

Even for the few who were saved, life remains impossibly hard. Of the five who escaped on the boat and were settled in the US, only Tommy has secured his asylum status. The rest continue to wait, banking on the kindness of strangers for jobs, struggling to further their education, living lives entirely different from what they imagined before 2019. President Joe Biden has done the bare minimum, offering a reprieve from deportation for Hong Kong residents in the US. It is a temporary fix that fails to address the issue with any certainty.

The focus in Washington has largely moved from Hong Kong to Taiwan. The island is under constant military threat from Beijing, which claims the territory as its own despite the Chinese Communist Party never controlling it. Given how events transpired in Hong Kong, with the US offering such vocal backing and then abandoning the cause in the time of most need, there is good reason to interrogate the sincerity of the politicians who have made Taiwan a new cause célèbre.

For the UK as well, the concerns about what has happened in Hong Kong appear to have largely receded, replaced by the insatiate demands of British businesses to get on with things as they were. Ministerial visits have resumed between the two places, a normalization of relations despite the UK having declared the Sino-British Joint Declaration breached and welcoming some 150,000 fleeing Hong Kongers to the country through the BN(O) scheme. British businesses have a "huge appetite to come back and reconnect" with the city, Brian Davidson, the UK consul-general to Hong Kong, said in an interview with the *South China Morning Post* in May 2023, urging governments to avoid "megaphone diplomacy."[1]

Recall Emily Lau, the Hong Kong journalist who pointedly questioned Margaret Thatcher before the Hong Kong handover. "Is it really true," she asked, "that in international politics the highest form of morality is one's own national interest?"

The spirit of resistance that encapsulated 2019 is more difficult to spot now but can be seen with some searching, particularly in Gwyneth. She has pleaded not guilty to the charges against her and, as evidenced by her calluses, continues writing from jail. Apart from the national security charge against her, she was also found guilty and sentenced for turning up at Victoria Park on June 4, 2020, the first time the yearly Tiananmen vigil was banned. In both trials she has used the courtroom as a platform to broadcast her beliefs, arguing with the judges and questioning their decisions like she did her university professors back in Amsterdam. She corrects the court's Cantonese translations and has instructed her lawyers to challenge prosecution witnesses with cross-examinations, hoping that the political motivations behind the national security case will be laid bare. Gwyneth's key argument: "On what grounds can the court try a leaderless movement?"

Reverend Chu is still in Taiwan, where journalists and academics sometimes visit to hear his oral history of the Hong Kong democracy struggle. The ranks of his generation of activists are dwindling, either because of jail or age, and he is one of the few still able to speak. He is writing his long-planned memoir, which will create another record against Beijing's gross distortion of history, although he has to protect his "brothers" now in jail by censoring sensitive parts. Authorities are still building their case against the Hong Kong Alliance, with a trial scheduled for late 2023. The National Security Department pulled the two-ton Pillar of Shame statue out from storage in May 2023 in connection with what it said was an attempt to incite subversion. Dorothy is Chu's congenial editor who corrects dates and reminds him of names that have slipped his mind.

Finn, once anonymous, is one of the most visible Hong Kong activists in the UK. He eventually graduated from his master's program at UCL in the summer of 2022, taking the stage with Catherine in the audience snapping photos and cheering. The two jointly organized a major conference on Hong Kong in March 2023, and Finn also helped set up a diaspora media outlet with veteran Hong Kong journalists who were forced out of the city when their publications closed under political pressure. Navigating the rifts and arguments within the diaspora brings back occasional anxiety attacks, but they are easier to manage with Catherine. Finn wants to start growing potted plants around their apartment, inspired for the first time to spruce up his living quarters with the green thumb he inherited from his parents.

Finn was with Catherine in the apartment on July 3, 2023, almost exactly three years to the day of the passage of the national security law and more than four since he first posted as "iwantlaamcau," when messages started flooding his phone. In Hong Kong, the police had convened a press conference announcing that he was one of eight overseas activists now formally wanted for offenses under the law. The government was offering a 1 million Hong Kong dollar bounty, the equivalent to $128,000 USD, for information that could lead to their arrest—ten times more than was offered for the capture of a child rapist authorities had been hunting for over a decade. John Lee, the chief executive, said these eight would be "pursued for life" unless they surrendered.

The closest precedent for China's brazen call to vigilante action against peaceful opposition activists was the aftermath of the 1989 Tiananmen crackdown, when authorities released the names of most wanted students and sent them fleeing to Hong Kong via Operation Yellowbird.

Finn looked at a copy of the warrant on his phone. The photo authorities had used of him was taken when he was just eighteen. His hair was floppier, cheeks rounder. He started to laugh. It felt almost ridiculous, a desperate, performative attack from a government frustrated at the limits of its control. "You can't even buy a public housing flat in Hong Kong with that bounty," Finn quipped. We asked about fear, anxiety—surely he recognized that physical attacks against him were now more likely. Just weeks prior, Hong Kongers in the city of Southampton had been assaulted by Chinese nationalists at a protest. The British police had been seemingly unable to control such occurrences, more frequent with the large influx of Hong Kong people into the UK. The mundane details of Finn's everyday whereabouts were now theoretically valuable, even if he could never be formally extradited from the UK to Hong Kong.

Finn replied that he had come to terms with the risk a long time ago. All he felt was validation, the bounty testament to what he had done for the movement.

We met up with Tommy again one night in February 2023. By then, the ninety-six codefendants in his rioting case from September 29, 2019, were on trial. Some would soon be sentenced for up to thirty-eight months in jail. Tommy was still living free in New York.

He picked us up in his car, which he sometimes used to drive for Uber when he wasn't busy with his other jobs. He sped through Queens, weaving in and out of traffic, ignoring the horns of other drivers. "New York City," he said, like a lifelong New Yorker passing on some street wisdom, "you need to be aggressive." We stopped to pick up ramen at a shop where his girlfriend, a Hong Konger he met at a protest in the city, worked between her art history classes at New York University. As we made our way to his apartment—he had moved from Bensonhurst to

Flushing—Tommy leaned forward and pointed out the windshield to the Chinese characters on the signs around him. "I tried to flee China only to end up in it," he laughed. He moved the following month to Whitestone because he felt that Flushing was too much like the mainland.

When we visited, Tommy lived with Aaron in a narrow basement apartment. Ray joined them for a while, bringing along a mattress and some trash bags of clothes after being evicted from his own place. He set up his bed near the doorway. When he lay down to sleep, his feet dangled in the kitchen. The three keep a photo from their journey taped to the wall. It shows the black bow of the boat with the ocean spread out in front of it, no land in sight.

Between slurps of ramen broth, Tommy told us he has become more interested in the history of the Hong Kong democracy movement and its links to the mainland. In New York, he met with a number of student leaders from the 1989 Tiananmen Square protests, and helped them curate the Hong Kong section of a June 4 memorial museum. It is the only such permanent exhibition in the world, after the one in Hong Kong closed alongside persecution of the Alliance. He also wanted to meet Reverend Chu.

But not everything in his life is work and activism. Tommy was departing early the next morning for New Orleans with his girlfriend to take in the Mardi Gras festivities. He still hadn't started packing.

As he drove us back to the subway station across Roosevelt Avenue, the streets of Queens, illuminated by flaxen streetlamps, rushed by the car windows. Tommy remarked that there was a lot of graffiti along the bridge we were crossing. "There's a Gwong Fuk Heung Gong," using the Cantonese version of "Liberate Hong Kong," the rallying cry of the 2019 movement.

"Was it you guys?" we asked. "Yeah," he replied. "Me and my girl."

He pointed it out as we passed, along with a "Free Hong Kong" sticker he'd slapped on a road sign, both barely visible in the mess of curly cursive lettering. "I think no one notices," he said with a laugh. "Only you—because I told you."

ACKNOWLEDGMENTS

OUR DEEPEST GRATITUDE IS RESERVED FOR TOMMY, THE CHU FAMILY, FINN Lau, and Gwyneth Ho: thank you for your trust in us. To say it was an honor to record your stories is an understatement. We know our asks of you—hours of time and the multiple video calls and in-person conversations—were at times difficult, requiring you to recount the most painful periods of your life in detail. Over the three years we worked on this project, the risk to all of you and your loved ones, particularly for Gwyneth, compounded as the situation in Hong Kong deteriorated. You all took a leap of faith that we would capture Hong Kong's story, and your place in it, with care. We hope we have not disappointed you. A special thanks to Tommy for providing the illustrations that accompany the section breaks. We are thrilled to have your vision as an artist reach a wider audience.

So many other Hong Kongers took the time to speak to us for this book, including Aaron, Kenny, Ray, Catherine Li, Glacier Kwong Chung Ching, Frances Hui, Ray Wong, Venus, Galileo Cheng, Mina, Dennis Kwok, Jeffrey Ngo, Nathan Law, Prudence, Kairos, and many others who cannot be named for their safety. Wu'er Kaixi and Cai Chongguo walked us through their dramatic escapes from China to Hong Kong after June 4, 1989. Others assisted on behalf of their former colleagues now in jail and helped us surmount seemingly impossible logistical hurdles. Gwyneth's friends, particularly Kathryn Lam and Sarah Van Meel, were beyond generous with their time and memories. Former pro-Beijing officials and police officers broke ranks to share with us the degradation of their institutions and their alarm as they watched Hong Kong turn unrecognizable. Beyond the book itself, dozens of pro-democracy activists and ordinary people during our five years in Hong Kong opened up to us about their wishes and desires for their home, tried not to laugh at our bad Cantonese, and taught us what it means to be a Hong Konger. We may not know all of your names or faces, but for the most formative, inspiring, and motivating years of our journalistic careers, we are grateful and forever indebted. We will see you all, someday, beneath the pot.

Starting this project was less daunting with the counsel and encouragement of Patrick Radden Keefe, Mei Fong, James Crabtree, Lauren Hilgers, and especially Josh Chin. Thank you for helping us believe in ourselves and providing guidance on the wild world of publishing. We are grateful to Tina Bennett, too, for her initial support, which gave us the confidence to keep pushing.

From the time we met Howard Yoon at his office in Washington, we knew we would have not only a tireless agent but a confidant who understood the story we were trying to tell the world. Thank you for being a fierce advocate for us and our book. We are grateful to the team at RossYoon for their support through this process. Chun Han Wong deserves a special mention for the introduction to Howard, and also for his decades-long role as a friend, sounding board, and model for ambitious and diligent journalism.

Our first editor, Sam Raim, saw our vision and found a home for us at Hachette Books, and Mollie Weisenfeld, tirelessly and with great empathy, carved a narrative out of too many words and was responsible for shaping this book into its final product. We are lucky to have editors who cared for our characters, and for the story of Hong Kong, as much as we did.

Over our time in Hong Kong, we got to know some exceptional reporters, some of whom helped us as researchers for this book. It is deeply regrettable that their continued ties to Hong Kong and China mean they cannot be named or publicly credited for their work and time, with the exception of Alicia Ying-Yu Chen, who helped us with reporting in Taiwan. Our meticulous fact-checker not only looked out for errors like dates but also ensured that our framing and positioning were as close to the truth as could be. We are appreciative of their help and also their friendship and humor through many frantic messages on Signal. This book is as much yours as it is ours. We are also thankful for the camaraderie of the wider Hong Kong journalist community, particularly our fellow malcontents formerly of the Foreign Correspondents Club of Hong Kong: Dan Strumpf, Eric Wishart, James Pomfret, Jessie Pang, Mary Hui, Neil Western, Dan Ten Kate, Geoffrey Crothall, Jerome

Taylor, and Jennifer Creery. Your moral fortitude and belief in our collective mission in the face of acquiescence keeps us going, and we are proud to have stood alongside you.

Numerous academics who have dedicated their careers to studying Hong Kong and China informed our understanding of the city, reporting, and book writing. Thank you to Sebastian Veg, Ho-fung Hung, Steve Tsang, Francis L. F. Lee, Eric Yan-ho Lai, Thomas E. Kellogg, Luwei Rose Luqiu, Jerome A. Cohen, Edmund W. Cheng, Lokman Tsui, Samson W. H. Yuen, Jeffrey Wasserstrom, Ching Kwan Lee, Chan Ka Ming, John P. Burns, David Ownby, Geremie R. Barmé, Michael C. Davis, and the late Suzanne Pepper. Joseph Torigian was instrumental in helping us understand how Xi Zhongxun helped shape his son Xi Jinping and his approach to Hong Kong.

We are thankful to our editors at both the *Washington Post* and the *Atlantic* for giving us the space and time to work on this book. Former managing editor Tracy Grant and Douglas Jehl at the *Post* graciously granted Shibani book leave, and Peter Finn, Shibani's editor, has continued to support ambitious work on Hong Kong. At the *Atlantic*, Timothy's former editor, Prashant Rao, as well as Yoni Appelbaum and Jeffrey Goldberg, never questioned the importance of the Hong Kong story and Hong Kongers, and gave prominence to deeply reported work. Mark Robinson, formerly of *Wired* magazine, commissioned and helped shape Timothy's ambitious pieces for the outlet.

Others deserve a special thanks for helping us kick-start our careers and teaching us what it means to be dogged yet empathetic journalists. For Shibani, that was Sandy Padwe at Columbia Journalism School, who, simply put, epitomizes every right value in our profession, and Patrick Barta at the *Wall Street Journal*, whose humor and fondness for llamas masks a quiet brilliance. For Timothy, thanks to the former staff of the *Myanmar Times*, particularly Thomas Kean, Geoffrey Goddard, and Sonny Swe, for their guidance early in his career and for providing a model of what unwavering dedication to journalism looks like, even under the most trying of circumstances.

Prashant Rao also helped read and provide advice on initial drafts of this manuscript, as did Jerrine Tan, Mike Chinoy, and Antony Dapiran.

We appreciate their care and effort, and were lucky to have them as confidants and as first eyes on this book. Keith Zhai guided us on some key aspects of China's approach to Hong Kong, graciously sharing his insights with us.

Finally, to our families: our time in Hong Kong, in the later years trapped by restrictions imposed by the pandemic and politics, took us away from you. Life kept happening even as the book demanded our attention, most harrowingly with the acute hospitalization of Timothy's mother in early 2023. Throughout, you remained proud of us and made sacrifices so we could keep going. We are so lucky, and so grateful. Thank you to our fathers, John McLaughlin and Deepak Mahtani, for inspiring our curiosity in the world; to our siblings, Andrew McLaughlin, Daniel McLaughlin, Dinika Mahtani, and their partners Kristin Luber, Caroline Wilson, and Andrew Mistry for being our biggest cheerleaders; but most of all, to our mothers, Doreen Byrne and C—for everything and more.

NOTE ON SOURCES

THIS BOOK WAS A PRODUCT OF DOZENS OF INTERVIEWS WITH THE CHU family, Tommy, and Finn over two-and-a-half years. Because Gwyneth was jailed at the time of writing, we relied on our previous interviews with her and interviews with her friends, professors, and colleagues, along with her own lengthy and extensive writing. Additionally, we interviewed more than a hundred others in Hong Kong, China, Taiwan, the United Kingdom, the United States, Canada, Germany, the Netherlands, Spain, and Brussels. We consulted hundreds of hours of video footage; documentaries; thousands of Hong Kong, British, and Chinese government statistics, records, and archives; academic papers; court and police documents; and primary sources, such as diaries. These supplemented our five years of reporting inside Hong Kong.

Sections on the 2019 protests and their aftermath are largely the product of our own reporting on the ground and our footage, supplemented and corroborated by major media outlets including but not limited to the *New York Times*, the *Wall Street Journal*, Reuters, Agence-France Presse, the *South China Morning Post*, *Hong Kong Free Press*, *HK01*, *Initium*, and NowTV. We were at all of the protests in 2019 and 2020 described in this book, as well as the mass arrests through 2021. If we used exclusive reporting from others, that is noted in the text or in the notes. Hong Kong's *Apple Daily*, *Stand News*, and *Citizen News* shuttered. They removed all their online content midway through our work on this book, and the government-funded *RTHK* removed a significant amount of content related to the 2019 movement. Some groups have worked to preserve some of this content, which we used as reference alongside internet sites that captured archived versions of these news websites.

A significant amount of reporting for this book—including but not limited to the chapters on Carrie Lam, the Hong Kong government, and diplomatic negotiations in the lead-up to June 2019; the attitudes of the Hong Kong Police Force; the July 21, 2019, attack in Yuen Long; and Joshua Wong's asylum bid—came from sources who wish to stay anonymous because of fears for their safety and retaliation from authorities inside Hong Kong and mainland China. For their protection, we have opted to exclude citations on materials from anonymous sources.

BIBLIOGRAPHY

Abbas, Ackbar. *Hong Kong: Culture and the Politics of Disappearance*. Minneapolis: University of Minnesota Press, 1997, reprinted 2008.

Baker, Hugh D. R. "Life in the Cities: The Emergence of Hong Kong Man." *China Quarterly* 95 (1983): 469–479.

Barmé, Geremie R. "An Anthem to Restore Hong Kong." *China Heritage*, September 12, 2019, https://chinaheritage.net/journal/an-anthem-to-restore-hong-kong.

Barmé, Geremie R. "I Am Brian Leung: They Cannot Understand; They Cannot Comprehend; They Cannot See." *China Heritage*, August 20, 2019, https://chinaheritage.net/journal/i-am-brian-leung-they-cannot-understand-they-cannot-comprehend-they-cannot-see.

Bird, Les. *A Small Band of Men: An Englishman's Adventures in Hong Kong's Marine Police*. Hong Kong: Earnshaw, 2020.

Carroll, John M. *Edge of Empires: Chinese Elites and British Colonials in Hong Kong*. Cambridge, MA: Harvard University Press, 2005.

Chan, Chi Kit. "China's Influence on Hong Kong's Media." In *China's Influence and the Center-Periphery Tug of War in Hong Kong, Taiwan and Indo-Pacific*, edited by B. C. H. Fong, J.-M. Wu, and A. J. Nathan, 121–137. London: Routledge, 2020.

Chau, Tak-huen, and Kin-man Wan. "Pour (Tear) Gas on Fire? Violent Confrontations and Anti-government Backlash." *Political Science Research and Methods* (2022): 1–11.

Chau, Wilton Chi Fung, and Koon Lin Wong. "Evolution and Controversies of Social Studies Education in the Hong Kong Context." In *Social Studies Education in East Asian Contexts*, edited by Kerry J. Kennedy, 50–68. London: Routledge, 2020.

Chen, Albert H. Y. "The National Security Law of the HKSAR: A Contextual and Legal Study." In *The National Security Law of Hong Kong: Restoration and Transformation*, edited by Hualing Fu and Michael Hor, 20–28. Hong Kong: Hong Kong University Press, 2022.

Cheng, Edmund W., Francis L. F. Lee, Samson Yuen, and Gary Tang. "Total Mobilization from Below: Hong Kong's Freedom Summer." *China Quarterly* 251 (2022): 629–659.

Cheng, Joseph S. "The Future of Hong Kong: Surveys of the Hong Kong People's Attitude." *Australian Journal of Chinese Affairs* 12 (July 1984): 113–142.

Cheung, Anthony B. L. *Can Hong Kong Exceptionalism Last? Dilemmas of Governance and Public Administration over Five Decades, 1970s–2020.* Hong Kong: City University of Hong Kong Press, 2021.

Chu, Yiu-ming. "Confessions of a Bell Toller: A Statement from the Defendant's Dock." *Hong Kong Free Press*, April 9, 2019, https://hongkongfp.com/2019/04/09/full-i-no-regrets-not-give-umbrella-movement-convenor-reverend-chus-speech-ahead-sentencing.

Chu, Yiu-wai. *Hong Kong Cantopop: A Concise History.* Hong Kong: Hong Kong University Press, 2017.

Cohen, Jerome A. "Hong Kong's Transformed Criminal Justice System: Instrument of Fear." *Academia Sinica Law Journal*, 2022 special issue. NYU School of Law, Public Law Research Paper no. 22–10, November 2021.

Cradock, Percy. *Experiences of China.* London: John Murray, 1994.

Dapiran, Antony. *City of Protest: A Recent History of Dissent in Hong Kong.* Melbourne: Penguin Random House, 2017.

Dapiran, Antony. *City on Fire: The Fight for Hong Kong.* Melbourne: Scribe, 2020.

Davies, Hugh Llewelyn. *Hong Kong 1997: Handling the Handover.* Self-published, 2016.

DeGolyer, Michael E. "How the Stunning Outbreak of Disease Led to a Stunning Outbreak of Dissent." In *At the Epicentre: Hong Kong and the SARS Outbreak*, edited by Christine Loh and Civic Exchange, 117–138. Hong Kong: Hong Kong University Press, 2004.

DeGolyer, Michael E., and Janet Lee Scott. "The Myth of Political Apathy in Hong Kong." *Annals of the American Academy of Political and Social Science* 547 (1996): 68–78.

Grant, Jonathan S. "Cultural Formation in Postwar Hong Kong." In *Hong Kong Reintegrating with China: Political, Economic and Cultural Dimensions*, edited by Lee Pui-tak, 159–176. Hong Kong: Hong Kong University Press, 2001.

Han, Minzhu. *Cries for Democracy: Writings and Speeches from the 1989 Chinese Democracy Movement.* Princeton, NJ: Princeton University Press, 1990.

Hong Kong Public Opinion Research Institute. Polls and data sets including "Popularity of Chief Executive," "People's Ethnic Identity," and "Appraisal of the Local News Media."

Hou, Guanghao. "A Mighty River Flowing Eastward: The Formation and Transformation of the Ethnic and National Identities of Situ Hua." *China Report* 54, no. 1 (2018): 81–98.

Hualing, Fu, Carole J. Petersen, and Simon N. M. Young, eds. *National Security and Fundamental Freedoms: Hong Kong's Article 23 Under Scrutiny.* Hong Kong: Hong Kong University Press, 2005.

Hung, Ho-fung. *City on the Edge: Hong Kong Under Chinese Rule*. Cambridge: Cambridge University Press, 2022.

Hung, Ho-fung. "Identity Contested: Rural Ethnicities in the Making of Urban Hong Kong." In *Hong Kong Reintegrating with China: Political, Economic and Cultural Dimensions*, edited by Lee Pui-tak, 181–196. Hong Kong: Hong Kong University Press, 2001.

Jiang, Shigong. *China's Hong Kong: A Political and Cultural Perspective*. Singapore: Springer, 2017.

Kaufman, Jonathan. *Kings of Shanghai: Two Rival Dynasties and the Creation of Modern China*. London: Little, Brown, 2020.

Lang, Graeme, Catherine Chiu, and Mary Pang. "Impact of Plant Relocation to China to Manufacturing Workers in Hong Kong." In *Hong Kong Reintegrating with China: Political, Economic and Cultural Dimensions*, edited by Lee Pui-Tak, 109–124. Hong Kong: Hong Kong University Press, 2001.

Lau, Siu-kai. "The Hong Kong Special Administration Region Government in the New Political Environment." In *Hong Kong Reintegrating with China: Political, Economic and Cultural Dimensions*, edited by Lee Pui-Tak, 59–75. Hong Kong: Hong Kong University Press, 2001.

Law, Nathan, with Evan Fowler. *Freedom: How We Lose It and How We Fight Back*. London: Bantam, 2021.

Lee, Ching Kwan. *Hong Kong: Global China's Restive Frontier*. Cambridge: Cambridge University Press, 2022.

Lee, Ching Kwan. "Take Back Our Future: An Eventful Sociology of the Hong Kong Umbrella Movement." In *Take Back Our Future: An Eventful Sociology of the Hong Kong Umbrella Movement*, edited by Ching Kwan Lee and Ming Sing, 1–33. Ithaca, NY: Cornell University Press, 2019.

Lee, Francis L. F. "Mediascape and Movement: The Dynamics of Political Communication, Public and Counterpublic." In *Take Back Our Future: An Eventful Sociology of the Hong Kong Umbrella Movement*, edited by Ching Kwan Lee and Ming Sing, 100–122. Ithaca, NY: Cornell University Press, 2019.

Lee, Francis L. F., and Joseph M. Chan. *Memories of Tiananmen: Politics and Processes of Collective Remembering in Hong Kong, 1989–2019*. Amsterdam: Amsterdam University Press, 2021.

Lee, Francis, Hai Liang, Edmund W. Cheng, Gary K. Y. Tang, and Samson Yuen. "Affordances, Movement Dynamics and a Centralized Digital Communication Platform in a Networked Movement." *Information, Communication & Society* 25, no. 12 (2021): 1699–1716.

Lee, Francis L. F., Samson Yuen, Gary Tang, and Edmund W. Cheng. "Hong Kong's Summer of Uprising: From Anti-extradition to Anti-authoritarian Protests." *China Review* 19, no. 4 (2019): 1–32.

Liang, Hai, and Francis L. F. Lee. "Thread Popularity Inequality as an Indicator of Organization Through Communication in a Networked Movement: An Analysis of the LIHKG Forum." *Chinese Journal of Communication* 15, no. 3 (2022): 332–354.

Lilley, James, with Jeffrey Lilley. *China Hands: Nine Decades of Adventure, Espionage, and Diplomacy in Asia.* New York: PublicAffairs, 2004.

Lim, Louisa. *Indelible City: Dispossession and Defiance in Hong Kong.* New York: Riverhead, 2022.

Lim, Louisa. *The People's Republic of Amnesia: Tiananmen Revisited.* New York: Oxford University Press, 2014.

Loh, Christine. *Underground Front: The Chinese Communist Party in Hong Kong.* Hong Kong: Hong Kong University Press, 2018.

Loh, Christine, and Civic Exchange, eds. *Functional Constituencies: A Unique Feature of the Hong Kong Legislative Council.* Hong Kong: Hong Kong University Press, 2006.

Luqiu, Luwei Rose. *Covering the 2019 Hong Kong Protests.* Cham: Palgrave Macmillan, 2021.

Moore, Charles. *Margaret Thatcher: The Authorized Biography.* New York: Alfred A. Knopf, 2016.

Ownby, David. "Jiang Shigong: Probing the Imaginary World." In *Reading the China Dream,* 2020, www.readingthechinadream.com/jiang-shigong -probing-the-imaginary-world.html.

Patten, Chris. *The Hong Kong Diaries.* London: Allen Lane, 2022.

Pompeo, Mike. *Never Give an Inch: Fighting for the America I Love.* New York: Broadside, 2003.

Sheridan, Michael. *The Gate to China: A New History of the People's Republic & Hong Kong.* London: William Collins, 2021.

So, Alvin Y. "Hong Kong's Problematic Democratic Transition: Power Dependency or Business Hegemony?" *Journal of Asian Studies* 59, no. 2 (May 2000): 359–381.

Summers, Tim. *China's Hong Kong: The Politics of a Global City.* Newcastle upon Tyne: Agenda, 2019.

Szeto, Wah. *A Mighty River Flowing Eastward: An Autobiography of Szeto Wah* 大江東去:司徒華回憶錄. Hong Kong: Oxford University Press, 2011.

Tai, Benny. "30 Years After Tiananmen: Hong Kong Remembers." *Journal of Democracy* 30, no. 2 (April 2019): 64–69.

Tsang, Steve. *A Modern History of Hong Kong: 1841–1997.* London: I.B. Tauris, 2007, reprinted 2019.

Veg, Sebastian. "The Rise of Localism and Civic Identity in Post-handover Hong Kong: Questioning the Chinese Nation-State." *China Quarterly* 230 (2017): 323–347.

Vines, Stephen. *Defying the Dragon: Hong Kong and the World's Largest Dictatorship*. London: Hurst, 2021.

Wasserstrom, Jeffrey. *Vigil: Hong Kong on the Brink*. New York: Columbia Global Reports, 2020.

Watson, James L. "Rural Society: Hong Kong's New Territories." *China Quarterly* 95 (1983): 480–490.

Wong, Joshua, with Jason Y. Ng. *Unfree Speech: The Threat to Global Democracy and Why We Must Act, Now*. New York: Penguin, 2020.

Yew, Chiew Ping, and Kin-ming Kwong. "Hong Kong Identity on the Rise." *Asian Survey* 54, no. 6 (November/December 2014): 1088–1112.

Yuen, Samson. "Transgressive Politics in Occupy Mongkok." In *Take Back Our Future: An Eventful Sociology of the Hong Kong Umbrella Movement*, edited by Ching Kwan Lee and Ming Sing, 52–73. Ithaca, NY: Cornell University Press, 2019.

Zhou, Taomo. "Leveraging Liminality: The Border Town of Bao'an (Shenzhen) and the Origins of China's Reform and Opening." *Journal of Asian Studies* 80, no. 2 (May 2021): 337–361.

Zhu, Han. "Beijing's 'Rule of Law' Strategy for Governing Hong Kong: Legalisation Without Democratisation." *China Perspectives* 1, no. 116 (2019): 23–34.

NOTES

PROLOGUE

1. Hong Kong Police Force statistics, presented at press conference, via *Hong Kong Free Press*, https://hongkongfp.com/2019/12/10/hong-kong-police-used-crowd-control-weapons-30000-times-since-june-6000-arrests.

INTRODUCTION

1. Sources include a transcript of Anthony J. Blinken in a conversation with Condoleezza Rice and Jim Mattis at Stanford University via the State Department, October 17, 2022, www.state.gov/secretary-antony-j-blinken-at-a-conversation-on-the-evolution-and-importance-of-technology-diplomacy-and-national-security-with-66th-secretary-of-state-condoleezza-rice; and a leaked memo from General Mike Minihan, obtained by multiple media outlets, including the *Guardian*, February 2, 2023, www.theguardian.com/world/2023/feb/02/us-general-gut-feeling-war-china-sparks-alarm-predictions.

CHAPTER 1

1. Jonathan Kaufman, *Kings of Shanghai: Two Rival Dynasties and the Creation of Modern China* (London: Little, Brown, 2020), 16–19.

2. Steve Tsang, *A Modern History of Hong Kong: 1841–1997* (London: I.B. Tauris, 2007), 11.

3. Reverend Chu Yiu-ming's mitigation before the court, April 2019, https://hongkongfp.com/2019/04/09/full-i-no-regrets-not-give-umbrella-movement-convenor-reverend-chus-speech-ahead-sentencing.

4. Anniversary book compiled by Hongkong Land Limited, *Hongkong Land at 125*, 2014, 85–88, https://hklandblob.blob.core.windows.net/assets/125_anniversary/mobile/index.html#p=1.

5. He Huifeng, "Forgotten Stories of the Great Escape to Hong Kong Across the Shenzhen Border," *South China Morning Post*, January 13, 2013, www.scmp.com/news/china/article/1126786/forgotten-stories-huge-escape-hong-kong.

6. Vaclav Smil, "China's Great Famine: 40 Years Later," *BMJ* 319, no. 7225 (December 1999), www.ncbi.nlm.nih.gov/pmc/articles/PMC1127087.

7. Taomo Zhou, "Leveraging Liminality: The Border Town of Bao'an (Shenzhen) and the Origins of China's Reform and Opening," *Journal of Asian Studies* 80, no. 2 (May 2021): 337–361.

8. Mao Zedong, "A Study of Physical Education," April 1917, www.marxists.org/reference/archive/mao/selected-works/volume-6/mswv6_01.htm.

CHAPTER 2

1. Christopher Dewolf, "Hong Kong Crime Wave: Why the 1990s Were a Decade of Famous Gangsters and Spectacular Robberies," *Zolima Citymag*, September 14, 2018, https://zolimacitymag.com/hong-kong-crime-wave-why-the-1990s-were-a-decade-of-famous-gangsters-and-spectacular-robberies.

2. Stuart Heaver, "When Hong Kong's Fight Against Smugglers in Speedboats Turned Deadly," *South China Morning Post*, June 19, 2022, www.scmp.com/magazines/post-magazine/long-reads/article/3182104/when-hong-kong-was-hotbed-high-speed-smuggling.

3. Tad Szulc, "U.S. Backs U.N. Seat for Peking, Opposes Ousting Taiwan," *New York Times*, August 3, 1971, www.nytimes.com/1971/08/03/archives/us-backs-un-seat-for-peking-opposes-ousting-taiwan-old-policy-ended.html.

4. Huang Hua letter to the United Nations Special Committee, March 9, 1972, A/AC.109/396, https://digitallibrary.un.org/record/3895944?ln=en.

CHAPTER 3

1. Interview with Lord Charles Powell of Bayswater.

2. Powell interview.

3. Margaret Thatcher, *The Downing Street Years* (London: HarperPerennial, 1995), 265.

4. Joseph S. Cheng, "The Future of Hong Kong: Surveys of the Hong Kong People's Attitudes," *Australian Journal of Chinese Affairs* 12 (July 1984), www.jstor.org/stable/2158991.

5. Frank Cooper, record of conversation at No. 10 Downing Street, December 23, 1982, www.margaretthatcher.org/document/138829.

6. Christopher S. Wren, "China Affirms Its Hong Kong Deadline," *New York Times*, November 10, 1983, www.nytimes.com/1983/11/10/world/china-affirms-its-hong-kong-deadline.html.

7. Steve Tsang, *A Modern History of Hong Kong: 1841–1997* (London: I.B. Tauris, 2007), 221.

8. Powell interview.

9. Margaret Thatcher, interview with Bernard Shaw, CNN, June 29, 1997, http://edition.cnn.com/WORLD/9706/30/thatcher.transcript.

10. Record of a meeting between Margaret Thatcher and Deng Xiaoping at the Great Hall of the People in Beijing, December 19, 1984, www.margaret thatcher.org/document/136839.

11. Hong Kong Housing Authority, *Heritage Impact Assessment on Chai Wan Factory Estate at No. 2 Kut Shing Street, Chai Wan, Hong Kong*, April 2023, www .amo.gov.hk/filemanager/amo/common/form/HIA_Report_CWFE.pdf.

12. Interview with Chan Kin-man.

CHAPTER 4

1. John Pomfret, "Minority Student Galvanizes Students at One School," *Associated Press*, April 28, 1989.

2. "Editorial," *People's Daily*, April 26, 1989, http://tsquare.tv/chronology /April26ed.html.

3. Francis L. F. Lee and Joseph M. Chan, *Memories of Tiananmen: Politics and Processes of Collective Remembering in Hong Kong, 1989–2019* (Amsterdam: Amsterdam University Press, 2021), 55.

4. Szeto Wah, *A Mighty River Flowing Eastward: An Autobiography of Szeto Wah* 大江東去:司徒華回憶錄 (Hong Kong: Oxford University Press, 2011), 295–296.

5. Steve Vines, "Million March in Hong Kong to Support Beijing Students," *Guardian*, May 22, 1989.

6. Kevin Hamlin, "Hong Kong Marchers Back Peking Protest," *Independent*, May 22, 1989.

7. Eric Ellis, "Beijing's Bush Telegraph," *Sydney Morning Herald*, May 27, 1989.

8. Olivia Cheng and Siaw Hew Wah, translated by *China Change*, "The Life and Death of the Hong Kong Alliance in Support of Patriotic Democratic Movements of China," July 29 2022, https://chinachange.org/2022 /07/30/the-life-and-death-of-the-hong-kong-alliance-in-support-of -patriotic-democratic-movements-of-china-part-one.

9. *Ta Kung Pao*, May 28, 1989.

10. "Upheaval in China; 200,000 at Hong Kong Rally Pledge to Continue Struggle," *New York Times*, May 28, 1989, www.nytimes.com/1989/05/28/world /upheaval-in-china-200000-at-hong-kong-rally-pledge-to-continue-struggle .html.

11. Dan Williams, "8-Hour March Belies Hong Kong Apathy," *Los Angeles Times*, May 29, 1989, www.latimes.com/archives/la-xpm-1989-05-29-mn -688-story.html.

12. Sheryl WuDunn, "In Quest for Democracy, a Mini-city Is Born," *New York Times*, May 31, 1989, www.nytimes.com/1989/05/31/world/in-quest-for -democracy-a-mini-city-is-born.html.

13. Han Minzhu, *Cries for Democracy: Writings and Speeches from the Chinese Democracy Movement* (Princeton, NJ: Princeton University Press, 1990), 347.

14. "Soldiers Blocked Again in Beijing," *St. Louis Post-Dispatch*, June 3, 1989.

15. Timothy Brook, interview with *Frontline PBS*, April 2006, www.pbs.org /wgbh/pages/frontline/tankman/interviews/brook.html.

16. Francis L. F. Lee and Joseph M. Chan, *Memories of Tiananmen: Politics and Processes of Collective Remembering in Hong Kong, 1989–2019* (Amsterdam: Amsterdam University Press, 2021), 59–61.

17. Martin Lee, interview with *60 Minutes Australia*, 1989, https://youtu.be /OTD10NhMeJo.

18. "Hemlock," "Hong Kong on the Day of the Tiananmen Massacre: Rumours, Unlikely Protests and a Brutal Reckoning," *Hong Kong Free Press*, June 4, 2019, https://hongkongfp.com/2019/06/04/hong-kong-day-tiananmen -massacre-rumours-unlikely-protests-brutal-reckoning.

CHAPTER 5

1. Szeto Wah, *A Mighty River Flowing Eastward: An Autobiography of Szeto Wah* 大江東去:司徒華回憶錄 (Hong Kong: Oxford University Press, 2011), 339.

2. "Sun Yee On Incorporated," *South China Morning Post*, October 13, 1993, www.scmp.com/article/46411/sun-yee-incorporated; David W. Chen, "Hong Kong's Movie Industry Plagued by Gangsters," April 20, 1992, https://apnews .com/article/9fb7174ef981b762744f60cb5cad4515.

3. Interview with Jean Pierre-Montagne in *Opération Yellow Bird*, a 2016 documentary directed by Sophie Lepault.

4. Interview with Wu'er Kaixi.

5. Memorandum of Conversation, Chairman Deng Xiaoping with Brent Scowcroft and Lawrence S. Eagleburger, July 2, 1989, www.thewire china.com/wp-content/uploads/2020/06/Deng_Scowcroft_July_2_1989 _Meeting.pdf.

6. No. 10 Downing Street record of conversation between Margaret Thatcher and George Bush, by Charles Powell to Stephen Wall at the Foreign and Commonwealth Office, June 5, 1989, www.margaretthatcher.org /document/149468.

7. James Lilley with Jeffrey Lilley, *China Hands: Nine Decades of Adventure, Espionage, and Diplomacy in Asia* (New York: PublicAffairs, 2004); Orville Schell, "The Odyssey of Comrade Fang," *Los Angeles Times*, October 7, 1990, www.latimes.com/archives/la-xpm-1990-10-07-tm-2958-story .html.

8. Interview with Ray Burghardt.

9. Jeffie Lam, "'Operation Yellow Bird': How Tiananmen Activists Fled to Freedom Through Hong Kong," *South China Morning Post*, May 26, 2014, www.scmp.com/news/hong-kong/article/1519578/operation-yellow-bird-activists-recall-flights-freedom-through-hong.

CHAPTER 6

1. Christopher DeWolf, "Kowloon Tong History: Hong Kong's Original Garden City and Its Unusual Path," *South China Morning Post*, November 5, 2018, www.scmp.com/lifestyle/travel-leisure/article/2171675/kowloon-tong-history-hong-kongs-original-garden-city-and.

2. "Guidelines on Civic Education in Schools," Hong Kong Education Department, 1996, 6.

3. International Telecommunications Union, *Broadband as a Commodity: Hong Kong, China Internet Case Study*, May 2003, www.itu.int/ITU-D/ict/cs/hongkong/material/CS_HKG.pdf.

4. Edward A. Gargan, "Tung Chee-hwa: Shipping Tycoon Chosen to Govern Hong Kong," *New York Times*, December 12, 1996, https://archive.nytimes.com/www.nytimes.com/library/world/121296hongkong-leader.html.

5. Erik Guyot, "Tung Chee Hwa Admits China Aided His Shipping Firm in '80s," *Wall Street Journal*, October 24, 1996, www.wsj.com/articles/SB846091379312344500; Hugh Llewelyn Davies, *Hong Kong 1997: Handling the Handover*, self-published, 2016, 389.

6. Jane Steer, "When Bill Clinton Became the First Serving US President to Visit Hong Kong," *South China Morning Post*, July 2, 2020, www.scmp.com/magazines/post-magazine/short-reads/article/3091482/when-bill-clinton-became-first-serving-us.

7. Regina Ip, "Hong Kong Needs Laws to Protect National Security by Secretary for Security," 2003, www.basiclaw23.gov.hk/english/focus/focus5.htmenglish/focus/focus5.htm.

8. Keith Bradsher, "Plan to Crack Down on Dissent Stirs Debate in Hong Kong," *New York Times*, November 3, 2002, www.nytimes.com/2002/11/03/world/plan-to-crack-down-on-dissent-stirs-debate-in-hong-kong.html.

9. Elaine Wu, Gary Cheung, and Joseph Lo, "Premier Points to a Better Tomorrow," *South China Morning Post*, July 2, 2003, www.scmp.com/article/420399/premier-points-better-tomorrow.

10. Alexis Lai, "'National Education' Raises Furor in Hong Kong," *CNN.com*, July 30, 2012, https://edition.cnn.com/2012/07/30/world/asia/hong-kong-national-education-controversy/index.html.

11. Joshua Wong with Jason Y. Ng, *Unfree Speech: The Threat to Global Democracy and Why We Must Act Now* (New York: Penguin, 2020), 31–33.

CHAPTER 7

1. Nicholas Kristof, "Looking for a Jump-Start in China," *New York Times*, January 5, 2013, www.nytimes.com/2013/01/06/opinion/sunday/kristof-looking-for-a-jump-start-in-china.html.

2. Interview with Joseph Torigian.

3. Sebastian Veg, "The 'Restructuring' of Hong Kong and Rise of Neo-statism," *Tocqueville21*, June 27, 2020, https://tocqueville21.com/le-club/the-restructuring-of-hong-kong-and-the-rise-of-neostatism.

4. Christine Loh, *Underground Front: The Chinese Communist Party in Hong Kong* (Hong Kong: Hong Kong University Press, 2018), 205–206.

5. Hung, Ho-fung. *City on the Edge: Hong Kong Under Chinese Rule* (Cambridge: Cambridge University Press, 2022), 137.

6. Jiang Shigong, *China's Hong Kong: A Political and Cultural Perspective* (Singapore: Springer, 2017), 102–134.

7. Harry Harrison, cartoon, in "Beijing Reasserts Its Total Control over Hong Kong in White Paper," *South China Morning Post*, June 10, 2014, www.scmp.com/news/hong-kong/article/1529300/beijing-reasserts-its-total-control-over-hong-kong-white-paper.

8. June Cheng and Erica Kwong, "Hong Kong's Freedom Fighter," February 13, 2021, https://wng.org/articles/hong-kongs-freedom-fighter-1617296810.

9. Joyce Ng and Patsy Moy, "Keep up the June 4 Struggle—Last Words of 'Uncle Wah,' Szeto Wah, 1931–2011," *South China Morning Post*, January 3, 2011, www.scmp.com/article/734657/keep-june-4-struggle-last-words-uncle-wah.

10. Joshua But, "Occupy Central Hong Kong Supporters Ready to Block Traffic and Go to Jail for Democracy," *South China Morning Post*, March 28, 2013, www.scmp.com/news/hong-kong/article/1201371/occupy-central-supporters-ready-block-traffic-and-go-jail-democracy.

11. Peter So and Chris Lau, "'The Sun Rises as Usual': Beijing Official's Response to Occupy Central," *South China Morning Post*, October 2, 2014, www.scmp.com/news/hong-kong/article/1607247/sun-rises-usual-beijing-officials-response-occupy-central.

12. Edward Leung Tin-kei campaign video, February 1, 2016, www.facebook.com/100067447335871/videos/1682451435342095.

13. Benny Tai, "30 Years After Tiananmen: Hong Kong Remembers," *Journal of Democracy* 30, no. 2 (April 2019), www.journalofdemocracy.org/articles/30-years-after-tiananmen-hong-kong-remembers.

CHAPTER 8

1. Carrie Lam, remarks at a media session, March 26, 2017, www.info.gov.hk/gia/general/201703/26/P2017032600607.htm.

2. Xi Jinping, speech marking the 20th anniversary of Hong Kong's return to China, *China Daily*, July 1, 2017, www.chinadaily.com.cn/china/hk2 othreturn/2017-07/01/content_29959860.htm.

3. Carrie Lam, interview with Reuters, July 14, 2017, www.youtube.com /watch?v=PCFkRocjWys.

4. Kenneth Lau, "Lam Bares the 'Bad Records' in Her Life," *Standard*, May 3, 2016, www.thestandard.com.hk/section-news/section/11/168864 /Lam-bares-the-%60bad-records'-in-her-life.

5. Stuart Lau, "The Search for the Real Carrie Lam, Hong Kong's Leader in Waiting," *South China Morning Post*, March 25, 2017, www.scmp.com/week-asia /politics/article/2081938/search-real-carrie-lam-hong-kongs-leader-waiting; Carrie Lam's office, February 23, 2017, www.facebook.com/carrielam2017 /photos/a.174633419705278/174633639705256/?type=1&theater.

6. Interview with Lee Wing-tat.

7. Carrie Lam speech at the 194th Congregation and Prize Presentation Ceremony at the Li Ka Shing Faculty of Medicine, University of Hong Kong, November 21, 2015, www.med.hku.hk/-/media/HKU-Med-Fac/about/mfn /MFN—Special—194th-Congregation.ashx.

8. Carrie Lam's office, February 23, 2017, www.facebook.com/photo/?fbid =174633439705276&set=a.174633419705278.

9. Timothy McLaughlin, "The Leader Who Killed Her City," *Atlantic*, June 18, 2020, www.theatlantic.com/international/archive/2020/06 /carrie-lam-hong-kong-china-protest/612955.

10. Ella Lee, "I Won't Become Heartless: Carrie Lam," *South China Morning Post*, January 17, 2017, www.scmp.com/article/403831/i-wont -become-heartless-carrie-lam.

11. Luisa Tam, "'Good Fighter' Plus 'Peacemaker,' but Can Carrie Lam Hold up the Sky?," *South China Morning Post*, December 15, 2016, www.scmp.com/news/hong-kong/politics/article/2054855/good -fighter-plus-peacemaker-can-carrie-lam-hold-sky.

12. Olga Wong, "Tearful Carrie Lam Says She Put Reputation on the Line," *South China Morning Post*, September 8, 2012, www.scmp.com/news /hong-kong/article/1031942/tearful-carrie-lam-says-she-put-reputation -line.

13. *South China Morning Post*, liveblog of student government talks, October 21, 2014, www.scmp.com/news/hong-kong/article/1621141/live-hong -kong-students-prepare-meet-government-officials-democracy.

14. Nikki Sun, "'Invisible Hand' Interfering in Hong Kong Chief Executive Race, NPP Deputy Chair Michael Tien Says," *South China Morning Post*, January 17, 2017, www.scmp.com/news/hong-kong/politics/article/2062740

/invisible-hand-interfering-hong-kong-chief-executive-race?module=hard
_link&pgtype=article.

15. Carrie Lam, interview with the BBC, June 21, 2017, www.youtube.com
/watch?v=srp_UPG5VAA.

16. Carrie Lam, interview with the *Financial Times*, March 2018, www
.ft.com/content/d81d82ba-2392-11e8-ae48-60d3531b7d11.

17. Interview with Kurt Tong.

18. Alexandra Stevenson, "Chinese Canadian Billionaire Sentenced
to 13 years for Financial Crimes," *New York Times*, August 19, 2022, www
.nytimes.com/2022/08/19/business/chinese-canadian-billionaire-xiao-jianhua
-sentenced.html.

19. For more, see Alex W. Palmer, "The Case of Hong Kong's Missing Booksellers," *New York Times Magazine*, April 3, 2018, www.nytimes
.com/2018/04/03/magazine/the-case-of-hong-kongs-missing-booksellers
.html.

20. Interview with Matt Pottinger.

21. Michael Lipin, "Hong Kong's No. 2 Gets Positive Reviews for Rare Washington Visit," *Voice of America*, June 15, 2016, www.voanews.com/a/hong-kong
-carrie-lam-gets-positive-reviews-in-washington-visit/3376644.html.

22. Donald J. Trump, interview with *South China Morning Post*, August
19, 1993, www.scmp.com/magazines/style/news-trends/article/3108142
/when-donald-trump-visited-hong-kong-future-us-president; Farah Stock-
man and Keith Bradsher, "Donald Trump Soured on a Deal, and Hong
Kong Partners Became Litigants," *New York Times*, May 30, 2016, www.ny
times.com/2016/05/31/us/politics/donald-trump-hong-kong-riverside-south
.html.

23. Jeffie Lam and Alvin Lum, "In a First, Hong Kong Leader Carrie Lam
Donates Money to City's Biggest Pro-democracy Party," *South China Morning
Post*, March 21, 2018, www.scmp.com/news/hong-kong/politics/article/2138115
/first-hong-kong-leader-donates-money-citys-biggest-pro.

24. Ellie Ng, "'CY Leung's Crony Network': Gov't Think Tank Slammed for
Rising Role in Adviser Appointments," *Hong Kong Free Press*, June 14, 2017,
https://hongkongfp.com/2017/06/14/cy-leungs-crony-network-govt-think
-tank-slammed-rising-role-appointing-personnel-advisory-bodies.

25. James Pomfret, "Unscheduled Departure: China's Legal Reach Extends
to Hong Kong Rail Station," *Reuters*, September 4, 2018, www.reuters.com
/article/us-hongkong-china-rail-idUSKCN1LK0J4.

26. Carrie Lam speaking at the YPO Hub in Davos, March 4, 2020, youtu.be
/pVA3P4RqkaE.

27. HKSAR v. Chan Tong-kai, hearing at the High Court of the Hong Kong Special Administrative Region, April 12, 2019.

CHAPTER 9

1. Interview with Kathryn Lam.
2. Lam interview.
3. Interview with Sarah Van Meel.

CHAPTER 10

1. Democratic Alliance for the Betterment and Progress of Hong Kong (DAB) press conference, February 12, 2019, www.youtube.com/watch ?v=CBpiutiyqDU.

2. John Lee Ka-chiu, article on behalf of the Hong Kong Security Bureau, February 28, 2019, www.sb.gov.hk/eng/articles/articles_2019_02_28.html.

3. Kris Cheng, "Hong Kong's New One-Off China Extradition Plan Seeks to Plug Legal Loophole, Says Chief Exec. Carrie Lam," *Hong Kong Free Press*, February 19, 2019, https://hongkongfp.com/2019/02/19/hong-kongs -new-one-off-china-extradition-plan-seeks-plug-legal-loophole-says-chief -exec-carrie-lam.

4. Nathan Vanderklippe, "China Charges Canadians Michael Kovrig and Michael Spavor with Espionage," *Globe and Mail*, June 19, 2020, www .theglobeandmail.com/world/article-china-charges-michael-kovrig-and -michael-spavor-with-spying.

5. Holmes Chan, "In Pictures: 12,000 Hongkongers March in Protest Against 'Evil' China Extradition Law, Organisers Say," *Hong Kong Free Press*, March 31, 2019, https://hongkongfp.com/2019/03/31/pictures -12000-hongkongers-march-protest-evil-china-extradition-law-organisers -say.

6. Interview with Matt Pottinger.

7. Owen Churchill and Alvin Lum, "Hong Kong's Former No 2 Anson Chan Meets Mike Pence in Washington as US Report Criticises Beijing 'Intervention' in City's Affairs," *South China Morning Post*, March 23, 2019, www.scmp.com/news/hong-kong/politics/article/3002953/hong-kong -lawmakers-and-former-no-2-hit-us-capital-report.

8. Minutes of Legislative Council meeting, May 9, 2019, www.legco.gov.hk /yr18-19/chinese/counmtg/hansard/cm20190509a-translate-c.pdf.

9. Interview with Kurt Tong; interview with Jeff Nankivell.

10. Christopher Bodeen and Yanan Wang, "Extradition Bill Pushes Hong Kong to a Political Crisis," Associated Press, June 10, 2019, https://apnews

.com/article/asia-pacific-carrie-lam-ap-top-news-international-news-hong
-kong-70c87c10413e452d8338a760b48ece47.

11. Interview with Dennis Kwok.

12. Rupert Dover, interview with *South China Morning Post*, June 10,
2020, www.scmp.com/news/hong-kong/law-and-crime/article/3088482
/police-commander-gives-inside-account-what-led-firing.

13. Chris Lau, "Hong Kong Police Facing High Court Challenge over Officer's 'Jesus' Comment During Extradition Bill Protest," *South China Morning Post*, June 19, 2019, www.scmp.com/news/hong-kong/law-and-crime
/article/3015184/hong-kong-police-facing-high-court-challenge-over; Javier
C. Hernandez et al., "Did Hong Kong Police Abuse Protesters? What Videos
Show," *New York Times*, June 30, 2019, www.nytimes.com/2019/06/30/world
/asia/did-hong-kong-police-abuse-protesters-what-videos-show.html.

14. Carrie Lam interview with TVB, video via *South China Morning Post*, June 13, 2019, www.scmp.com/video/hong-kong/3014253/carrie
-lam-addresses-extradition-law-controversy.

15. Interview with Jasper Tsang.

16. Transcript of Alice Mak Mei-kuen, obtained by *Oriental Daily*, translated
by Language Log, https://languagelog.ldc.upenn.edu/nll/?p=43351.

17. Kwok interview.

CHAPTER 11

1. Francis Lee, Hai Liang, Edmund W. Cheng, Gary K. Y. Tang, and Samson
Yuen, "Affordances, Movement Dynamics and a Centralized Digital Commu-
nication Platform in a Networked Movement," *Information, Communication &
Society* 25, no. 12 (2021): 1699–1716.

2. Hong Kong Public Opinion Research Institute, October 11, 2022, www
.pori.hk/wp-content/uploads/2022/10/pr_2022oct11.pdf?fbclid=IwAR
18Ruc-2IZKtNIEFhpBtQlzwMc9HnQlm5Ik6xpRtMhnti7mry9JlfDFFbI.

3. Kris Cheng, "Chinese Media Mogul Revealed as Owner of Hong Kong
Broadcaster TVB, in Potential Regulatory Breach," *Hong Kong Free Press*, May
11, 2017, https://hongkongfp.com/2017/05/11/chinese-media-mogul-revealed
-owner-hong-kong-broadcaster-tvb-potential-regulatory-breach.

4. Timothy McLaughlin and Eric Cheung, "Burning Threads: How a Raucous Internet Forum Became Ground Zero for the Hong Kong Protests," *Rest
of World*, April 2020, https://restofworld.org/2020/lihkg-hong-kong-protests
-forum.

5. Lee et al., "Affordances."

6. SensorTower data, August 2019, https://sensortower.com/blog/hong-kong
-protests-app-downloads.

7. Brian Wong, "Hong Kong Protester 'Raincoat Man' Wrote Note Blaming Government, Took Out Life Insurance Ahead of Fatal Fall, Inquest Hears," *South China Morning Post*, May 11, 2021, www.scmp.com/news/hong-kong /law-and-crime/article/3133070/hong-kong-protester-raincoat-man-wrote -note-blaming.

8. Hong Kong Observatory, www.weather.gov.hk/en/wxinfo/pastwx /mws2019/mws201907.htm#:~:text=July%202019%20was%20much%20 hotter,highest%20on%20record%20of%20July.

9. Carrie Lam, speech at reception in celebration of twenty-second anniversary of the establishment of the Hong Kong SAR, July 1, 2019, www.info.gov.hk /gia/general/201907/01/P2019070100238.htm.

10. Peter So, "Security Checks for All as Hong Kong's Legco Building Beefs up Protection," *South China Morning Post*, April 21, 2015, www.scmp.com/news /hong-kong/politics/article/1772848/security-checks-all-hong-kongs-legco -building-beefs.

11. *Stand News* live stream; Alvin Lum and Christy Leung, "The Only Unmasked Protester at Hong Kong Legco Takeover 'Has Fled the City,' but Whereabouts Not Confirmed," *South China Morning Post*, July 6, 2019, www.scmp.com/news/hong-kong/politics/article/3017530/only-unmasked -protester-hong-kong-legco-takeover-has-fled.

12. *Stand News* live stream, via Facebook post, www.facebook.com /watch/?v=459441244847661.

13. Transcript of remarks by Carrie Lam at a media session, July 2, 2019, www.info.gov.hk/gia/general/201907/02/P2019070200193.htm?fontSize=1.

CHAPTER 12

1. Gerry Shih, "China's Backers and 'Triad' Gangs Have a History of Common Foes. Hong Kong Protesters Fear They Are Next," *Washington Post*, July 23, 2019, www.washingtonpost.com/world/asia_pacific /chinas-backers-and-triad-gangs-have-history-of-common-foes-hong-kong -protesters-fear-they-are-next/2019/07/23/41445b88-ac68-11e9-9411-a608f9d0c2d3_story .html.

2. Independent Police Complaints Council, "Incident Day—Sunday 21 July 2019 Yuen Long," May 2020, www.ipcc.gov.hk/doc/en/report/thematic_report /Incident%20Day%20%E2%80%93%20Sunday%2021%20July%202019%20 Yuen%20Long.pdf.

3. James Pomfret, Greg Torode, and David Lague, "Chinese Official Urged Hong Kong Villagers to Drive off Protesters Before Violence at Train Station," Reuters, July 26, 2019, www.reuters.com/article/us-hongkong -extradition-gang-insight-idUSKCN1UL0LK.

4. Emma Yeomans and Richard Lloyd Perry, "Cambridge Restaurateur 'Seen with Hong Kong Thugs,'" *Times of London*, July 25, 2020, www.the times.co.uk/article/cambridge-restaurateur-seen-with-hong-kong-thugs-khv xj9nnp.

CHAPTER 13

1. Liu Xiaoming, interview with BBC, June 13, 2019, www.youtube.com /watch?v=SMTc8ml5yoo.

2. Shibani Mahtani and Timothy McLaughlin, "Hong Kong Leader Carrie Lam Is Facing the Wrath of Her People. Beijing May Be Even Angrier," *Washington Post*, June 21, 2019, www.washingtonpost.com/world/asia_pacific /hong-kong-leader-carrie-lam-is-facing-the-wrath-of-her-people-beijing-may -be-even-angrier/2019/06/21/69df9b40-928a-11e9-956a-88c291ab5c38_story .html.

3. Interview with Jasper Tsang.

4. Austin Ramzy and Tiffany May, "China Warns Hong Kong Protesters Not to 'Take Restraint for Weakness,'" *New York Times*, August 6, 2019, www .nytimes.com/2019/08/06/world/asia/hong-kong-china-protests.html.

5. "US Wages Global Color Revolutions to Topple Govts for the Sake of American Control," *Global Times*, December 2, 2021, www.globaltimes.cn /page/202112/1240540.shtml.

6. James Pomfret and Greg Torode, "Amid Crisis, China Rejected Hong Kong Plan to Please Protesters," Reuters, August 30, 2019, www.reuters.com /article/us-hongkong-protests-china-exclusive-idUSKCN1VKoH6.

7. Interview with Michael Tien.

8. Ellie Ng, "Protesters Claim They Were Paid to Attend Pro-Beijing Rally in Support of China's Ruling on Oath Row," *Hong Kong Free Press*, November 14, 2016, https://hongkongfp.com/2016/11/14/protesters-claim-they-were-paid-to -attend-pro-beijing-rally-in-support-of-chinas-ruling-on-oath-row.

9. Johnny Tam, "Beijing Upset After Martin Lee and Anson Chan Meet Joe Biden at the White House," April 7, 2014, www.scmp.com/news/hong-kong /article/1466666/beijing-upset-after-martin-lee-and-anson-chan-meet-joe -biden-white.

10. "Game Targeting Hong Kong 'Traitors' Popular on Mainland Social Media," *Global Times*, December 4, 2019, www.globaltimes.cn/content/1172323 .shtml.

11. Interview with David Stilwell.

12. Interview with Ivan Kanapathy.

13. Kris Cheng, "In Pictures: New Hong Kong Protest Ads Urging Int'l Help Appear in 11 Newspapers Worldwide," *Hong Kong Free Press*, August 19,

2019, https://hongkongfp.com/2019/08/19/pictures-new-hong-kong-protest
-ads-urging-intl-help-appear-11-newspapers-worldwide.

14. Interview with Jeffrey Ngo.

15. Interview with Glacier Kwong Chung-ching.

16. Ngo interview.

CHAPTER 14

1. "China 70th Anniversary: Pigeon Ban and Lockdowns as Count-
down Begins," BBC, September 24, 2019, www.bbc.com/news/world-asia
-china-49806653.

2. Steven Lee Meyers, "Tanks, Missiles and No Pigeons: China to Celebrate 70th Birthday of the People's Republic," *New York Times*, September
28, 2019, www.nytimes.com/2019/09/28/world/asia/china-national-day-70th
-anniversary.html; "Beijingers Sweat It Out During Rehearsals for National
Day Parade," *Global Times*, September 5, 2019, www.globaltimes.cn
/content/1163738.shtml.

3. Gerry Shih, "Chinese State TV Cancels Broadcasts of NBA Presea-
son Games and Sponsors Drop out in Dispute over Hong Kong Comments," *Washington Post*, October 8, 2019, www.washingtonpost.com
/world/asia_pacific/chinese-state-tv-cancels-broadcasts-of-nba-preseason
-games-and-sponsors-drop-out-in-dispute-over-hong-kong-comments/2019
/10/08/28f9dfd4-e9b8-11e9-bafb-da248f8d5734_story.html.

4. Jonathan White, "Houston Rockets Return to China Screens, 15 Months
After Hong Kong Tweet Ignited NBA Controversy," *South China Morning Post*,
January 11, 2020, www.scmp.com/sport/china/article/3117175/houston-rockets
-return-china-screens-15-months-after-hong-kong-tweet.

5. Ted Cruz, interview with *Face the Nation*, CBS, October 14, 2019, www
.youtube.com/watch?v=F90L07Qa6iY&t=14s; Josh Hawley, Twitter post,
October 13, 2019, https://twitter.com/hawleymo/status/1183344431379779585
?lang=hu.

6. Shibani Mahtani, "Hong Kong Protesters Plead for American Protection as Police Crackdown Intensifies," *Washington Post*, October 14, 2019,
www.washingtonpost.com/world/hong-kong-protesters-plead-for-american
-protection-as-police-crackdown-intensifies/2019/10/14/0e936fec-ee37
-11e9-bb7e-d2026ee0c199_story.html.

7. Jennifer Creery, "Explainer: From 'Five Demands' to 'Independence'—
The Evolution of Hong Kong's Protest Slogans," *Hong Kong Free Press*, June
25, 2020, https://hongkongfp.com/2020/06/25/explainer-from-five-demands
-to-black-cops-to-independence-the-evolution-of-hong-kongs-protest
-slogans.

8. Timothy McLaughlin, "How Hong Kong's Protests Turned into a Mad Max Tableau," *Wired*, December 21, 2019, www.wired.com/story/how-hong-kongs-protests-turned-into-a-mad-max-tableau.

9. Nancy Pelosi, "Remarks at Bill Enrollment Ceremony for the Hong Kong Human Rights and Democracy Act of 2019," November 21, 2019, https://pelosi.house.gov/news/press-releases/pelosi-remarks-at-bill-enrollment-ceremony-for-the-hong-kong-human-rights-and.

10. David J. Lynch, "Trump Says He Might Veto Legislation That Aims to Protect Human Rights in Hong Kong Because Bill Could Affect China Trade Talks," *Washington Post*, November 22, 2019, www.washingtonpost.com/business/2019/11/22/trump-says-he-might-veto-legislation-that-aims-protect-human-rights-hong-kong-because-bill-would-impact-china-trade-talks.

11. Interview with Keiji Fukuda and Gabriel Leung.

12. Mandy Zhou, Lilian Cheng, Alice Yan, and Cannix Yau, "Hong Kong Takes Emergency Measures as Mystery 'Pneumonia' Infects Dozens in China's Wuhan City," *South China Morning Post*, December 31, 2019, www.scmp.com/news/china/politics/article/3044050/mystery-illness-hits-chinas-wuhan-city-nearly-30-hospitalised.

CHAPTER 15

1. Tsai Ing-wen at a campaign rally, January 10, 2020, www.youtube.com/watch?v=gloGoJzRD4E.

2. Victor Ting, "China Coronavirus: Hong Kong Medical Experts Call for 'Draconian' Measures in City as Research Estimates There Are Already 44,000 Cases in Wuhan," *South China Morning Post*, January 27, 2020, www.scmp.com/news/hong-kong/health-environment/article/3047813/china-coronavirus-hong-kong-medical-experts-call.

3. Clara Ferreira Marques, "Hong Kong Is Showing Symptoms of a Failed State," *Bloomberg*, February 9, 2020, www.bloomberg.com/opinion/articles/2020-02-09/coronavirus-hong-kong-shows-symptoms-of-a-failed-state.

4. Joe Pompeo, "'This . . . Invisible Sense of Danger': Doing Journalism in the Coronavirus War, Italian Front," *Vanity Fair*, March 19, 2020, www.vanityfair.com/news/2020/03/doing-journalism-in-the-coronavirus-war-italian-front.

5. Interview with Jasper Tsang.

6. Statement from the National People's Congress, May 22, 2020, www.npc.gov.cn/npc/c30834/202005/e235c7a3ebea43ca98aa80032590e924.shtml.

7. CrimeRate.co.uk data, 2023, https://crimerate.co.uk/london/richmond-upon-thames.

CHAPTER 16

1. Eva Dou and Shibani Mahtani, "With Hong Kong Security Law, China Writes Broad International Powers for Itself," *Washington Post*, July 1, 2020, www.washingtonpost.com/world/asia_pacific/with-hong-kong-security-law-china-writes-broad-international-powers-for-itself/2020/07/01/cf1e2c0a-bb61-11ea-97c1-6cf116ffe26c_story.html.

2. Dou and Mahtani, "With Hong Kong Security Law, China Writes Broad International Powers for Itself."

3. Transcript of Hillary Rodham Clinton in conversation with Dr. Robin Niblett, director, Chatham House, October 11, 2013, www.chathamhouse.org/sites/default/files/public/Chatham%20House/111013Clinton.pdf.

4. Interview with Miles Yu.

5. Interview with Matt Pottinger.

6. Donald J. Trump, speech at the Rose Garden, May 29, 2020, https://trumpwhitehouse.archives.gov/briefings-statements/remarks-president-trump-actions-china.

7. Interview with Jeffrey Ngo.

8. Pottinger interview.

9. Interview with Ivan Kanapathy.

10. Ngo interview.

11. John Lyons, "American Citizen Says He Was Denied Refuge in Hong Kong's U.S. Consulate," *Wall Street Journal*, November 8, 2020, www.wsj.com/articles/u-s-citizen-says-he-was-turned-away-after-seekingrefugein-u-s-consulate-in-hong-kong-11604863457.

12. Interview with Glacier Kwong Chung-Ching.

13. Glacier Kwong Chung-Ching interview.

14. Glacier Kwong Chung-Ching interview.

15. Kimmy Chung and Chris Lau, "Hong Kong Elections: Beijing Accuses Occupy Protest Leader Benny Tai of Breaking National Security Law Through Primary Poll," *South China Morning Post*, July 14, 2020, www.scmp.com/news/hong-kong/politics/article/3093175/hong-kong-elections-beijing-issues-strongest-condemnation.

16. Xinqi Su, "Under Beijing's Watchful Eye, Hong Kong Activist Joshua Wong Treads a Fine Line," Agence France-Presse, September 13, 2020.

CHAPTER 17

1. Yoshiyuki Ogasawara, "The Pratas Islands: A New Flashpoint in the South China Sea," *Diplomat*, December 10, 2020, https://thediplomat.com/2020/12/the-pratas-islands-a-new-flashpoint-in-the-south-china-sea.

2. *Ta Kung Pao*, August 11, 2020, www.takungpao.com.hk/news/232109
/2020/0811/485097.html.

3. Cited in multiple news articles, including Jack Lau and Danny Lee, "Campaigners for 12 Hongkongers Arrested While Fleeing to Taiwan Demand Government Discloses Details on 'Police Spy Plane,'" *South China Morning Post*, October 8, 2020, www.scmp.com/news/hong-kong/politics/article/3104765/campaigners-12-hongkongers-arrested-while-fleeing-taiwan. However, this information cannot be independently verified because it was a leak to *Apple Daily*, a now-defunct media outlet.

4. *Ta Kung Pao*, August 29, 2020, www.takungpao.com.hk/news/232109/2020/0829/491799.html.

CHAPTER 18

1. Vivian Wang, Austin Ramzy, and Tiffany May, "With Mass Arrests, Beijing Exerts an Increasingly Heavy Hand in Hong Kong," *New York Times*, January 6, 2021, www.nytimes.com/2021/01/06/world/asia/china-hong-kong-arrests.html.

2. Hong Kong government press release with responses from John Lee Ka-chiu to media, January 6, 2021, www.info.gov.hk/gia/general/202101/06/P2021010600555.htm?fontSize=1; Shibani Mahtani and Theodora Yu, "'Total Submission': With Mass Arrests, China Neutralizes Hong Kong Democracy Movement," *Washington Post*, January 6, 2021, www.washingtonpost.com/world/asia_pacific/hong-kong-arrests-national-security-law/2021/01/06/c3ccc248-4fbe-11eb-a1f5-fdaf28cfca90_story.html.

3. James Pomfret and Jessie Pang, "Besieged Barrister," Reuters, November 10, 2022.

4. Timothy McLaughlin, "Beijing Keeps Trying to Rewrite History," *Atlantic*, November 27, 2021, www.theatlantic.com/international/archive/2021/11/pillar-of-shame-tiananmen-square-massacre-symbol/620810.

5. "Artist Says University of Hong Kong May Allow Retrieval of Removed Tiananmen Statue, Though Shunned by Crane Firms," *Hong Kong Free Press*, April 8, 2022, https://hongkongfp.com/2022/04/08/artist-says-university-of-hong-kong-may-allow-retrieval-of-removed-tiananmen-statue-though-shunned-by-crane-firms.

6. University of Hong Kong Council statement on the removal of a statue from campus, December 23, 2021, www.hku.hk/press/press-releases/detail/23802.html.

7. "Arthur Li Voices Firm Opposition to External Interference in HKSAR Affairs," CGTN, May 28, 2020, https://news.cgtn.com/news/2020-05-28/Arthur-Li-voices-rejection-to-external-interference-in-HKSAR-affairs

-QR5cYpmMYo/index.html; "'Pillar of Shame' Is a Lie, Says HKU Council Chair Arthur Li," *Standard*, January 1, 2022, www.thestandard.com hk/breaking-news/section/4/185387/'Pillar-of-Shame'-is-a-lie,-says-HKU -Council-chair-Arthur-Li.

AFTERWORD

1. Jeffie Lam, "Turning a New Page: Britain Wants to Reinvigorate Ties with Hong Kong and to Have Less Megaphone Diplomacy, Consul General Says," *South China Morning Post*, May 4, 2023, www.scmp.com/news/hong-kong /politics/article/3219296/turning-new-page-britain-wants-reinvigorate -ties-hong-kong-and-have-less-megaphone-diplomacy-says.